They're Playing My Song

They're Playing My Song

Fifty-Two Great Songwriters Discuss Their Craft

BRUCE POLLOCK

excelsior editions
State University of New York Press
Albany, New York

Cover Credit: Susanna Hoffs, 2015. Photo: Justin Higuchi from Los Angeles, CA, USA, Creative Commons Attribution 2.0 Generic license.

Published by State University of New York Press, Albany

© 2025 State University of New York

All rights reserved

Printed in the United States of America

No part of this book may be used or reproduced in any manner whatsoever without written permission. No part of this book may be stored in a retrieval system or transmitted in any form or by any means including electronic, electrostatic, magnetic tape, mechanical, photocopying, recording, or otherwise without the prior permission in writing of the publisher.

Links to third-party websites are provided as a convenience and for informational purposes only. They do not constitute an endorsement or an approval of any of the products, services, or opinions of the organization, companies, or individuals. SUNY Press bears no responsibility for the accuracy, legality, or content of a URL, the external website, or for that of subsequent websites.

EU GPSR Authorised Representative:
Logos Europe, 9 rue Nicolas Poussin, 17000, La Rochelle, France
contact@logoseurope.eu

Excelsior Editions is an imprint of State University of New York Press

For information, contact State University of New York Press, Albany, NY
www.sunypress.edu

Library of Congress Cataloging-in-Publication Data

Name: Pollock, Bruce, author, interviewer.
Title: They're playing my song : fifty-two great songwriters discuss their
    craft / Bruce Pollock.
Description: Albany : State University of New York Press, [2025]. | Series:
    Excelsior editions | Includes bibliographical references and index.
Identifiers: LCCN 2024057618 | ISBN 9798855803402 (pbk. : alk. paper) | ISBN
    9798855803419 (ebook)
Subjects: LCSH: Composers—Interviews. | Lyricists—Interviews. | Rock
    musicians—Interviews. | Popular music—History and criticism. | Rock
    music—History and criticism. | Popular music—Writing and publishing.
Classification: LCC ML3470 .P6517 2025 | DDC 782.42164092/2—dc23/eng/20241203
LC record available at https://lccn.loc.gov/2024057618

To Barbara, for everything . . . and more.

Contents

Acknowledgments	xi
Introduction	1
Fred Parris / the Five Satins (1980): "(I'll Remember) In the Still of the Night"	4
John Lee Hooker (1984): "Boom Boom"	15
Felice and Boudleaux Bryant (1974)	19
Doc Pomus (1974)	30
Neil Sedaka (1980)	35
Hank Ballard (1980): "The Twist"	42
Gerry Goffin (1974)	52
Jackie DeShannon (2012): "Put a Little Love in Your Heart"	55
Phil Ochs (1974)	59
Buffy Sainte-Marie (1974)	64
Paul McCartney (1990)	72
Keith Richards (1985)	76
Pete Townshend (1974)	83

John Sebastian (1974)	92
Jimmy Webb (1989)	98
Frank Zappa (1974)	102
Laura Nyro (1984)	109
Paul Simon (1976, 1985)	112
Jerry Garcia (1984) and Robert Hunter / Grateful Dead (1974)	118
Valerie Simpson (2009)	123
Lou Reed (1974)	127
Tim Rice (1974): "Jesus Christ, Superstar"	132
Melvin Van Peebles (1974)	137
Don McLean (2020): "American Pie"	143
Neil Smith / Alice Cooper (2012): "I'm Eighteen"	148
Steven Tyler / Aerosmith (1985, 1987): "Dream On" and "Walk This Way"	151
Linda Creed (1974)	154
Donald Fagen / Steely Dan (1985)	157
Randy Newman (1974)	161
John Prine (1974)	167
Bruce Springsteen (1973, 1984)	172
Allen Toussaint (2014): "Southern Nights"	178
Chris Frantz / Tom Tom Club (2014): "Genius of Love"	183
Marc Campbell / the Nails (2012): "88 Lines About 44 Women"	188
Neil Peart / Rush (1986)	197

Mike Watt / Minutemen (2012): "History Lesson, Pt. 2" 207

Billy Steinberg (2012): "Like a Virgin" 213

Narada Michael Walden (2012): "Freeway of Love" 219

Julie Gold (2013): "From a Distance" 224

Andy Partridge / XTC (1988) 232

Kool Moe Dee (2001) 238

Dave Alvin / the Blasters (2013): "4th of July" 242

Susanna Hoffs / the Bangles (2012): "Eternal Flame" 248

Sophie B. Hawkins (2019): "Damn, I Wish I Was Your Lover" 252

Todd Thomas / Arrested Development (2001): "Tennessee" 257

Travon Potts (2001): "Angel of Mine" 260

Shelly Peiken (2018): "What a Girl Wants" 263

Tom Higgenson / Plain White T's (2020): "Hey There Delilah" 267

Stephan Moccio (2015): "Wrecking Ball" 272

Kevin Kadish (2018): "All About That Bass" 277

Index of Song Titles 281

Contents | ix

Acknowledgments

To the many songwriters who gave me their time and stories over the years and the many editors and publications that saw fit to print them.

Introduction

Straight out of City College in New York, I landed a staff writing job at the plucky tabloid *Rock Magazine*, responsible for articles, interviews, and spritely comments every two weeks. The first person I chose to interview was the music publishing magnate and soon to be host of his own *Rock Concert* series on TV, Don Kirshner, who pioneered the Brill Building sound with his staff of Gerry Goffin and Carole King, Barry Mann and Cynthia Weil, Neil Sedaka and Howie Greenfield, among others. Forget about journalistic integrity, my plan was to slip him some of my lyrics after the interview was concluded.

In his twenty-seventh-floor office, Kirshner began talking about re-creating himself as a cross between Bill Graham and Ed Sullivan as the host of *Rock Concert*. "We're going to try to do the show as real and sincere as possible," he said sincerely. "We're going to get the best lighting engineers, the best sound technicians. The only problem is, if that tube doesn't generate the excitement of a rock concert, we're going to be in trouble."

When it came time for me to write the piece in *Rock*, I tossed reality out the window and went with my original image of Donnie Kirshner before I met him, the ultimate street kid and Golden Ear, rather than the somber businessman I confronted that day. In a fit of inspiration, I dubbed him a Legend on His Old Block.

"To be a legend on your old block one must not only be a graceful dancer, but a sprinter as well, able to outdistance life by a city-mile," I may have slightly overstated in my opening graph. "Someone who not only keeps the rhythm but creates it. Donnie Kirshner, who played baseball and basketball in college, has been creating the city rhythm for years. His universal ear has led him into enough gold to pave the Grand Concourse.

Although he sings not a note, Kirshner has scaled the walls of the middle class and advanced himself to an awe-inspiring plateau in the life of a city person—king of the asphalt hill."

A few weeks after the article came out, I got a call from Kirshner's press agent, who had set up the interview. He told me his client was thrilled with my portrayal. "You're the first person to capture the real Donnie," he gushed.

Soon after the Kirshner article appeared, I started getting calls from his office gifting me with courtside Knicks tickets, which I courteously accepted. Later, I received a note from Walter Wager, a bigshot at ASCAP, who was one of the early fans of my writing. He said he passed along my stuff to Sy Peck, an editor at *The New York Times*, and that I should be hearing from him soon. This led to an assignment to review Bruce Springsteen's second album, *The Wild, the Innocent, and the E Street Shuffle*, in the hallowed pages of the *Sunday Times*, section 2. Wager then recommended me to his editor at Macmillan, resulting in my first book, *In Their Own Words: Twenty Successful Songwriters Tell How They Write Their Songs*, which was one of the first of its kind, presenting interviews with Randy Newman, Frank Zappa, Phil Ochs, and Buffy Sainte-Marie, among others.

Thinking better of presenting Kirshner with my lyrics, I became obsessed with songs and songwriters. For fourteen years, from 1985 to 1999, I compiled and edited a reference book on each year's most important songs, called *Popular Music*. In 1997, I put together what I felt was the ultimate (yet discriminating) compendium of the 7,500 most important songs in rock and roll history, *The Rock Song Index*, which was thoroughly revised and rearranged for volume 2 in 2005.

This collection includes interviews with fifty-two songwriters—many reprinted for the first time and some augmented with new material—with the writers talking about their art and craft, the creative process, and, in many cases, specific classic songs, like "In the Still of the Night," "From a Distance," "The 4th of July," and "Graceland." Although they took place over the course of fifty years, I have arranged these interviews in roughly chronological order based on the development of rock and popular music. I've given dates for the original interviews and added endnotes to briefly update an artist's subsequent life and career. Some of these interviews are derived from my popular column "They're Playing My Song," which appears on the website songfacts.com, along with excerpts from my book, *When Rock Was Young*, as well as selected interviews published in the *Saturday Review, USA Today, Rock Magazine, Modern Hi-Fi and Music*, and my column "On Songwriting," that appeared in *Guitar for the Practicing Musician*.

Fred Parris / the Five Satins (1980)

"(I'll Remember) In the Still of the Night"

The name Fred Parris seems fated to be bound forever with the song "In the Still of the Night," one of the most enduring and evocative of the singles to bridge the channel from rhythm and blues to rock 'n' roll in 1956. It is at the center and along the perimeter of Fred Parris's story, a tale as old as rock 'n' roll, probably as old as rhythm and blues. Its chance creation defines his career, glorifies it, and limits it. He's never been able to duplicate that song's success, yet when he's tried to run and hide from it, the song has always found him. It's gotten him jobs when he's been down; it's lured him out of comfortable work. When the song first hit, he was in no way able to take full advantage of the fame it might have offered. Even more to the point, he was to be denied the greater part of the riches it should have accrued. He has spent his life in the grasp of that song, going so far as to engage in legal action in the attempt to recover his due. And recently there has been a rumor that he never really wrote the song in the first place.

A not-dissimilar fate befell many of the classic groups and writers from this supposed golden era of rock 'n' roll. It was a world populated by hungry footloose kids, dreamers, romantics, naïfs in the ways of big business. They just wanted to record their song, get it out, get it heard, and revel in the approval of their peers. It was obvious they didn't know about agents, managers, royalty statements, and the nuts and bolts (and screws) of a show business career. Rock 'n' roll to them was not a career at all—it was a lark, an accident. Some of the biggest groups of the era, the pioneers whose influence has reached second and third generations, whose records consistently made the charts, came away from their glory years bittersweet, unable to prove anything conclusively, to get their hands on the necks of any culprits, and for all their success, curiously short of bankable funds.

In his hometown of New Haven, Connecticut, Freddy Parris entertained other dreams, mainly of curveballs and shutouts. Through high school he pitched with a variety of sandlot teams.

"That's when the Braves were in Boston," he says. "One day they had tryouts at City Stadium and I did pretty well." But his parents wouldn't hear of his leaving school to play ball. In the meantime, a new sound was beginning to take him away from that of horsehide on leather.

"My friends started turning me on to groups like the Clovers, the Dominoes, and the Spaniels," says Parris. "The songs were easy to sing. I knew the music was kind of sloppy, but there was just something about it that caught my ear, something about those four chords . . ."

Those four chords would usher in an age of harmony. In almost any ethnic neighborhood in the early fifties, in housing project and candy store and schoolyard, wherever baseball cards were being flipped or traded and pennies pitched, there was that sound: caterwauling in courtyards, cascading down the sides of buildings from the rooftop, sinuously drifting out of open basement windows. It was to be heard on the street corners under lamplight or moonlight, or under boardwalks or elevated train lines in the summer, or inside hallways and under stairwells in the winter—an urban, rattling, reckless sound, blending with the sirens and the traffic. In threes and fours and fives, hardly ever twos, they gathered—mini-gangs, basketball teams, sidewalk social clubs—their heads close together, hands behind their backs, the odd finger sings bass, to serenade the urban passing throng, city girls, and the very moon of love. Most of these serenades would never be preserved. Most of these singers would never leave the street. But in their dreaming voices, their ceaseless quest for harmony, lay the seeds of the future.

By the time it became obvious that Fred Parris's destiny was to be in rock 'n' roll, in a life if anything more uncertain than pro baseball, it was too late for his parents to prevent it. He was out of school, of age, about to join the army. He's already formed a group, the Scarlets, and recorded with a label in New York. "Dear One" and "I've Lost" had made him something of a celebrity in the neighborhood, respected for his vocalizing and writing ability.

"We were probably like the only recording group around," says Parris. "Kids just weren't in the business then. We were big shots because of that. We were cocky and enjoyed all the glory." Those two records went

Figure 1. Fred Parris, 2007. Photo: Debra Marafiote / Pmarafio, Wikimedia Commons, CC0 1.0.

on to achieve positions on national rhythm and blues charts, which was icing on the cake.

"When I started receiving royalties for what I'd done, which to me was nothing, I said, well there's no sense in me going any further, I might as well do this. I'm getting rich. Then we got lucky with 'In the Still of the Night,' and it was too late to change my mind."

When the song finally broke from the R&B underground to splash across the pop charts in the autumn of '56, Parris was about as far from the center of the acclaim as you can get—he was a buck private stationed in Japan. In fact, only two of the Five Satins who toured the country in the first rush of the song's success had taken part in the original sessions that produced it in the basement of St. Bernadette's Church in New Haven.

"I assumed I was still part of the group," says Fred, a silent, frustrated partner to all this stateside activity. "One of the guys wrote me a letter asking for material, but they weren't really counting on me being back at all. I didn't send them any, because I felt cheated."

Certainly, Armed Forces Radio didn't help ease his long-distance agony. Introducing his song one Saturday on the popular dance-party program as one of the most requested records in army history (Fred had been doing a lot of bragging), the deejay proceeded to play Ella Fitzgerald doing Cole Porter's "In the Still of the Night," a standard that had nothing to do with Parris's gem of rhythm and blues. Adding salt to the wound was a magazine article that subsequently circulated around the base, detailing the life and times of a group calling themselves the Five Satins. "I'd told everybody in camp that I was in the group and then the article comes out and there's nothing in it about me. The picture that went along with it really blew a hole in me, because I knew all the guys. I knew they weren't doing what they were supposed to."

The only thing somewhat alleviating the stress of being so far from the scene of his success were the weekly letters he received from his manager, Marty Kugell, on the progress of his baby in the realms of Tin Pan Alley. With sales figures like 150,000, then 200,000 copies bouncing in front of his eyes, Fred could be forgiven his constant daydreams. "I was counting the money," he recalls. "Boy, you know, I'm going to buy a house, a Cadillac. And I ended up with nothing."

Actually entitled "I'll Remember (In the Still of the Night)," in deference to Porter, the song was released on Kugell's own Standord label, which he ran out of his house. At this time, there were as many one-shot labels as one-hit artists—hole-in-the-wall operations as starry-eyed and foot-leather foolish as the hopeful neighborhood groups who came to audition for them, demos in hand, five-part harmonies at the ready. A box of gummed labels, a cheap master, and you were in business, with a legitimate shot at selling a thousand or so records in New York, Connecticut, and Massachusetts. Kugell himself had signed up at least a hundred exponents of such local talent in Connecticut alone.

None, however, would achieve the success of the Five Satins, whom Kugell had first come upon in their earlier incarnation as the Scarlets. There wasn't any rock 'n' roll on the radio to speak of then, only rhythm and blues. Because records achieved so little airplay, record stores would allow prospective buyers to sample their wares before deciding on a purchase. Many groups inhabited the immediate vicinity of the record store, to provide a little added incentive. Kugell first heard "Dear One" by the Scarlets in an even more intimate way. It was loaned to him by a clothes presser in his father's dry-cleaning establishment; the man's son just happened to be a member of the group. Something of a high school impresario already, Kugell promised him that he'd listen to his son's group the next time they rehearsed.

Since the Scarlets were at that point the property of Uncle Sam, their rehearsals were few, if any. Whenever someone found himself home on leave, there were usually four other local cats to surround him. Groups were fluid, careers nebulous; the sound was all that mattered. At the Scarlets' first paid gig, shortly before their record was released on Bobby Robinson's Red Robin label, they received all of two dollars a man. "Half of which we spent on uniforms that consisted of red ties, because we all had blue suits," Parris recalls. To make a living of this nonsense was unthinkable.

On the occasion Kugell caught up with them, the Scarlets were represented by Fred Parris, in from Philadelphia, where he was stationed, shortly to be bound for Japan. Duly impressed, Kugell set up a recording session for Parris, which occurred on one of the coldest nights of the year, at a VFW hall. None of the backup musicians Kugell had invited down to the session happened to make it, so "All Mine" was done a cappella. Thereafter, with Fred facing imminent embarkation, Kugell sought to get all of his work down on tape. He staged sessions every Sunday at St. Bernadette's Church, accompanied by whoever was around, sober and willing to sit in.

"One of the guys in the Scarlets, Al Denby, was in on those sessions," Fred recalls. "He became one of the Satins. He must have been home on leave. We picked up two other guys from the neighborhood. There were different guys each week. There were really only *four* Satins," says Fred, "but you couldn't call yourself the Four of anything in those days. It was uncool. You had to be the Five." (Like the Five Keys, the Five Crowns, or the Five Royales.) "So we signed up a piano player when we went on the road."

These frantic sessions resulted in the album *The Five Satins Sing*, which contains just about the sum total of Parris's early work, including the initial single released on the Standord label, the up-tempo "The Jones Girl," backed with the slower, more intense ballad, "In the Still of the Night." Eventually, of course, the latter was flipped over, thus allowing "shoo doo't 'n shoo be doo" a permanent place in the lexicon of rock 'n' roll, right up there with "sha-bop sha-bop" (from "I Only Have Eyes for You" by the Flamingos) and "dom-de-dom-dom, de-dang-de-dang-dang, de-ding-de-dong-ding" (from "Blue Moon" by the Marcels), although in fact that particular legendary riff was lifted in its entirety from the middle of an existing R&B hit, "Night Owl" by Tony Allen. But six months after its release, "In the Still of the Night" was virtually dead, achieving airplay only in Springfield, Massachusetts, and Dallas, Texas. Kugell's bills were overdue at the distributor and the presser. So when Al Silver, president of the mighty independent label Herald/Ember, home of the Turbans and the Nutmegs, phoned with an offer to distribute the platter, a deal to split net proceeds fifty-fifty seemed like a two-out homer in the last of the ninth. When the net was finally determined, however, Kugell recalls that his first royalty check from Herald/Ember, representing royalties, amounted to $365.69, paid in full.

Greeted with this paltry sum on his return from Japan, sheepish smiles all around, glad hands transferring the blame like a hot coal, and a group calling themselves the Five Satins at the Apollo Theater in nearby Harlem, Freddy Parris was understandably irate. He felt deceived, denied, swindled. He was unable to trust his manager, his record company, or his friends. The measure of his inner turmoil and paranoia can be seen in the series of apparently contradictory moves he next engaged in. Feeling he deserved the Five Satins name at the very least ("I thought it up. I started the group. I wrote the song. I sang it."), he nonetheless released his first song after returning home under the name of Fred Parris and the Scarlets. It was the obscure "She's Gone" which went nowhere on Marty Kugell's Klik label. Although Kugell was in the process of suing Al Silver and Herald/Ember Records, Parris signed a new contract with them, and put together his own Satins, a group which included Jim Freeman, who was at the time a part of the same bogus Satins who had sold him out while he was in Japan. (With Parris back in the States, the other Satins rather quickly disbanded.) He then broke off all ties with Kugell; they would not speak to each other for ten years. Meanwhile, he had ballooned up to 240 pounds, up from his GI weight of 185. Before taking his new Satins on the road, Fred suddenly returned to Japan to marry a Japanese woman. He stayed four months, then brought her back to New Haven. Although the marriage would last fifteen years, according to Fred it was never on solid ground.

"Rather than blame the music or anything, I would blame myself," he says. "I was the one who chose to do this, and I guess I wasn't ready to settle down, make that sacrifice. Unfortunately, I didn't find that out until after I was married."

He must have found supreme respite on the road then, as rough as it was. Away from family and friends, contracts and royalty statements, he fell into the camaraderie of the boys on the bus: Frankie Lymon and the Teenagers, Huey Smith and the Clowns, Hank Ballard and the Midnighters. "It was an entirely different life than what I was used to," he recalls. "It was all sort of off the top of your head. 'Hey, I got you guys a gig.' 'Okay, we'll be there. Maybe we can get an advance on next week's pay. As soon as we get through we can go out, meet some girls, have some fun.' There were always girls who would wait at the stage door for you to come out. They kept up with your career; I think that's all they did. They might hang around with you, even go with you if you were going to California. Then they'd stay out there and latch onto somebody else. It was a very free-living thing. That's all we worried about in those days."

There were the one-nighters and the theater tours. Theater tours were better; they lasted six days, six shows a day starting at noon. The show broke Thursday, then moved to another town along the circuit: the Apollo in Harlem, the Earl in Philadelphia, the Royal in Baltimore, the Howard in Washington. Even in the North the acts would put up at Black hotels. "It wouldn't make sense to go ten miles out of your way to stay at a hotel you couldn't afford," Parris explains. "You were only making $750 a week for five guys, and that included room and board. So you ended up staying in one room most of the time. Living conditions left a lot to be desired. Usually you set something up in the neighborhood with a lady in a restaurant, who let you eat on credit until the end of the week. The food was always delicious."

Sets were only about fifteen minutes, enough time to do your hit, the flip side, and the follow-up. But the groups took pains with their performances. For one thing, they dressed to the hilt, in iridescent suits, white shirts, and shined shoes. "We never had any problems with anyone looking sloppy," Fred notes. Then you had your good dancing groups, like the Cadillacs, the El Dorados, or the Dells. "My group was just adequate. We did what was expected. We never looked at our overall career and said, 'We should do this or that.'"

Neither did most of the acts on the bus. It was impossible to foresee, for instance, that Bo Diddley would still be an attraction twenty years later, or that Chuck Berry would wind up revered. "I don't think Chuck was looked on as such a star in those days," Parris suggests. "He became sort of a cult figure when the Beatles came up. What made him was the white audience, because Black people, I've found, don't like oldies. They like things that are happening right now; if it was last week, forget it."

Although the Five Satins continued to release records, eventually leaving Herald/Ember and moving on to Chancellor, Warner Brothers, Roulette, Checker, Atco, and others, it was always "In the Still of the Night" that came to the rescue when times were slow. It made the charts in 1959 and again in 1960, each time reviving the group's fading career. It has since been recorded by many acts, from Dion and Belmonts to John Sebastian, and occasionally it provides Fred Parris with a surprisingly hefty royalty check, but the bulk of the royalties due him will probably never be seen.

"For me it was always a struggle," he says. "It was never a situation where I was comfortable. We kept on working even when the Beatles came here in 1964, with the whole British invasion. We all learned instruments. I started playing bass. The club owners got a real break when the Beatles came in. They no longer had to hire two groups, a singing group and a band, because everybody began to play their own instruments."

But the arrival of the Beatles signaled the end to rock 'n' roll's age of innocence. The Beatles were sophisticated, hip. They brought with them visions of megabucks. Soon would come the advent of the rock 'n' roll lawyer. Anyway, by the mid-sixties most urban street corners were becoming too unsafe for midnight harmonizing. Fledgling rock groups moved indoors, tethered to their amplifiers. Phil Spector showed them the advantages of multitracking in the recording studio. For a time it became a seller's market in the rock 'n' roll business—that is, for all but the original harmony groups who were still out there somewhere looking for that perfect, pure, sweet, high note they'd left in a doorway long ago.

Slowly Fred Parris's career dwindled to a part-time job. To put food on the table for his wife and three kids, Parris took a variety of outside positions. He built guns at High Standard. He was a chemical analyst for Olin. He became a sales representative for Roskin Distributors.

"I've had a diversified past," he says. "But if you're just going to say, that's it, I quit, then you're not going to do it anymore. If you want to be in it, you've got to keep doing it. Whenever things were right, I'd go out again." And, for certain, "In the Still of the Night," possibly the number one oldie in New York City, wasn't going to let him fade into the nine-to-fives. When the Five Satins appeared at a revival concert at Madison Square Garden in 1969, the response was overwhelming. Most people assumed they'd been dredged up from the pits.

"One story had it that they found us working a carwash," says Fred. "They tried to make us as low as possible. But I was making a pretty good living at Roskin and just singing on the side. When this came up, there was suddenly a demand for us. I was being booked on tours, working almost seven nights a week, going to Philly and Boston and Washington, plus working during the day. I had to quit my job."

Again, the song had sealed his fate, but this time the ending was a happy one. "Given our track record, we've played many more places than we should have," says Fred. "I've been to Lake Tahoe and Puerto Rico. A lot of the other guys on the circuit were a little bit jealous. In New York, they're still in love with the Satins, the doo-wop sound. But we also genuinely put on a class show. When you've got an hour to do in a club, you can't stand there all night and sing 'In the Still of the Night.'" Even the occasional bus tours are more tolerable. "No one's starving now," says Fred. "We don't all have to sleep in the same room."

It was *the song*, in fact, that got him to the doorstep of the president. The Five Satins, Danny and the Juniors, the Coasters, and Bobby Lewis went on a tour sponsored by the Young Republicans for Nixon. They were put up at the best hotels, wined and dined by senators and governors, introduced to Tricia and Julie, given a peek at the Oval Office. "We were supposed to meet President Nixon, but he'd already left for San Clemente," says Fred. "They gave me a box of presidential cufflinks, which I still haven't opened."

One day, circa 1972–1973, newly divorced and trying to get back into shape, Parris happened on his one-time friend and manager, Marty Kugell. "It was a matter of running into him on the street, and after this much time we'd forgotten our differences." Through Kugell, Parris immediately reinstated his suit for back royalties against the current owners of the Herald/Ember copyrights (Herald/Ember having gone bankrupt years before). It is a delayed, complicated, and no doubt quixotic quest for justice, still winding on with the outcome possibly years in the future. "I'm certainly not counting on it," says Parris. "I'm hoping someday it'll come through, but I figure I'll just let it alone."

Until two years ago, Fred Parris was still making a nice living with the Five Satins, playing the oldies circuit—a string of small nightclubs, taverns, and high school auditoriums. The circuit caters to the growing number of dedicated, paunchy, pushing-forty nostalgia freaks who gather to pay homage to the echoes of their good times. But Fred, a student of today's changing music scene, finally tired of such a noncreative, repetitious life. "There was pressure building up," he says of his decision to

12 | They're Playing My Song

disband the Satins. "I felt I wasn't doing what I wanted to do musically, and in order to do that I had to stop touring. Audiences see you only as an oldie. They want to see you the way you were. Maybe I'll never make it again, but if I have to stick to oldies, I'd rather go out and dig a ditch."

Recently remarried, down in weight to a svelte 185, Parris finds his later work worlds apart from simple, innocent doo-wop. He's been putting most of his time into a theatrical concept, musically complex, lyrically grand. Supposedly there's been some interest. A script is being prepared to go along with it. "I've taught myself a lot of techniques," he says. "Right now I have a little Farfisa organ that I use; I'm hoping to get a bass soon. I use a four-track machine and I do all the harmonies myself, so that if I put a new band together, the parts will be very easy for the singers to learn. They'll all be individualized on tape. That's the way I would have done it then, had the equipment been available. If I'd had these kinds of tools to work with, I'm sure we woulda done a much better job. I could have put everything on tape exactly as I wanted it. But as it went down, I'd have to tell everybody what I wanted at rehearsals; the guys were local musicians who couldn't pick up too quick, and I would end up saying, 'Ah, okay, what the hell, let it go that way.'"

Local musicians, a disorganized scene, a chaotic career, claims and counterclaims, lost love, lost royalties, and one record after another that was released with hope invariably going straight down the tubes . . . And now even Fred's centerpiece, "In the Still of the Night," had been suddenly threatened—as have so many early classics—by at least one alleged author. It's no wonder Fred's glad to see that none of his kids have eyes for rock 'n' roll. "My youngest son occasionally likes to play my old stuff. He asks me a lot of questions about it, but I don't think he has any designs on following in my footsteps. I prefer it that way. Performing's a rough life. I like what my kids are doing now, because they're all pretty serious about school."

Fred Parris, in fact, seems to have learned from them. He has plans himself for returning to school, to study the craft of this thing that has been, in good times and bad, his living.

"I should have studied before," he says, "but I never took it seriously. Now it's a necessity. It's too late to start over at anything else." He laughs. "I don't know too many teams that would want me now. Except the Mets. They need me."

Fred Parris / the Five Satins (1980) | 13

Before his death in 2022, Fred went out with several more iterations of the Five Satins. As late as 1997, his song "(I'll Remember) In the Still of the Night" remained a fixture atop the annual WBCS-FM list of the Top 100 Oldies

John Lee Hooker (1984)

"Boom Boom"

"I used to play at this place called the Apex Bar in Detroit. There was a young lady there named Luilla. She was a bartender. I would come in at night and I'd never be on time. Every night the band would beat me there. Sometimes they'd be on the bandstand playing by the time I got there. I'd always be late and whenever I'd come in she'd point at me and say, 'Boom boom, you're late again.' She kept saying that. It dawned on me that that was a good name for a song. Then one night she said, 'Boom boom, I'm gonna shoot you down.' She gave me a song but she didn't know it.

"I took that thing and I hummed it all the way home from the bar. At night, I went to bed and I was still thinking of it. I got up the next day and put one and one together, two and two together, trying to piece it out—taking things out, putting things in. I finally got it down right, got it together, got it down in my head. Then I went and sang it, and everybody went, Wow! Then I didn't do it no more, not in the bar. I figured somebody would grab it before I got it copyrighted. So I sent it to Washington, DC, the Library of Congress, and I got it copyrighted. After I got it copyrighted I could do it in the bar. So then if anybody got the idea to do it, I had them by the neck, because I had it copyrighted. About two months later I recorded it. I was on VeeJay then. And the record shot straight to the top. Then, after I did it, the Animals turned around and did it. That barmaid felt pretty good. She went around telling everybody 'I got John Lee to write that song.' I gave her some bread for it, too, so she was pretty happy."

If, as the saying goes, "The blues had a baby and they called it rock and roll," then John Lee Hooker was lucky he was never slapped with a massive paternity suit. Bands like the Rolling Stones, ZZ Top, and J. Geils all looked up to Hooker as a musical father figure at some point in their career, while Canned Heat, George Thorogood, and the Blues Brothers all borrowed generously from his sizzling guitar style. John Lee Hooker continued to burn his boogie across the stages of America and Europe until his death in 2001 at the age of eighty-three. In the nineties he even fulfilled one of his fondest goals by recording some personal favorites, "I Cover the Waterfront" on 1991's *Mr. Lucky* (in a duet with Van Morrison) and the Brook Benton classic "Kiddio" on 1995's *Chill Out*. In '89 and '91 some of rock's best blues singers and players paid tribute to Hooker, recording duets with the great man on *The Healer* (featuring Bonnie Raitt, Carlos Santana, Los Lobos, Canned Heat) and *Mr. Lucky* (Albert Collins, John Hammond Jr., Keith Richards, Johnny Winter, and Ry Cooder).

"I'm doing the same thing as I used to, but it's more modern," Hooker told me in 1985. "I'm playing the same basic beat, but I build different instruments around it. I can do lots of different styles if I want to. I can play ballads, country and western, but I don't do it. If I start to do that I would lose my blues audience. I would lose my fans. They know me from playing the blues and the boogie. When I sit at home, I can play beautiful ballads like 'I Cover the Waterfront.' I can do Brook Benton's style really good. I like 'A Rainy Night in Georgia.' I love 'I Left My Heart in San Francisco.' When I heard that song, I couldn't help it. I said, I gotta do it as a blues. So I wrote 'Frisco.' I love Tony Bennett. I just love his voice. I want to meet him so bad.

"There are certain types of songs that fit my music just like that. I turn it around and it becomes mine," he said. "You can write something for me and I may love it, but I've still got to change it to where it fits me. I listen to the radio all the time and I pick up on new things. A lot of blues artists inspire me. Some of the old blues songs are so good and so sweet and so mellow I'd like to do a whole album of them. My mind's made up to do it, but I haven't done it yet. I could sing 'Hoochie Coochie Man.' I wouldn't do it like Muddy did it. I do a lot of Howling Wolf's stuff. It's like that song by Otis Spann: 'Don't Let the Blues Die.'" As far as I can tell, however, he never did get to record that classic blues album he dreamed of, although at least one or two classics of the genre appear on all of his albums, as well as the tunes he turns into blues classics with his fingers.

Figure 2. John Lee Hooker at the Long Beach Blues Festival, 1997. Photo: Masahiro Sumori, Wikimedia Commons, CC BY-SA 3.0.

Clearly, the blues informed every one of his songs and interpretations. "The blues come from way back," he told me. "When the world was born, the blues was born. As the world progressed the blues got more fancy and more modern. They dressed it up much more. They got lyrics now that they didn't have then. But they're still saying the same thing. The greatest music of all comes from the blues—spirituals, rock, country and western. Everything comes from that root. When the blues first came out, it was only among Black people. We used to sing them in the cotton fields, on the farms. They didn't care about lyrics, they whistled the blues, hummed the blues, moaned the blues. They didn't have set words—they didn't rhyme. But you have to roll with the times."

Ironically, as a songwriter, Hooker claimed he found it very difficult to work when he actually had the blues. "A lot of people think blues singers write when they're sad and lonely. They think you gotta be down and out to write the blues—hungry, broke. It's not true," he said. "I write when I've got a good feeling, when I'm happy. When things are going well for you, you write. You have to be in the groove to write. You can't be upset and worried and write the blues. You've got to have a clear mind. The songs are sad, and they think you're sad when you're writing them, but you're not. You're just in a good mood for writing blues. When you write like that, you're not writing for yourself. There are millions of people out there. Maybe some of them are sad, and when they hear the words you said, the song will hit them. Goddamn, my old lady just left me. Anyone in the world who's been in that position will buy it. I'm not feeling that way, but I'm writing it for the people who are. Sometimes you feel something deep down and write it to get it out, get it off your chest. But I cannot write a song when I'm feeling blue. I can't think when my mind is on my troubles.

"Some songs are much harder to write than others. It just depends on what type of a song it is. On some you get it down right away. Ballads are a little bit harder. You have to go over some of the lines to get them right. If I get an idea, I'll think about it and get it together and then I'll pick up a guitar and phrase it. I'll play it once to get the sound, the feeling, the beat. Then I'll get the band I'm playing with and work on it in the studio. If I wake up in the middle of the night with a good idea, I'll start talking into the tape recorder. I have one right by my bed. Sometimes I'll take it with me in my car. Before tape recorders I just had to keep it all in my head."

Hooker recorded an album with Van Morrison in 1997, entitled Don't Look Back. *"Boom Boom" was included in the* Rolling Stone *magazine list of* Songs That Shaped Rock and Roll. *Hooker passed away in 2001.*

Felice and Boudleaux Bryant (1974)

This husband-and-wife country songwriting team have been at it for more than twenty-five years, proving the old adage, the family that plays together, stays together. Their family of songs comprises perhaps the largest body of work in the field today. Known internationally for their million sellers with Don and Phil Everly, the Bryants have written songs for such other artists as Roy Clark, Bob Luman, Elvis Presley, Eddy Arnold, Charlie Pride, Carl Smith, and the Osbornes.

The interview with the Bryants took place at the Essex House Hotel in Manhattan where they were staying prior to delivering a lecture on songwriting as part of the 92nd St. YMHA Great Lyricist Series. Although it was a fancy hotel suite, during the course of the interview I felt as if I were a guest at the Bryants' own home, outside of Nashville.

> FELICE: My writing was venting my feelings because I couldn't talk to my elders. I always wrote; I wrote letters and poetry that I would tear up so that they couldn't be found. I wrote all the time, even if it was only doodling. I had to have someone to talk to, so I talked to myself.

> BOUDLEAUX: If I'm too close to a subject emotionally, I don't like to write about it. I keep it to myself. I like to write though and if we write something I really enjoy, I can get emotionally involved in it after it's done. But if I had a deep emotional experience, I doubt seriously that I would try to set it to words.

A songwriting team, Felice and Boudleaux Bryant: a team of opposites merging each other's writing strengths into a hit combination. Felice, emotional; Boudleaux, realistic—he writes to live, she lives to write. But, of course, it's not quite so simple.

> BOUDLEAUX: We work in many, many ways. Sometimes the lyrics come first, sometimes the melodies come first. Sometimes we work together and sometimes we work separately. Most of the time we work together.

> FELICE: For a long time I had these ideas, but I couldn't tell anything about them while they were in my head, so I'd have to write them out, the words. I don't read music. I don't play an instrument. The words themselves will have a musical value. That's how I can compose a melody. Then he'll write the music down, or I'll turn on the tape machine. It's only then that I can evaluate the idea.

At the start Felice sang at amateur shows, usually coming in second or tied for first. Boudleaux was a professional musician, playing everything from country music to society swing. After they were married they moved to Moultrie, Georgia, where they began writing songs for fun, seriously.

> BOUDLEAUX: We started writing for the hell of it, for fun, and after we had about eighty songs we thought, this looks like it could be a good thing. But we originally wrote them for our own amusement and we'd show them to our friends.

> FELICE: Some people cut stones and polish them. We wrote songs. The family used to say, "Oh, ain't that *good*. Just listen, that's a neat song." They were encouraging like you are to a child. "That's nice honey, now go to your room."

> BOUDLEAUX: They enjoyed the songs, but they didn't have any more idea than we did about how to get through the closed door.

> FELICE: We didn't look for the door. Then all of a sudden I said to Boudleaux, I said, we're not fantastic, but we're not bad. Let's do something with them. And that's when he started writing letters.

BOUDLEAUX: I wrote about twenty letters a day to everybody I could think of, people I had known, people I didn't know. We'd get names and addresses out of *Billboard* magazine. We sent songs out all over the world for a couple of years without any results except rejections and unopened returns.

FELICE: My heart would crack with every rejection. I thought, well maybe we're not that good, because I was counting on the fact that the powers that be really knew, cause if they didn't know they wouldn't be there. I didn't realize that it's all guesswork in their department too. But it would antagonize Boudleaux when people would say, this isn't structured properly. I mean their criticism was strictly their own opinion. You don't come up to Boudleaux and say, "Man, you don't know what you're doing."

BOUDLEAUX: I'd been in the music business long enough to know they weren't lousy songs.

FELICE: He hangs his teeth and stays in there.

BOUDLEAUX: Some of those early songs were good and some weren't. The same thing is true for the songs we write now. You don't ever really know for an absolute fact that a song is rotten. Occasionally you make a judgment from a personal taste standpoint, but I think every song we write—that we finish—is crafted fairly well, some better than others of course, but you can't make any kind of absolute judgment as to whether a song is good or bad. Some of the ones that we ourselves have liked personally the least have been songs that other people have flipped out on, and some of them have been pretty good hits. And some songs that we absolutely just were crazy about and loved and thought were just the best we'd ever written didn't do a thing, and we still have them sitting around.

FELICE: And there's still magic connected with them. Until somebody else feels that same magic those songs will stay in the book. We have some songs on the books that are twenty-five years old, and still, when we do them the magic is there, for us.

Felice and Boudleaux Bryant (1974) | 21

BOUDLEAUX: People come to our house to listen to songs and we bring out the books. We write in five-hundred-page legal ledgers, and we'll go through songs at random.

FELICE: People want to see our old songs because they want to see what the years of experience have done to us.

BOUDLEAUX: What they really hope to do is stumble across a good song that's been overlooked, because each person who listens to a song has his own idea about what constitutes a good song. One of our biggest songs was shown over thirty times before it was ever cut and that was "Bye Bye Love." It was even shown the very morning of the same day the Everly Brothers heard it in the afternoon. It was shown that morning and turned down and the fella said, "Why don't you show me a good *strong* song?" So . . . nobody really knows what a good song is.

In 1949, however, somebody recognized a good song when they heard one, as written by the Bryants.

BOUDLEAUX: There was a fellow I had worked with in Detroit, Rome Johnson, who had gotten on record as a country singer and we showed him a few of our songs and he flipped out on one of them, said he wanted to do it and he called Fred Rose of Nashville and told him about the song and we sent the song to Fred Rose. As a result of this conversation, Fred Rose didn't let Rome do it, but had Little Jimmy Dickens do it and it was a smash country record, just a stone smash and that's all there was to it. It was called "Country Boy." After about a year of traveling around we went to Nashville and started making contact with the various artists who were recording there. And from then on we've done nothing but write.

FELICE: At that time, in the field that we flopped into, the artists wrote and performed all of their own material. Then, after a while, the road got to them; they couldn't think, they couldn't doodle around on the front porch with a guitar, they couldn't stroll through the woods and get inspired. So

22 | They're Playing My Song

Boudleaux and I were the first people who came to Nashville who didn't do anything but write. We were the factory—what an "in" you know?

BOUDLEAUX: There were many other writers in town, but they had to work at other things.

FELICE: We had to be very careful back then at what we wrote, because we could get almost anything and everything recorded.

BOUDLEAUX: There's one thing that happens after you've been writing and you're solidly into it, and that's that occasionally you will show a song that you don't particularly like yourself.

FELICE: And Boudleaux gets very angry because I'll say to the artist, "Well, I don't like that one."

BOUDLEAUX: I think that's a ridiculous remark to make to an artist, because it might have an effect, and the song could be ideal for the artist. I think you should keep an absolutely impartial attitude. Just let them react to it and if they react positively, maybe you've got a pretty good chance. We had a song not long ago that we both thought would have been an absolute smash for Hank Snow, who hadn't then really had a smash in a long time. It was not the style of song he customarily does.

FELICE: Our song wasn't in the style he usually did, but it was his.

BOUDLEAUX: It wasn't the sort of thing Hank Snow's ever done, but it was the kind of thing I could hear in my mind being done by him, because he does have a very distinctive voice and this song was just the sort of thing that I thought would be an absolute total smash done in his way.

FELICE: Now there was magic that we felt that he didn't.

BOUDLEAUX: He didn't do the song and it still hasn't been done yet. But since that time, he has had a number one country record, so I must acknowledge that he knows what he's doing.

Felice and Boudleaux Bryant (1974) | 23

FELICE: And we haven't thought of anybody to show the song to. The song just said, "Gimme to Hank!"

BOUDLEAUX: Once in a while you're able to bring a thing like that off. We had a song last year, "Come Live with Me." The minute it was done I said that's a Roy Clark song, absolutely no way otherwise. It happened that *Hee Haw* was filming at the time and I got hold of Roy and showed it to him at the studio with fifteen secretaries sitting around typing. He couldn't hear it too well, so we went to a little cubbyhole office and I played it again . . . and he just fell out.

FELICE: He fell in love with a chord change.

BOUDLEAUX: It happened that his record producer was there and we showed it to him. They called a session just for the song, did it within a week and it was out a few weeks later. It went to number one.

FELICE: Whenever we've had this feeling and the artist has gone along, we've had a hit. And when the artist doesn't go along, that's so painful, because you can see it so clearly, like in a crystal ball.

BOUDLEAUX: We once high-pressured a guy into doing a song. The name of the song was "Let's Think About Living," and it was an all-out smash, but this cat hated it. Bob Luman hated that song.

FELICE: That was another one of those things that we saw that the artist didn't. We've had about five of them in twenty-five years. But in each song that is shown to an artist, you've got to remember his enthusiasm and you've got to remember that this is the hook he wants to hang on. If *you* looked at me and you said, "Felice, this is important to me. I have a heavy date and I want her to like me. I want to make an impression. Does this shirt look right?" By God, I'm gonna tell you what I think. I'm gonna say, "Blue would really work on you." And if Boudleaux is peddling a red shirt that day, he's gonna be madder than hell.

24 | They're Playing My Song

BOUDLEAUX: Because they might like red as well as they do blue, and they might look just as good in it. When it comes to songs, I believe that you don't know if the song's good or not any more than anyone else does. If it's crafted well, if the rhymes are true, if the thought is expressed in a fairly comprehensible way and the melody is singable, who knows, it might be the best song that ever came down the pike.

FELICE: I know, but the whole thing is, it only has cost us paper and pencil, which is nothing. Brown paper sacks we used to write on, and that costs nothing. But if you came to us and you had your sights on something, if I didn't believe in this paper bag here, I'd say, "Man, we've got one over there that might be better."

I stepped in at this point to ask Boudleaux to describe what makes a song a country song.

BOUDLEAUX: There are various kinds of limiters. By that I mean a country limiter would be colloquialisms that are peculiar to say, the South or the Southwest, a rural atmosphere. It doesn't necessarily mean the song won't be a national hit, but it does definitely mean that it's a country song. It can be identified as a country song, whereas some songs, even though they are done as country songs by a country artist in the beginning, cannot actually be identified with any authority as country songs because they don't have any limitations on them whatsoever. A lot of songs that have these limiting qualities about them just absolutely don't ever escape their limitations. For example, if there's a song about chitlins and gravy and all that sort of business, that song is not likely to break out and be done by a pop artist.

We've had songs ourselves that have been done as country, as pop, and as rhythm and blues. There are a lot of R 'n' B songs that are rhythm and blues only because of the interpretation that's given to them. Now if a record is R 'n' B only by virtue of its interpretation, then that song often is done by country artists too. More often you'll find the transition goes the other way. The song will start off as a country song.

Felice and Boudleaux Bryant (1974) | 25

I wanted to know how country music has been affected by the changing times.

BOUDLEAUX: There's more permissiveness in sexual connotations.

FELICE: Kris Kristofferson brought the bedroom onto the Opry stage.

BOUDLEAUX: We had one song that was banned on some radio station because it had the word "wiggle" in it. And we had a song called "Jackass Blues" that was banned on all the stations.

FELICE: It's like a family. Did you ever notice that the rest of the kids can get away with that thing and you can't? Well Boudleaux and I still can't get away with anything suggestive. They've put a collar on Boudleaux and for some reason they think we have no sex life.

BOUDLEAUX: We've got a lot of turndowns because there was something maybe just a little suggestive, however "Jackass Blues" was written up by a famous columnist, Walter Winchell I think. He said it was the dirtiest record he ever heard. A few more papers picked up on his remark and it sold an enormous amount of records.

FELICE: That was our first *underground* record.

I then talked with Felice about certain technical problems of the trade.

FELICE: We save every scrap of paper, never throw anything away. We've got several ideas where there's just four lines and it's said right there; to stretch it would be wrong. It's not long enough to record; it's not anything. It's just a little whatever the hell it is and it's perfect.

We had a title for years. Boudleaux's sister had a maid, twenty-three, twenty-four years ago. She worked like a dog but her husband sat home. She spent her life working hard and coming back home to this man who did nothing. When we asked her why she did it, she said the line; she said, "O honey,

I makes the livin' and that man makes the livin' worthwhile." What an idea! What a title! And we have attacked that idea three or four times and never came up with anything that was as good as that title. And just to use a title and put trash around it is a sin.

I had told this story so many times. The other night in Nashville we found out that the title of the new Roy Clark album is *I Make the Living and My Woman Makes the Living Worthwhile*. I have not heard the song but I'm dying to hear it to see what he did with it and will I like it, because that's the strongest title in the world and if you can't do it justice, leave it alone.

I asked if they worked every day.

BOUDLEAUX: We used to and we still do a little bit. We'll at least talk about something or maybe try to germinate some ideas. But we don't work as hard as we did.

FELICE: Well, if the pressure's on, if a request has been made and a session is coming up . . .

BOUDLEAUX: We get a lot of requests from either the A 'n' R man or the artists themselves. The A 'n' R man might say, "I'm doing so and so in a couple of weeks; have you got anything?" And we'll check through our books and if we don't have anything that we think is what they're looking for, we'll try to write something. We've had a lot of success that way, actually. The material that we wrote for the Everly Brothers happened that way. The first song they did, "Bye Bye Love," had already been written, but then we had about five in a row that were multimillion sellers that we wrote specifically with them in mind. They weren't captive artists either. You know, they were looking at material all over the place. We just got lucky enough to have the songs that were absolutely ideal for them.

I wouldn't just think of somebody and write the song for that person without having had some contact with the person, without the artist having asked for the song. In writing for specific artists, you have to take a number of things into

Felice and Boudleaux Bryant (1974) | 27

consideration. You have to know what their audience consists of. Whether or not they're appealing to a middle-aged group or a young group, young adults or teenagers. And as nearly as possible if you can write a song that has a universal type of feel to it, you're in business.

But generally, if you give a song to an artist and you don't know much about the artist's style, you know that there are many possible interpretations that could be given that song, so you're generally surprised one way or another, either pleasantly or otherwise.

FELICE: You've turned your child over to a couple of strangers and they have an idea of how to raise your kid and then all of a sudden here's this kid with a swollen belly, and you don't know how it got that way.

BOUDLEAUX: There's one thing I know that happens with us when we first finish a song. If we like it pretty well, we'll sing it over and over. She'll do it. I'll do it. We'll do it together if it's harmonizable. And we'll do it till we're almost sick of it, then we'll put it away until we show it; we'll forget it, and after we show it and it's done and recorded, we just about totally forget it.

FELICE: It's fallen out of our top ten. The thing is, we have to erase the board to go onto the new song and not be hung up on the last thing. And when a song becomes a hit, something else takes over right then and there. You get the feeling that it isn't your song. It's your song till you put it out there on the street and then you've cut the cord, man, you've mopped its face with the apron for the last time. And when it's doing what it's doing, you don't even feel like you wrote it. Your name is there but it doesn't mean anything. All of a sudden it's not yours anymore.

As a closing comment, Felice summed things up like this.

FELICE: John Loudermilk will tell you that he made a study of our material, trying to find out where the key was, and he

28 | They're Playing My Song

found it, he said. And I said, "Yeah? Show it to me. What does it look like?" Because I still don't know what it is.

In addition to penning twenty-four hits for the Everly Brothers, Boudleaux (who died in 1987) and Felice (who died in 2003) also had songs recorded by Ray Charles, Elvis Presley, Buddy Holly, Bob Dylan, the Beach Boys, Emmylou Harris, and Nazareth.

Doc Pomus (1974)

Jerome Felder aka "Doc" Pomus (with Mort Shuman), Jerry Leiber (with Mike Stoller), Chuck Berry, Fats Domino, Buddy Holly, and a handful of others were the seminal figures during the transition period from rhythm and blues and rockabilly into rock 'n' roll. While Berry, Holly, and Domino were essentially singer-songwriters, Pomus and Leiber made their livings ghostwriting words for Elvis Presley and the many acts that followed his glittering footsteps into the brave new world of pop music.

In person Pomus is a cross between Doctor John and Burl Ives, a big man, bearded, confined to a wheelchair due to childhood polio. Behind the scenes in the music business he is truly a venerated figure, the pro's pro, a veteran of many bags. In the late fifties his creations spurred such groups as Dion and the Belmonts and the Drifters to huge success. When the Beatles arrived in 1964, leading the British revolution in a takeover of the Brill Building, ancient gathering place for New York City staff songwriters, Doc and the others broke ranks and seemed to disappear. He never gave up writing; however, the hits just stopped coming—an example of the winds that blow hot and cold in the songwriting arena. But he continued to collaborate with such cult figures as Willy DeVille and Dr. John, producing, some said, his finest work.

The interview with Doc Pomus took place in an uptown Manhattan coffeehouse near his West Seventy-Second Street residence. It was a spirited discussion, lasting well into the evening dinner rush.

"Early success is tough to live with—success is tough to live with anytime, it's almost as tough as failure," he said. "My experience has been it's always tougher for me to take success because most of my life has been filled with failure and I found it very easy to live with. It was only when I started getting successful—I was in my thirties—that I found it impossible. I must have blown a half a million dollars, all because of one thing—I couldn't cope with success. It's a madness. You know, up until the time I was thirty-two years old my good years were when I was able to buy a suit, you know, this was a real good year. Then suddenly you're going into a store and having ten made to order.

"I've gone through the other side too. What happens is that you start imagining you know what a hit record is and suddenly that song that you swore is a hit song isn't a hit, and it destroys you, absolutely destroys you.

"The thing that scared me most, from a personal viewpoint, is that I had a marriage that broke up and I got out of the business. So, I had to go back to writing because I had blown all my money and the first couple of months I didn't know what the hell I was doing. It was a really bad period. But when I got back into it I thought I was doing some good tunes, but nothing was happening and it went on and on . . . for a couple of years. Now when I look back on those songs I realize there was nothing wrong with them, it was just a question of today the markets are so limited. When you're on a streak, you never even think of it. Catch almost anybody who's got a number of hit songs and he'll show you fifty songs that you'll think are just as good that nothing happened to. As for myself, almost without exception, every hit song I've ever written has been rejected by ten or fifteen artists. I mean rejected seriously, where an artist will say, how can you think that this song is going to be a hit? So by this time, I don't say a word. I just write them and do what I can with them."

Before becoming a full-time songwriter, Doc was a music critic. He had some fiction published. Mostly he was a singer. "I used to write a lot of songs for blues singers like Joe Turner and Ray Charles. Funny, it was always easier for me to make a living writing than singing. I used to write to survive because I was always making records that weren't successful. Finally, when I was about thirty, I started to realize that singing was a losing battle, so I began to concentrate on writing. And two or three years later I suddenly started getting hits all over the place."

The first song he wrote that made nationwide noise was "Youngblood," by the Coasters. "The first song you could call a rock 'n' roll song was something by Fabian, 'I'm a Man.' In the old days, there were always people to help you. Leiber and Stoller were a great help to me, fantastic fellows. Also, Otis Blackwell. Otis introduced me to Hill and Range publishing, and they were the first publishers I signed up with. Leiber and Stoller helped me get a Lavern Baker recording and for a fact they helped me in rewriting certain songs.

"You know, I met John Lennon last year at a BMI dinner, in fact we spent the whole dinner together. One of the biggest kicks I had was when Lennon told me that one of the first songs the Beatles ever did was a song I wrote called 'Lonely Avenue.' You never know if other writers are aware of you. And he was telling me originally all they wanted to do was reach a point, like Morty and myself or like Carole King and Gerry, where they could make enough money to survive writing songs. Then when all that success happened; look at him—he can't cope."

Doc talked about his working habits.

"I write all the time. At first I used to write the melodies and lyrics, and the funny thing is I considered myself more of a melody writer than a lyric writer. Eventually I became a lyric writer, not even involved with melodies at all. That's why, when I hear some of my old songs, I can't believe I wrote both, because it's a whole different frame of reference. I couldn't visualize myself being alone writing a song now. There's a certain type of solitary thing that I can't do anymore. I prefer to be in a room and keep throwing ideas back and forth.

"Generally I've started with a premise and we worked on the premise. It would be a title or an idea or approximately a title, and then you'd get some pictures. Whenever I have an idea, I always write it out, but I never know beforehand whether it's very commercial or not. When I'm through, I know if it's a good song or if it isn't a good song. Some of my favorite songs would have no reason at all to be hits, they're just ideas that I liked that I worked through.

"I've written some very personal songs. 'Lonely Avenue,' that Ray Charles recorded, is about myself. And I have a couple of personal ones that nobody has seen except the publisher. But that's the nature of the process. When I get an idea, sometimes it's personal, sometimes it's an idea that's out of context. I just write the idea. But I'll tell you this, if you don't have a good melody I don't give a damn how good your lyric is. Whereas if you have a real strong melody, sometimes the lyrics can subordinate. Also, you're driven by a good melody, you'll write better lyrics. I got spoiled because the fellow I was working with all those years, Mort Shuman, was absolutely brilliant and it's just a shame that he doesn't want to be involved with popular songs anymore. So, unfortunately, you're at the mercy of your cowriter, which has bothered me for the last four or five years. Let me put it to you this way: Doing this for so many years, you develop a facility, and generally if I'm under contract to a firm, they'll put me with somebody who might not have even had a song published, let alone a hit song. And I'll be about three times as fast as he is and then I start getting depressed when there are lags along the way.

"I like to work with a song in parts. I'm not really geared to write the complete song. But I wind up writing about two-thirds of the song anyway simply because I'm working with someone who can't do anything. Or else you're subject to all the hang-ups of the cat. You know, if they don't have proper bowel movements that morning, forget about it. In my experience ninety percent of the guys you sit with, before you can actually do the first note, you gotta listen to their stories for about two hours. I'm just not in the mood for it anymore. And this is also with people who have great reputations. It's bad enough going through it with them, but

Figure 3. Doc Pomus, ca. 1947. Photo: William P. Gottlieb, Library of Congress. Public domain.

imagine when you have to go through it with an amateur. I remember there was a time about five years ago when I was under contract to Screen Gems and they had some heavy writers there and this one guy came over to write with me, and before we got a song going he spent two hours playing all his hits for me. I couldn't believe it. I knew all his hits and he knew all my hits, but he had to go through them all for two hours. We never wrote a song.

"I'll tell you something else; it's not necessarily true that the best songs are the ones that come easy. Some of the best songs I've written were hard to write, others were easy. 'Save the Last Dance for Me' was written in about thirty minutes, and yet another tune we wrote for the Drifters, 'I Count the Tears,' took us two weeks to write."

His most famous single record, "Teenager in Love," by Dion and the Belmonts once had three different versions in the British top ten during the same week. "I don't even remember writing 'Teenager in Love,'" he said. "It was an assignment. We wrote the other side of that record too and I always liked it better. It was a song called 'I've Cried Before.'

"The scariest thing is when you think you've found the formula and suddenly you realize there's no such animal," he said. "Catch anybody who's got a hit song and he'll show you fifty songs that you think are just as good that nothing happened to."

Doc Pomus's last appearance on the charts was the B. B. King recording of "There Must Be a Better World Somewhere" in 1981. He passed away in 1991.

Neil Sedaka (1980)

Influenced by doo-wop groups like the Penguins, the Nutmegs, and the Harptones; rhythm and blues crossovers like Chuck Berry, Little Richard, and Fats Domino; and the Latin rhythms of La Playa Sextet, Machito, and Tinto Puente, Neil Sedaka was among the first to sign on with Aldon Music, helmed by Donnie Kirshner and Al Nevins. He was following in the footsteps of his friend and neighbor, Carole King (née Klein).

"I met Carole either on a street corner or through a mutual friend," said Sedaka. "She would follow me around every time I appeared at a wedding or a bar mitzvah. Then we started going out socially and we were very close for a couple of years, until she met Gerry Goffin. She had a group, too, called the Cosines. Her mother told me that I was a bad influence on her, because she would neglect her schoolwork to write songs and to chase me from bar mitzvahs to weddings. And my mother would say, 'Why do you like her?' Because she was a chain-smoker. To my mother that was the worst, a sixteen-year-old girl who's a chain-smoker. I said, 'I'm intrigued with her.'"

Despite his string of hits, Neil Sedaka was an outcast in the teen idol era. "I had a lot of good years, but no one knew what I looked like," he told me. "I wasn't in too many of the teenage magazines. They went for the very pretty boys; I was too skinny. I didn't have the thing Fabian or Frankie Avalon had. They were in movies already. I was just a voice. I never did the Dick Clark tour. I was on *The Ed Sullivan Show* once. I played the Copacabana once. I played the Steel Pier in Atlantic City. Then came the bow tie and tuxedo—everybody wanted to be Bobby Darin. So I played the Twin Coaches, the Holiday House. They didn't want to take a chance on me bombing in the United States, so my first gigs were in the Philippines and Japan." When "Oh Carol" was number one in several international markets, he was the first American popstar to play Brazil. "I headlined with a group of Brazilian musicians who didn't speak English. We had arrangements for eight songs. That was the extent of the act."

Instead he held on to his day job at Aldon Music, later moving to their posh Fifth Avenue offices when Kirshner and Nevins sold out to Screen Gems. "I always worked the same way," said Sedaka. "I wrote the melody, or a good part of it, and Howie [Greenfield] would stand there and write the lyrics at the same time. I would sing them out, and if they didn't fit, he'd revise them. I learned to write a song in every beat, in every feel. I would study the records on the radio so I could play the top ten hits fluidly. There were assignments. I was in the office writing every day. We'd all wait until we came back with our demos and everybody used to sit in the office and listen. I remember Carole's demo of 'Will You Love Me Tomorrow.' It was marvelous. I came in with 'Breaking Up Is Hard to Do,' and Barry Mann and Cynthia Weil said it was very mediocre." It only turned out to be Neil's biggest hit, in 1962 reaching number one.

Looking back over the years, the charts, the numbers, Sedaka can recall names and positions much in the same manner an old ballplayer, one of the Boys of Summer, perhaps, can remember, down to the inning and the score, his opposite-field home runs with more than one man on. "'The Diary' just missed top ten. My second record, 'I Go Ape,' was a flop in this country, but a hit in Europe. My third record, 'Crying My Heart Out for You,' was a total flop. 'Oh Carol' started the string. Then there was 'Stairway to Heaven,' 'Run Samson Run,' 'You Mean Everything to Me,' 'Little Devil,' 'Happy Birthday, Sweet Sixteen,' 'Calendar Girl,' 'Breaking Up Is Hard to Do,' 'Next Door to an Angel,' and then they died away." Sedaka's recap contains a slightly selective memory lapse, for, during the stretch he's recalling, from 1959 to 1962, he also released "Sweet Little You" and "King of Clowns," both of which failed to make the top forty. Nevertheless, of the eleven records he had out in those four years, six made the top ten, and "Little Devil" just missed, at number eleven—an impressive streak.

Through it all, Neil still lived in Brooklyn. "I retained the same friends," he says, "I felt like a big fish in a small pond and I liked that, it was good for my ego. I felt uncomfortable being with celebrities. I never really indulged myself or had money so to speak. My mother took it all. She knew a gentleman who became my manager. I bought myself one car every year. When I traveled, it was for singing; I never went on vacations, was never into clothes. I did it for the power and the fame. I liked being

Figure 4. Sam Lender and Neil Sedaka. Photo: Carl Lender, Wikimedia Commons, CC BY 2.0.

recognized when I went into a place where they knew me from *The Ed Sullivan Show*. But I stayed the same old Neil; I never changed."

But something was changing. Every day the wheels of the top forty spun, and someone who was previously accustomed to being a winner could just as suddenly find himself on the outside looking in. "It was gradual," says Neil, speaking of the knowledge that the streak was over, maybe for good. "After 'Next Door to an Angel' was 'Alice in Wonderland,' which made top twenty. Then 'The Dreamer,' which only got into the forties. And my brother-in-law at the time—married to my sister—said, 'You know it's going to end.' I said, 'I know it,' but it was not easy to accept. At that time Neil Diamond became popular, and his parents were right across the street. They owned a clothing shop on Brighton Beach Avenue called Diamonds. And everybody said, 'Well, whatever happened to *you*? Neil Diamond is doing so great.' But little by little the records stopped, and I got over it," he says softly. "I got over it."

Neil Sedaka (1980) | 37

He was twenty-three at the time, just married, at the point in a young man's life when the future, if still indistinct, is definitely ahead. His was retreating, dancing backward into the past, vanishing into the air like a radio station sucked off the currents as the automobile ceaselessly blunders west. "I had made a great deal of money, but a lot of it went astray because of mismanagement, because of bad investments. I had an accountant, Allan Klein, who made me buy a building in Birmingham, Alabama, for $150,000. That went down the drain. I didn't have charge of my money. I was married to my wife and we were living in a fantasy. My money, my entire life was being run by Donnie Kirshner, Al Nevins, my mother, and my mother's friend."

Dutifully, maybe desperately, he clung to the songwriter's trade. When Don Kirshner sold Aldon Music to Screen Gems in 1963 for a few million clams, Sedaka and Greenfield, along with Carole and Gerry and the rest of the crew, changed offices, moving east to Fifth Avenue. Ironically, this post-chart period turned out to be one of his most prolific in terms of writing. "I wrote with three lyricists, five days a week," says Neil. "I was writing with Carole Sager, Howie Greenfield, and Roger Atkins. I said I could write like Paul McCartney, and I did write like Paul McCartney, but it was very hard to get records when I wasn't singing the songs. I made one record for Colgems, which was a part of Screen Gems, called 'Rainy Jane,' produced by myself and Howie Greenfield, and it was terrific. I heard it once, I think, on WNBC. The only time I'd hear myself on the radio was when an oldie would come on. So I felt, well this is it, I'd better get resigned to the fact that I had my shot and it'll never happen again."

Through the rest of the sixties Sedaka penned singles sporadically, but his songs did show up on albums by Johnny Mathis, Peggy Lee, the Partridge Family, and the in-house group, the Monkees. He also had "Working on a Groovy Thing" and "Puppet Man," which were top-twenty items for the Fifth Dimension in 1970 . . . the first signs of what was to be a long and grueling, often humiliating climb back to the very top. Carole King's landmark *Tapestry* album of 1971 was another harbinger that the wheel was about to spin again.

"When I heard that album it blew me away," he says. "I said, 'Oh my God, that's my style, the piano, the voice, the whole approach to melody—we grew up together.' And I begged Donnie Kirshner to let me do an album for RCA. I wrote probably the best collection of songs I ever wrote in my life. I was going to do it like Carole, with a small group. But Donnie called me in, and he said, 'You're a classical artist. You have

38 | They're Playing My Song

to have a big symphonic thing.' And he called in Lee Holdridge, who's a brilliant arranger, and the songs came out sounding like magnificent things that should have been on the Broadway stage. The album was too classy, and it was against the market; RCA was not about to promote it. So *Emergence* was a flop, and it shattered Howie Greenfield and me, and we split up for two and a half years."

This was no mere professional parting here, after twenty years. This was childhood's end. "It was very sad," Sedaka recalls. "Howie moved to California. Just before he left we wrote two songs; one was called 'Our Last Song Together,' the other was 'Love Will Keep Us Together,' which I think was kind of like his plea. We both cried."

For the performer and the lyricist, the tears, like the tides and the tables, would turn, but not before a painful hegira to the lower depths. Greenfield faced down a two-year silence. Sedaka pocketed his ego and knelt before imposing club owners, more unknown than he'd ever been as a teenager. "The original record of 'Oh Carol' had been rereleased by RCA and was a hit in England. So I picked up my wife, my two kids, and Mary the housekeeper, and we moved to London. I got a job at a real toilet in Manchester." Then he was introduced to an area group called Hotlegs, which had a studio in Stockport. "They were marvelous," Sedaka recalls. "I sat down and recorded a whole album with them. I spent $6,000 and recorded an album called *Solitaire*. It had 'Solitaire' on it, 'That's Where the Music Takes Me,' 'Standing on the Inside.' And I brought it back to Donnie, and he said, 'Well, I'm not sure.' He got RCA to put it out—on a shoestring. Nothing happened. But I knew when I heard the record that I was on the right track."

His second album in England was entitled *The Tra La Days Are Over*, also recorded with Hotlegs, who were by then better known as 10cc. It marked another step forward along the comeback route. But the light at the end of the tunnel had to come from America; his self-enforced exile required the kind of hero's welcome only a hit record could provide. And who else could give him and his career the kind of boost that was needed—a blurb, a pat on the back—but his chain-smoking buddy from the old neighborhood, his songwriting stablemate turned LA superstar, Carole King. She was divorced from Gerry Goffin but hopefully still funky enough to remember Andrea's Pizza Parlor.

"I saw her when I went to LA to record another album for England," Sedaka recounts. "She said, 'What are you doing here?' Like she owned LA. I said, 'I'm recording at Clover studios,' and she said, 'Oh, that's nice,'

Neil Sedaka (1980) | 39

almost resentful. She didn't want to know of the past, or have anybody infringing on her territory." The album, *Laughter in the Rain*, produced the single of the same title that was a smash in England (and which in 1975 became a number one song for Sedaka in the US).

"By that time Elton John and I were pretty close," Sedaka says. "We had met many times at Bee Gees concerts; we were both friendly with Maurice Gibb. One night at my apartment in London we had a big party and I took Elton and [his manager] John Reid aside. I said, 'I'm frustrated. I have a hit in England. I'm now a concert artist in England. You've got to help me.' It just so happened that they were in the process of opening Rocket Records. I said, 'Don't pay me. I don't want any money. Just put out a compilation album, some of the things I did with 10cc, some of the things I did in LA. All I want is your endorsement.' And that's what he did. The album was *Sedaka's Back*, and he wrote on the jacket, 'Neil Sedaka's songs are great . . .' "

The next time Sedaka went to Los Angeles, it was to headline at the Troubadour. "I took over the town," he modestly exclaims. "Every producer in town was there." The comeback was complete; the hero was home. "I wanted it with a vengeance," Sedaka says. "Donnie Kirshner said I would never make it again; that drove me. My old manager said I'd never make it again; that drove me. Carole King; that drove me. I knew I was good, and I spent hours at the piano. I wasn't afraid of it. My voice was a great help to me, too, because I knew that nobody could sing those songs like me, nobody. The critics in LA couldn't believe that anybody could write and sing with such enthusiasm, with such spirit, and with this vengeance."

Sedaka, it appears, would agree with Frank Sinatra about the loveliness of the second time around. "It felt much better," Neil concurs. "I was now managing my own affairs. Everything creative was in my hands. I had a more well-rounded performing career. I broke into Vegas. I had that experience opening for the Carpenters, where I blew them off the stage. Leba and I, when we went to England, had to call on radio stations. I had to schlep to those places. I had to lower myself, humble myself. Now I appear on TV practically whenever I want." And the crowning touch, the icing on the cake, or, if you're from Brooklyn, the foam on the egg cream, was the BMI award for Most Performed Song of the Year, on the Captain and Tennille's recording of "Love Will Keep Us Together."

Sedaka palms the award proudly. "It was the dream of a lifetime. I mean, I'd been going to that BMI dinner since I was a kid. I got six awards in one year, including the Most Performed Song of 1976." He looks down

40 | They're Playing My Song

at the award, then corrects himself, "1975, I mean, beating out 'Rhinestone Cowboy.' I was afraid of 'Rhinestone Cowboy.'"

The slight error in chronology cools the moment, reminds him his valiant comeback is even further down the pike than he'd recalled. He resumes his seat on the couch, rather like the 1979 New York Yankees. He muses a while on that song, laden with sentiment, symbol of his odyssey in rock 'n' roll. "It was such a smash," he says, "why didn't I put it out myself as a single? After 'Laughter in the Rain' came out, I had ten other songs on *Sedaka's Back*, but I picked 'The Immigrant,' because it was a beautiful song and a beautiful record, and it made number twenty-two—after a number one."

He leans forward, at the edge of a painful conclusion. "I just can't last more than three or four years on the chart. I just can't. The last three years my records have stopped selling, and I'm eating my *kishkas* out. Thank God I have a performing career. But, being a record person, I feel very frustrated at this point. I have two albums out on Elektra Records that have not sold, and I'm discouraged.

"Even though I have fame, I have money, I have a wonderful family, I feel very unhappy, because it's always the records that have driven me. It becomes a way of life—what am I on ABC, what am I on KHJ? Unless you see it go up on the charts, you've failed. I was lucky enough to have it all those years; perhaps it'll never come again. Perhaps I don't have that creative spark anymore. Perhaps I'm not hungry enough. I could be bigger. I could be richer. But I just started writing again last week, after not writing for almost a year, and it scares the hell out of me."

∽

Neil Sedaka has rerecorded many of his early hits and become a popular nightclub performer. His memoir, Laughter in the Rain, *came out in 1982.*

Hank Ballard (1980)

"The Twist"

He was floating in a swimming pool the first time he heard it on the radio, flat on his back in Miami, Florida, in the summer of 1960. "I thought it was me," Hank Ballard recalls. "I was sure it was me. I was wondering why they were playing it on the radio. I didn't find out it wasn't me until a few weeks later." By that time Chubby Checker's version of the song Hank Ballard had written and recorded in 1958 (as the flip side of his hit "Teardrops on Your Letter"), entitled "The Twist," was on its way to its first appearance in the number one slot on the top forty (it would be back again in 1962); Chubby Checker was dancing his way to a career-two-three-four. "They did a pretty good job duplicating my record, man, note for note, gimmick for gimmick, phrase for phrase. Dick Clark auditioned about twenty people before he picked Chubby Checker. And I could have sworn it was me; that's how close he came to my sound."

In 1958 Hank tried to convince Syd Nathan, then president of his label, King Records, that "The Twist" indeed had hit potential. But with the ballad side, written by Henry Glover, vice president of the label, heading for the top of the rhythm and blues chart, it wasn't difficult to fathom the reasoning behind King's reluctance to jump on it. "The members of my group, the Midnighters, were doing the dance," Hank says. "They were twisting, so that's where I got the idea of writing the song. But the company thought it was just another record." A couple of years later, however, Dick Clark, the man who'd persuaded Danny and the Juniors to rewrite their "Do the Bop" (turning it into the future standard "At the Hop"), once again heard intimations of immortality on a piece of dented plastic. Thereafter he programmed Chubby's version on "The Twist" relentlessly on his *American Bandstand* program.

"I can't complain," says Hank, magnanimous in retrospect. "It's one of the best copyrights I have. Dick Clark did me a favor; otherwise the song would never have been heard. I made a lot of money on that song. Of course, it was just a drop in the bucket compared to what Chubby made." In fact, the sudden renewed prominence of the aging flip side did much to fan the brushfires of resentment among the members of his group, the original inspiration for the lyric. Their manager at the time, Connie Dinkler, was convinced that Hank had been ripped off. "She spent so much money trying to overshadow Chubby Checker," Hank recalls with a rueful laugh. "She'd tell photographers to keep the camera on me. Oh boy, what's she say that shit for? There was a lot of dissension in the group about that, a lot of jealousy. But even she couldn't get around Dick Clark. He was too powerful. He was like a teenage god."

Meanwhile, Clark was playing Ballard's "Finger Poppin' Time," essentially a remake of "The Twist," which became a top ten item, reviving his flagging career. "A lot of people don't realize that when 'The Twist' broke for Chubby Checker, we got hot too. We were working 365 days a year. We had to beg for time off." After 1965 Hank Ballard would have all the time off he wanted to contemplate dance steps he might have championed. By then his original group would be long gone too.

"What happened is that they all became Muslims and their whole attitude changed about music. They didn't want to work anymore white dates; they didn't want to sign a white autograph. They became fanatical and I couldn't deal with them." Hank won the Midnighters name in court. He picked up a Cincinnati group that had his old act down cold, and what remained of the beat went on without his original sidemen. "I was mentally prepared for the decline," he says. "You have to save your mind. If you start thinking you're a god up there, you're in trouble. I'm not just into money. I get a lot of spiritual enjoyment out of my profession."

Back in Miami now, where he wrote "The Twist" in 1958, and where he returned for a weekend in 1979 and decided to stay, ensconced in none of the trappings of royalty (or even royalty deposed), Hank and his second wife occupy a small apartment in a sun-bleached armada of buildings off Biscayne Boulevard, probably not dissimilar to apartments he's lived for most of his life in New York City, Atlanta, Nashville, and Detroit. Born in Detroit in 1936, he moved to a small town outside of Birmingham, Alabama, with his brother when he was seven years old to live with an aunt and uncle, after his father, a truck driver, died.

"But I was a runaway at fourteen, man," he exclaims across a dining room table, color TV providing the background music. "That part of the family was heavy into religion. They used to beat me if they caught me humming the blues in the house. They couldn't understand. I was not allowed to sing anything but gospel. I had to get out of that." After the eighth grade he dropped out of school and returned to Detroit to live with another set of relatives. "I was never really family oriented," says Hank. "I have about ten thousand relatives, but I live more like a drifter." Alabama wasn't a total loss, however. "I got my gospel roots down there," Hank affirms.

Detroit in the early fifties was quite a funky town. You had the Four Tops imitating the Four Freshmen backing crooner Billy Eckstine. Berry Gordy was still on the assembly line, heading toward a career in the ring. He used to spar with Hank's brother. When Berry began to exhibit other career leanings, a Ballard first cousin, Florence, was part and parcel of his success, putting Motown on the musical map as a member of the *quartet* called the Supremes. (The fourth girl, Barbara, would drop out before the hits started to happen, to become a nurse; Florence would leave in 1967, at a dizzying plateau of stardom, and die tragically, on welfare, years later, while lady Diana sang the blues on the silver screen.) Berry also signed the Four Tops to his fledgling label.

"Berry Gordy made rock singers out of them," Hank Ballard recalls. "I couldn't believe it was the Four Tops when I first heard them. I didn't think they could holler that loud."

At sixteen, courtesy of the Korean War, Hank was allowed to sign on with Ford Motors. There his singing aspirations were recognized by a fellow worker, who was part of a group called the Royals, one of whose members had just been taken into that distant fray. (Hank would visit Korea on the Uncle Sam charter, spending nine months there in peacetime service.) The Royals already had an R&B hit, "Every Beat of My Heart," written by Johnny Otis (later revived by Gladys Knight and—her cousins—the Pips). Hank, with no professional experience at all to that point, but plenty of amateur acclaim, auditioned, then won a place in the group. He appeared at the Fox Theatre in Detroit where his idol, Clyde McPhatter, was headlining with Billy Ward and the Dominoes. Soon Hank became lead singer and songwriter for the group. "They were a real sweet Sonny Til and the Orioles style," he says of the incipient Midnighters. "I had them change to a more driving, up-tempo thing. You know, let's get funky!"

Funky they got; so funky that their records, like "Get It," "Sexy Ways," and "Work with Me Annie," were banned from the radio. They were even arrested for giving lewd performances onstage. "The South was

Figure 5. Hank Ballard, 1988. Photo: Los Angeles Times Photographic Collection, OpenUCLA Collections, CC BY-SA 4.0.

our territory. We didn't do too much touring in the East. They were afraid of our act. Like the Apollo, they threw us out of the Apollo," he says, not bothering to repress the laughter. "We went to Philadelphia, we sold out for the whole ten days. The Apollo wouldn't let us do our act; now you can do anything. They let Richard Pryor come in there and do his act." But what, precisely, did the act consist of? "Doing dirty shit onstage," says Hank nostalgically, "like dropping your pants. I didn't do none of it," he claims, "it was just the group. We had so much negative publicity, then we see Sam and Dave on TV, Frank Sinatra, dropping their pants . . ." While this story would seem necessarily to be somewhat apocryphal, their racy reputation decidedly was not. "We were a very glamorous group, but mentally I didn't get into it. I'm very low-key. I don't care for all that glamour. It never does anything for me. I call it 'commercial admiration.' But as far back as I remember we had a white audience, because they loved those dirty records, man. We sold a lot of damn records. We used to play colleges. They'd yell, 'Get dirty!' " In his spirited recollection the cry sounds like a killer hook in some avant-garde disco cut. "Most of the stuff that Alice Cooper did, all that stage shit, we were doing that years ago. They weren't as liberal then about a lot of things. They're even cursing on records now."

In those days most of Hank's cursing was done in private, and mostly at his own expense. Foreshadowing the events of 1958–1960, Hank undoubtedly cursed his rotten luck when his group, the Royals, became confused with another R&B group, the Five Royales. As Chubby Checker was to succeed them in another decade, the Five Royales wound up capitalizing on a Hank Ballard song much more than Hank and his group ever did. Riding on their hit called "Baby Don't Do It," the Five Royales were inadvertently considered the group responsible for "Annie Had a Baby," well on its way to becoming a huge record. Although the Royals quickly changed their name to the Midnighters, the damage had been done. "The Royales had gone out on tour and really cleaned up. So the promoters didn't want to book us. We sounded similar, you know? The promoters didn't want to gamble on us, even though we were the originators."

The copyright, however, was Hank's, as was one-third of the proceeds on "Dance with Me, Henry" (probably Henry Glover, vice president of King Records), on which Georgia Gibbs scored with the mass-market listening audience. It was the answer song, edited edition, expletives deleted, of "Work with Me Annie," itself descended from Etta James's "The Wallflower," which contained the phrase, "Roll with me Henry," deemed too salacious for tender ears. ("Work with Me Annie" was based on a real Ballard ex-girlfriend Annie, who really did have a baby, as per yet another follow-up record, "Annie Had a Baby," written by Henry Glover; "Annie's Aunt Fanny," written by Ballard, closed the series and the soap opera.)

Songwriting has been good to Hank Ballard, but not as good as it could have been had he, like most modern self-contained singer-songwriter acts, insisted on maintaining a piece of the publishing rights. "The company I was with said there's no such thing," he laughs today. "King Records, shit, if you asked for publishing rights, they'd give you your contract back. I didn't know there was so much money involved in publishing. They would tell me, 'You've got to write a hundred songs before you can even get a BMI contract,' and I found out later all you had to do is write one song. On my early tunes I didn't even have a BMI contract. I got it later, but they didn't even tell me I had to apply for it."

46 | They're Playing My Song

Most fledgling performers knew nothing at all about management either. "Man, I hate to even think about the way we were took. But what can you do, man? We were ignorant, and they were beneficiaries of that. Very few people were lucky enough to find a manager like Elvis Presley had." Hank Ballard and the Midnighters were managed briefly by Jim Evans, who managed Wilson Pickett, among others. "Jim Evans came out to Detroit from New York," Hank notes, "and he tied us up in a contract where he was getting fifty percent of our money. We didn't know a god-damned thing about it. When we found out, we took him to court and got out of that contract, man. Jim Evans had about ten thousand acts then; he had everybody."

In those days, the manager's job seemed more secretarial than anything else. If the caller on the other end of the line was willing to pay the price, the manager would accept the date, take his cut, and let the chips fall where they might. Such niceties as career-planning and longevity, routing, and proper accommodations were unheard of. Besides, what did it matter if the next gig was five hundred or seven hundred miles away? Chances are the few Black hotels in the vicinity would be filled with truck drivers, salesmen, or maybe a semipro ball team, anyway. Thus were the act encouraged to spend their nights on the road. This attitude toward Black performers prevailed until Berry Gordy, at Motown, put some structure and guidance into the business and made the artists feel a bit more secure, esteemed as human beings with a lifespan of more than six months to a year.

"They had these houses where you could go to where people would put you up for the night," Hank Ballard recalls, leading into a particularly gruesome flashback, an episode illustrating the awful necessity in those days of having to cover so much ground so quickly between jobs. "I was with Jesse Belvin the day he got killed. About an hour prior to him having that accident, I had gotten out of his car because I didn't like his driving. He was passing on hills and curves, going a hundred miles an hour. Next thing I knew they had a head-on collision. His wife could have lived, but she didn't want to live after losing him. The guy in the backseat, one of the Moonglows, was the only survivor, but he wound up getting hooked on painkillers at the hospital, on morphine, and he had an overdose at a hospital in Harlem soon after."

Such things as cover records, phony contracts, and misdirected royalties momentarily paled. Memory drifts to the good time at the beginning, tours through the Midwest with Alan Freed, then only a small-fry promoter starting to get hot. Six dates with Chuck Willis in Cleveland, Akron, Youngstown, and Cincinnati were the first professional gigs for Hank and the group. "Alan Freed broke things wide open when he started packaging a lot of acts and taking them into ball stadiums. They didn't have promoters like that before him. It was a big high for me, being independent. I liked being self-employed, yeah. But when I first went on the road, I didn't like it. I was almost tempted to go back to Ford Motors. You could see it was an abnormal way to live. Then it became normal."

Eventually, though, thoughts return to the same bottom line. "What I'm doing now is what I should have been doing then, you know? I should have had my own production company and everything. But we didn't know anything, and there was nobody that was ever going to tell you about it, because you had some dues you had to pay. But I don't hold anybody responsible for my being ripped off but myself. I just read the paper the other day where Bo Diddley said he sold all of his copyrights. Otis Blackwell sold the copyright on 'Fever' to Henry Glover for fifty dollars. Glover also bought 'Dedicated to the One I Love' from Lowman Pauling of the Five Royales for two or three hundred dollars. I can understand the circumstances. Circumstances can make you do a lot of things. I once bought a hit for twenty-five dollars." He chuckles, working his way back to the famous high, satisfied laugh. "I bought it from some guy who was locked out of his hotel in New York. It was 'Switch-a-Roo,' I think. I only gave the guy twenty-five dollars. It did almost half a million records."

According to a certain, possibly marginal, reference source, the writers of "Fever" are listed on the version recorded by Peggy Lee as Davenport and Cooley; years later when the McCoys revived it, Cooley had been mysteriously dropped from the credits, though the publishing company remained Lois. There is no record of who got credit for the original put out by Little Willie John in 1956. Lowman Pauling, along with Ralph Bass, is listed under the Shirelles' remake on the Royales' "Dedicated to the One I Love," but when the Mamas and Papas put it out in 1967, the name Ruff was inexplicably added, and the publishing company had changed from Armo to Trousdale. Go sort it out. You run into a maze of Chinese boxes, doors opening onto empty hallways, laundered signatures, and floating back accounts. And you can't ask Lowman Pauling anymore; he's been dead five years.

In time you could wind up like Bo Diddley, encountered at a hotel room in New York, staring fixedly at a succession of color TV game shows

48 | They're Playing My Song

while outlining his elaborate systems for the eventual recovery for his vanished money. "I don't think the public likes that I was ripped off," he muttered bitterly, proceeding to reveal how the club owners, managers, publishers, record companies, and booking agents of America were having at him still. "I just want to get what I deserve from my product. Just give me mine and I'll be happy."

To which, months later, in Miami, Hank Ballard would reply: "The way I figure it, you're responsible for your own ass."

When King Records was sold to Fort Knox Music in 1967, after Syd Nathan died, Hank Ballard was set free. "The company just wasn't up to par with promotion—they had very poor promotion. But it was one of those things where I had a good rapport going with them and I was afraid to make another move. We always had plenty of work, even when we didn't have a record out. We were red hot for a good ten to twelve years." Of course life with King, as with all families, was sometimes less than sweet. "Syd Nathan was the stingiest man in the world," Hank cackles, lovingly caustic. "Nobody could get as much out of one dollar as Syd Nathan could. Just to prove a point once he said, I'm going to show you how I can conserve $20,000 a month. So he started cutting back on everything, even the electricity. You'd go in the toilet and there weren't no light on!"

Yet Hank's career after King's demise reads like a litany of near misses, botched chances, and strikeouts with the bases loaded. He went in with James Brown, for whom he'd originally helped get a contract at King. "I wanted to be with Polydor so bad," Hank says, "and I figured if I got with James Brown's production company, that would be like a stepping stone. I was with James for a year and a half, but he killed it off. He stopped a hit record on me. That's what fouled it up. I had a record going so hot called 'In the Love Side,' on Polydor. All of a sudden we had 250,000 records gone. I did *Soul Train* and sales started coming; James got so paranoid and nervous because he didn't have anything going at the time that he called every jock in the country and told them to take it off their lists. I told him, 'That's it for me.' I just walked away from it." Next Hank moved to Nashville and did some work for Shelby Singleton.

"I'd grown up listening to country music—Marty Robbins, Hank Williams. I always did want to get country into R&B. The Commodores, that's the groove I was trying to get into. I did a tune for SS Records by Kris Kristofferson, 'Sunday Morning Coming Down.' Now that was a masterpiece, man. I know it because Jerry Wexler heard it and tried to buy the master from them. The record was never released. SS Records was in

Hank Ballard (1980) | 49

trouble with the Mafia at the time. Shelby Singleton had to go into hiding for a year, man; they were after him. I did an R&B version of the song that was really pretty. I have a copy of it and I'm going to record it over."

By 1980 the downslide seems to have extended far longer than the up slide ever did. But Hank regards it with remarkable perspective "You have to condition yourself for the decline," he says. "I've never had a star complex, thinking you're god. How the hell are you going to be a god when you got a top one hundred out there? Everybody with a hit record thinks they're a god overnight; you got a hundred gods! I've never tried to rise above ordinary people. I like ordinary people. I've never been on that star trip, but I've seen a lot of my associates destroy themselves. Take Clyde McPhatter. He was my idol; I was crazy about Clyde McPhatter. But he had an emotional problem that he never did outlive. He drank himself to death. Little Willie John, same thing."

Which doesn't mean Hank Ballard has given up on the thought of making music. In April 1979, for instance, he broke a four-year performing fast to headline several nights at the Howard Theater in Washington, DC, along with the Flamingos and Baby Washington. "I was scared," he admits. And shocked by the turnout, a full house each night, complete with ovations. "I had a hang-up about working in oldie shows. I just didn't want to get into that oldie thing; I wanted to play contemporary, you know?"

The success of the show has given him the incentive to think about a return engagement somewhere down the road, hopefully on the heels of a smash. "I want to concentrate now on having a big hit record," he says. "I'm going to do what Neil Sedaka did, come back with a big record, come back with a hit, man." Toward that end he closed up shop in New York City, after eight largely fruitless years there, and headed out where the weather suited his casual clothes. In Miami his prospects immediately improved when he ran into another legend from the seminal rock 'n' roll days of the fifties, Luther Dixon, arranger and producer of many of the Shirelles' classics, just back from an extended sabbatical in Jamaica.

"I had a studio started when I met Luther here," Hank says, "but I was running kind of short of funds and I needed some extra money, so I brought him in. He had a lot of contacts over at Criteria Studios in Miami, and we decided to form a joint venture. Luther has a monster catalog, about five hundred to six hundred songs. I have close to two hundred. You can survive as long as you're writing. If a hit don't happen you'll just keep writing." Their production company's first effort was Hank's "Freak Your Boom Boom," released a little late for the disco derby. "We got a

50 | They're Playing My Song

good reaction on 'Freak Your Boom Boom,'" says Hank, chuckling. "A lot of people in Europe had thought I was dead." Now they're producing Chuck Jackson on a song written by Bob Marley.

"Chuck's been down here rehearsing. We think we can get a hit on Chuck. Everybody else is coming back. Dionne Warwick is back with a hit. But it's a more competitive scene today," he acknowledges. "Most of the time in the past you could just walk up to a microphone and start singing any damn thing. I know James used to do that a lot, and Jimmy Reed. You have to be more meticulous now. The public ain't buying unless it's good. They want a good track and good lyrics. At one time you could get away with just a good track. You got to have both now. Disco is damn near completely out. The beat is still there, but the lyrics are different. Rock 'n' roll is coming back, same as it was twenty to twenty-five years ago. On the radio it sounds like fifties music."

While most of this new rock 'n' roll is being played by kids who weren't even born when Hank Ballard was out there—getting banned from the airwaves and public stages for being lewd and crude, blazing off-color trails with "Sexy Ways" and "Annie Had a Baby"—some, you can be sure, is the fevered product of ageless vets closer to forty-five than sixteen. And like this latest swing back to rock 'n' roll seems to prove, they were never gone at all, only waiting, enduring, on the outskirts of major cities, at the edges of subsistence. "You know," says Hank Ballard, always ready to see the bright side, "they made a survey and found out that seventy percent of all records are now sexually oriented. If you listen, you'll hear sex in nearly every damn thing. Even Helen Reddy had a song out—'Make Love to Me.' Boy," he laughs his swooping laugh, "that was hot stuff."

Hank Ballard passed away in 2003. He was inducted into the Rock and Roll Hall of Fame in 1990.

Gerry Goffin (1974)

A reclusive figure since his midsixties heyday, rumored to have suffered a breakdown after signing a $100,000 contract with Screen Gems, Gerry Goffin, when I interviewed him, was working through a difficult relationship to the songs he created with his first wife, Carole King. "Irwin Schuster [head of Screen Gems Music] gave me a list of songs I wrote and I can't believe some of the titles," he said when I interviewed him.

"Does it seem like a whole other person wrote them?" I asked.

"I *know* I wrote them, that's what hurts."

It was this half-kidding, evasive tone that Goffin adopted for most of the interview.

"When did you start taking lyric writing seriously?"

"I never took it seriously."

"Do you think youth plays a great part in the productivity of a songwriter?"

"Stupidity helps."

After a while, he did start owning up to his legacy.

"I'm not gonna say whether my songs were good or bad. It's pretty good to be successful at songwriting. If the people like them, that's fine and I'm happy. There was a time when I used to cringe hearing them; now I don't anymore because I figure it was that time and it was okay. I mean, you've got to realize when I started writing songs. There's been several revolutions that have taken place in pop music since then, and I think they were all improvements. I've always thought, any way you looked at it, that the changes have been for the better. I mean, it's better than having assignments. Groups are writing now for their own personal feelings. It's a whole different thing. To me that's a little more honest, not that I didn't enjoy what I was doing."

Back in those days, "it was write a song for this group or write a song for so and so. That was our job, Carole and I, and it was a lot of fun. When you're young, you don't mind doing that so much. When you get a little older, you sort of rebel against that and you get a tendency to want not to write to a market. I can't write under deadlines anymore . . . but I respect people who can. Right now, I'm just writing what I feel like writing and I keep changing. If I want to write something commercial, I don't see anything wrong with it. If I want to write a song that I feel personally, I don't see anything wrong with that either.

His first solo album, *It Ain't Exactly Entertainment* (Adelphi Records), is a package containing sixteen originals, with not one being a typical top forty song. A good percentage of the songs could be termed "protest"—a type of writing that was most popular during the period Goffin was struggling to turn out gems for the Drifters, the Shirelles, and the Monkees. Also on the album are quite a few lyrics in which Goffin probably reveals himself to a greater extent than he will in any interview. One in particular, "Everything and Nothing," seemed, quite adeptly, to describe his ambivalent feelings as to his past achievements and his current prospects.

"There's also another thing," Goffin summed it up. "There's a certain magic that some records have and that some records don't have and that's not a quality you can capture unless everything is going right, and that's something that comes and goes and there's no formula for it. I'm talking about at a record session. There are so many personalities involved, so many variables. Sometimes you could write a mediocre song and it becomes a big hit. When you're writing something good, it always seems to be easy. Anytime it took me a long time to write a song it usually wasn't too good a song. When I say good, I mean something that's right, marketable, that has something to say. It has to go through a lot of different ears; different people have to decide if it's something that people want to hear. If it gets on the radio and if people want to hear it, they buy it. That's how I thought I could tell if a song was going to be a hit or not, or how big a hit it would be—by listening to it on the radio. I never listened at home; I used to always listen in the car. It was just something about the resonance of the car radio, usually with the good records you caught the sound of a hit single like 'Up on the Roof.'"

At pains to sum up his contribution to the literature of what it was like to be a teen in America in the late fifties and early sixties, Goffin gave the lion's share of the credit to another writer. "I think Chuck Berry wrote a more accurate picture than me," he said. "I didn't realize how good his

Gerry Goffin (1974) | 53

lyrics were—because I didn't listen to lyrics much, I mean I just sort of enjoyed them—until I got a job and had to write them every day."

∽

Not long after my interview, Goffin apparently snapped out of his slump, eventually winning an Academy Award nomination for his collaboration with Michael Masser, "Theme from Mahogany (Do You Know Where You're Going To)." In 1984 he scored with the international hit for Whitney Houston "Saving All My Love for You," also written with Masser. In 1996, he released the album Back Room Blood, *which included two collaborations with his idol, Bob Dylan, "Back Room Blood" and "Tragedy of the Trade."*

Jackie DeShannon (2012)

"Put a Little Love in Your Heart"

With a resume that includes touring with the Beatles as an opening act in 1964, a Song of the Year Grammy Award for "Bette Davis Eyes" in 1981, and induction into the Songwriter's Hall of Fame alongside Leonard Cohen, Laura Nyro, and Bob Marley in 2010, Jackie DeShannon is at something of a loss when it comes to picking out the one song that had the most impact on her career. "Well, I have several choices," she said. "As a songwriter, 'Dum Dum' by Brenda Lee was my breakthrough in 1961. As a singer, 'What the World Needs Now' was my first major hit in 1965."

Written by Burt Bacharach and Hal David, that song was among the many they sampled for Jackie before going into the studio. "When Hal suggested that Burt play 'What the World Needs Now,' Burt was not that enthused about showing it to me at that moment," Jackie said. "So we went on, played some more songs, and tried to decide on the four sides that we would record for the session. At that point Hal again suggested that Burt play 'What the World Needs Now.' And reluctantly, I think, he played it for me. Of course it was love at first hearing and first sight at those gorgeous words and fantastic melody. There were cornfields and wheat fields in my back yard where I grew up in Kentucky on a farm, and I heard a little bit of a gospel feel in the chorus. I thought it was a match made in heaven. The minute Burt heard me singing it, he said, 'Off to New York! We're off to New York!' That's where we recorded the song."

Although "What the World Needs Now" would hit the top ten in the spring of 1965, Jackie wasn't immediately able to follow it up. "I did have some chart records but there were a lot of issues with the record company, a lot of marketing things I wasn't happy with. For instance, 'Needles and

Pins' was top five in Detroit, top five in Chicago, and top five in every city it was played in. However, unless you're coordinated across the country and the song hits the charts at the same time, you can't get the big leaps. My record didn't have that, because it would be going down in Chicago while it was going up in some other city. So that was a problem.

" 'The Weight' was another story. I absolutely said, 'No way I'm going to do it, it's the Band's record, goodbye.' But the label kept calling me, so I finally said, 'Well, if you can get confirmation from the Band that they're not putting it out as a single and I can do it with their permission, then okay.' So, I recorded it. The record's going up the chart and all of a sudden, here comes the Band's single. Then Aretha Franklin's version comes out. So I was at a radio station talking to the program director, and there were two other people promoting the same record outside the door."

In terms of "Put a Little Love in Your Heart," she says, "I was just writing for this album that was up and coming, and that was one of the songs. My brother Randy was playing this little riff and I said, 'Gee, I really like that riff, that's great.' All of a sudden, 'Think of your fellow man / lend him a helping hand / put a little love in your heart,' came just like that. I owe some of that to my mom, because she was always saying that people should put a little love in their heart when things are not so good. I'd like to say it was very difficult, but it was one of those songs you wait a lifetime to write.

"So we went into the studio to record it and it took a long time to get the right feel. It was either too slow or too fast. The demo was so good that everything we worked on to try to recast it didn't feel right. It's just something that you feel and if it wasn't close to the same feeling, you just had to keep pushing on. Some people record the same song for days. After about eight hours we finally got it and I just felt that I had done probably one of my best vocals ever. But when I came back in to hear it somehow my vocal was erased. Somebody must have hit something. I called my mom and I said, 'You know what, I'm just heartbroken. I've probably done the best vocal *ever*—at least it felt to me that it was right on the button—and I have to go do it again.' So I went right back in there fast, before I lost the muse. When I got to hear the new vocal, I felt that, of course, I wished I could have had the other one. But who's to say? Maybe this was the better vocal.

"The song was released in June, even before the album was done. It was the first single. I was very fortunate. A program director in Atlanta, I believe, was the first person to go on it. And then other stations heard it and they went on it. I think by August it was doing pretty well. Of course, I was watching it every week as it went up the charts. It's so thrilling to be part of something like that. At around number thirty, WABC went on it in New York and that was it. Because WABC usually picked records for their Pick of the Week that were top five. But they went on it early and then the rest of the country went on it. The airplay was great, and in those days if you had a record in rotation, that could be very good money. I was actually able to buy a car for my dad, and I bought a house for my parents.

"A lot of people still know that song. It came out at a time when we were all trying to make things better in this world. Everybody was sort of pulling together. I believe around that time I put together a show. I did the Copa in New York and some other major places. I did quite a lot of touring with that song. I went to a lot of places where I would just ask people off the street, or if I was doing a show and I was early, I would ask someone that was setting up tables, 'Have you ever heard the song "Put a Little Love in Your Heart"?' And they'd always say, 'Oh, yeah.' I think it's been recorded by over sixty artists. Mahalia Jackson did a great job on it. Annie Lennox and Al Green weren't too bad either. I'm thrilled with everyone that recorded the song. It was in a Smart Balance commercial for the last two years. Someone called me and told me it was done on *American Idol*. It's definitely the gift that keeps on giving.

"After it peaked in the fall of 1969 we took 'Love Will Find a Way' from the album, and that did chart. But it's very difficult to follow a 'What the World Needs Now' or 'Put a Little Love in Your Heart.' You have to remember that I, being a woman at that time, did not have the kind of leverage that young women today have. They go in, they own their publishing, they're the producer, they're the writer, they're everything. In those days, I would go in with producers and they would agree with me before we got in the studio about the vision of the song. Then we would get in the studio and they'd change it all around and if you said anything, you were being difficult. Now the more difficult you are, the more they respect you. But it was hard to get that respect. I was producing demos all the time, but when I went in the studio with many, many different producers, a lot of things fell apart because it wasn't my vision. Having a hit certainly helped in the short term, but you have to remember, there's a heckuva lot of songwriters around and a lot of politics. A lot of different things that the public probably isn't even aware of that go on with getting songs in this movie, and getting songs in that television show. It's not just

Oh, let's sit down and pick the best thing. I'd rather not talk about those things. I don't want to go down that trail. I just feel very blessed to have had the success that I've had. Being chosen for the Songwriters Hall of Fame in 2010 really kind of capped it all off.

"Another highlight in my career is a song I just did for Africa. It's called 'For Africa, in Africa.' It's a song I wrote about pitching in and digging wells for clean water for Africa. I'm really proud of it. I actually sent a copy to Nelson Mandela. I have a lot of nerve, don't I? I wrote, 'My name is Jackie DeShannon and I'm the composer of the song "Put a Little Love in Your Heart." You have been such an inspiration to me and the rest of the world that I was inspired to write a new song, "For Africa, in Africa," for you and the organizations working to provide clean well water for Africa.' Then I put, 'This is a link to the video on YouTube. I hope you have the opportunity to hear this song. With love and admiration, Jackie DeShannon.' And I got a lovely, lovely note back. 'Dear Ms. DeShannon, we would like to take this opportunity to thank you for your correspondence and the song which you have sent to Mr. Mandela. Your kind thoughts are most appreciated and will be conveyed to Mr. Mandela.' How about that? Because they did not have to respond at all. I'm sure they get one or two notes, right? So I'm so very proud of that. Just to think that he would hear this song makes me feel tingly. I have such admiration for him. I mean, who in the world could withstand what he went through and come out with a smile, and forgiveness? That puts things into perspective. When you say I've given it everything I have, he's the example. So that's definitely the icing on the cake."

∿

Following something of a trend, DeShannon rerecorded many of her hits on the album When You Walk in the Room *(2001). A previous album,* You Know Me *(2000), contained new material.*

Phil Ochs (1974)

Although his life ended in 1976 in a haze of drugs and alcohol and depressive behavior, Phil Ochs was remarkably cogent about himself and his career when I spoke to him in 1974.

"For me songwriting was easy from 1961 to 1966 and then it got more and more difficult," he said. "It could be alcohol; it could be the deterioration of the politics I was involved in. It could be a general deterioration of the country. Basically, me and the country were deteriorating simultaneously and that's probably why it stopped coming. Part of the problem was that there was never any pattern to my writing. The point of discipline is to create your own pattern so you can write, and I haven't done that. I always make plans to do that. I'm now thirty-three and I may or may not succeed. But ever since the late sixties that's constantly on my mind—discipline, training, get it together, clean up your act. I haven't been able to do it yet, but the impulse is as strong as ever. To my dying day I'll always think about the next possible song, even if it's twenty years from now. I'll never make the conscious decision to stop writing."

When he arrived in Greenwich Village, the next possible song was usually about five minutes away, just waiting for the next social or political crisis. Each month at the Sunday Songwriters Workshop held at the Village Gate, crowds of expectant fans lined up to wait for another batch of Ochs's originals, and each month a new edition of instant current events analysis in song form would issue from him.

"This was the period when folk music was on the rise, when John Kennedy had just come in and Fidel Castro had just come in. Those forces just sort of took me over. I mean Kennedy got me superficially interested in politics, and Castro got me into serious politics, socialism, and anti-imperialism. He became the teacher of anti-imperialism of that time period by surviving. And at the same time, I started writing songs. I'll never know why, but out they came. My first regular song was called, 'The Ballad of the Cuban Invasion.' Those early songs were all sort of political, about Freedom Riders, Billy Sol Estes, the AMA. They just came out, no effort, no strain, absolutely no training, just bang-o—songs—one after another, and it lasted from 1961 to 1970."

Ochs began his songwriting career in, of all places, jail. "I was down in Florida and I was arrested for vagrancy. I spent fifteen days in jail and somewhere during the course of those fifteen days I decided to become a writer. My primary thought was journalism. I'd been to college for two years and I didn't have a major, so in a flash I decided—I'll be a writer, and I'll major in journalism. At school (Ohio State) my roommate was Jim Glover of Jim and Jean. He gave me a few guitar chords and that week I wrote a song. It was the impulse of journalism, you know, you've got to get that story in. The infatuation with folk music and fifties rock, the newness of politics . . . all fused in my first songs. In school, I had my own paper called *The Word*, which was a very radical paper, which is where I saw the fundamental weakness of journalism. I had an editorial saying, at the peak of the anti-Castro hysteria, that Fidel Castro is perhaps the greatest man that this century has produced in the Western Hemisphere. And this caused a giant storm, and I was taken off political stories in the local newspaper. So, I saw the way bureaucracy censors people. At the same time, I went to a journalism fraternity meeting where I saw the same people who sacked me swearing an oath of allegiance to Truth. I had one of my first impulses to murder, which I still haven't lost.

"I would sing the songs for Jim right away. I sang with him for six months in a group called the Sundowners. Sort of Bud and Travis stuff, early Seals and Crofts. He loved the songs. After we both quit school we split up. I got a job in a club called Faragher's in Cleveland, which was good training, considering that I'd only been playing a half a year. To go public with new songs at a point when new songs weren't fashionable, before Dylan had entered the scene, was a very tough experience. I was opening act to a lot of really good people like Judy Henske, the Smothers Brothers. Bob Gibson was a big influence on me musically. So, I quickly gained the professionalism onstage. I did my early political songs and a couple of, say, Kingston Trio things thrown in.

"Everybody said go to New York and I figured, well, New York is the tiger's den, I can't go up against those pros. But I went to New York and right away I met Dylan and I said, 'Oh my God, this is the guy!' As

60 | They're Playing My Song

soon as I heard him sing his first song I flipped out. And, of course, there were also a good ten or fifteen other people around who wrote songs. At that time songwriting was still unfashionable. I mean it was still the euphoria of ethnic folk or commercial folk. Folk being defined by age; songwriting being defined as pretense. You can't write a folk song, that argument. You can't use it for propaganda. You can't use folk music for politics was also a side argument. The breakthrough was Newport '63, with the Freedom Singers, Dylan, Baez, the songwriter's workshop, where it suddenly became the thing. It moved from the background into the foreground in just one weekend.

"After that I got an album out and I was completely prolific; I was writing all the time. Quickly followed by another album, followed by a concert. My thought throughout this whole period was, all right, here we have the form of a song, how important can a song be? Can it rival a play? Can it rival a movie? Can it make a statement that's as deep as a book? And by making a simple point can it reach more people than a

Figure 6. Phil Ochs, 1977. Photo: Kenneth Tash, Wikimedia Commons, CC BY-SA 4.0.

book ever can? I saw it with my own eyes; I sang the songs, they came through me, and I saw they had a political effect on the audience.

"I was writing about Vietnam in 1962, way before the first antiwar marches. I was writing about it at a point where the media were really full of shit, where they were just turning the other way as Vietnam was being built. It was clear to me and some others—I. F. Stone—but *The New York Times*, CBS, Walter Cronkite, and all those other so-called progressive forces chose to look the other way for several years before they decided it had gone too far. But it had already gone too far back then. People had seen the handwriting on the wall.

"It's always been a question of will it stand the test of time? That was one of the things in the very early days, before Dylan left politics, when he and I were writing political songs. There were two attacks: You can't write folk music, and you can't use folk music for propaganda. Besides, it's topical and it'll be meaningless two years from then. And so, to sing 'Small Circle of Friends' seven years later and still get the same response gives the lie to that attack. Whether the audience is hearing it for the first or the fifteenth time it still holds up. It could be nostalgia for some people, but on the other hand, there's some essential truth locked up in that song, and it's locked up to a thirteen-year-old kid that hears it today for the first time. He responds to it because the truth is there.

"I'd just like to add that I never had anything against Dylan when he stopped writing political songs. In that controversy, I was always completely on his side. The thing that's important about a writer is whether or not he's writing good stuff. It's not important if he's writing politics, left-wing, right-wing, or anything. Is it good, is it great, does it work? When Dylan made the switch, I said he's writing as good or better. And when he made his *Highway 61* album I said, this is it, his apex. But after his hiatus, when he came back and made his recent albums, at that point I couldn't go along with Dylan, because he'd reached his heights, and I couldn't accept what I considered lightweight stuff."

During the early to midsixties, Greenwich Village was a mecca for songwriters, some of them based there, others just passing through, among them Eric Andersen, Joni Mitchell, Jackson Browne, Tom Paxton, Patrick Sky, and Buffy Sainte-Marie. "That period in the Village was incredibly exciting, super-euphoric," Ochs said. "There was total creativity on the part of a great number of individuals that laid the bedrock for the next ten years. But everything goes in cycles, everything has a life span and I guess this life span just ran out. The important thing to bear in mind in terms of a whole life is, I mean you take a whole life, whether it's ten years or sixty years and say, what has this person done, what has he accomplished, if anything? He's now dead, what has he left behind him of value? And I think the people who made that contribution in the sixties can rest on that."

Ochs may have been creating his own epitaph with that statement, as his career never reached the heights it did during the heyday. "The old-time songwriters were more trained," he observed. "Everything I wrote was on instinct. There was some sort of psychic force at work in those songs and I don't know what it was. It's a strange way of giving birth; ideas giving birth in song form. And when the songs came they came fast. I don't think I ever spent more than two hours on any one song. Even 'Crucifixion' was done in two hours. But if I liked a song, I had total confidence in it and it doesn't matter if people said it's a great song or a lousy song. Hysterical praise or hysterical attacks didn't affect me at all. It's always been between me and my songs, not about the critics, not about the public, not about sales or anything else. 'Crucifixion,' 'Changes,' 'I Ain't Marchin' Anymore,' 'There but for Fortune,' and a couple of songs I liked that the general public didn't, such as 'I've Had Her,' 'Bach, Beethoven, Mozart; and Me,' are my personal favorites.

"I'm amazed that 'Changes' wasn't a hit. We've got about twenty recordings on it. Done by Roberta Flack or Anne Murray I'm sure it would be a number one song. 'There but for Fortune' was a hit, but it certainly wasn't written as one. Joan Baez just happened to pick it up and it caught on. I think 'Flower Lady' could catch at any time with the right group. At one time the Byrds were going to do it, that's one of my disappointments. I think if they had done it, it could have been a hit."

If you wanted to guess what Ochs's favorite recording of one of his song is, you'd be guessing for quite a long time. It's "The Power and the Glory," by the middle-of-the-road crooner and anti–gay rights activist Anita Bryant. "She did it on her patriotic record, *Mine Eyes Have Seen the Glory*. It's straight patriotic stuff and it's unbelievable, I mean really incredible. I think if a song has enough meaning it can survive anything."

∽

This was one of Phil's last interviews, made more chilling by his comments in the second paragraph.

Phil Ochs (1974) | 63

Buffy Sainte-Marie (1974)

Buffy Sainte-Marie came to prominence during the folk era, hoisted to underground approval by virtue of her classic "Universal Soldier" and her first album of unique and disturbing songs, entitled *It's My Way*. Before long she was a Greenwich Village fixture, playing on bills with Phil Ochs, Eric Andersen, and Tom Paxton. She and Joni Mitchell were certainly among the pioneering female songwriters of the decade.

Although some of her most deeply felt creations have related to her Cree Indian background ("Now That the Buffalo's Gone"), she has written of many other experiences—battles with drugs ("Cod'ine"), women's protest ("Babe in Arms"), personal freedom ("It's My Way"), and a new definition of romantic love ("Until It's Time for You to Go"). Back on the concert circuit in the seventies, after much time spent abroad, Buffy is now writing and singing . . . rock 'n' roll!

A natural artist and intuitive poet, Buffy Sainte-Marie is articulate as well as passionate on the subject of writing. The interview took place at a restaurant in Greenwich Village.

"I've always been an inventor and a creator of my own world, partly because of unavoidable isolation and partly because of solitude not imposed so much as chosen. I've always enjoyed being by myself and have also fallen into that kind of situation from the time when I was growing up to now, being on the road. The pattern of my life seems to be that I'm alone a lot.

"I don't sit down with a pencil and paper and write poems and songs and stories, but I always have poetic ideas and music going on in my head. It's like a constant radio station of my own. I hear the music and the words at the same time and I have to feel, in the case of a 'song,' that they're just wedded together. I can't notate music very well, so I have to remember things. If it's exciting enough for me to remember it, then it's exciting enough to share with people.

"It's something I'm able to do. It's totally a gift. It's not something I did because I was a singer and I needed some songs. I've always been able to do it and I've always appreciated it. I swear it saved my life a number of times because I've felt down, ill, unable to cope with things, especially when I was in high school; and the music, I don't understand it at all, but it's healed me on a number of occasions. And I've found that it's healed other people too.

"I can't force it. People have asked me to write movie scores and toothpaste commercials, things that I could really make a lot of money with—and I would love to divert that money toward some things that I would like to see done—but I'm really not very confident about being able to write on a schedule. I probably could do it if they caught me on the right day, but I couldn't promise I'd have a song by next Thursday at four p.m. I once wrote a whole series of commercials for Jell-O. All of a sudden I got these commercials for Jell-O in my head. Visuals and everything. But I never sent them in. It's like dreaming a dream. Sometimes the music will keep me up at night. It's just there and if it wants to play with me and I don't get up, it keeps me awake.

"When I say 'play' I mean *play*, because music for me is play no matter how serious it is, because I've never been forced to take lessons, I've never been forced to write, I've never been trained to write. It started out maybe just being a pastime, an escape from homework, an escape from doing things the way everybody wanted me to do them, which I never did very well and then I found I could invent my own music, keep myself company with it, express myself with it, but most of all *play* with it.

"In growing, I've never felt obligated to consistency in any form, including my own personality. A lot of people are created by their parents. I was adopted, which automatically gave me a sense of distance. The next personality people develop is usually as a result of a lover, so they realize they can be something else other than what their parents created, what their high school playmates created. All of a sudden they have two personalities available to them. The Women's Movement has shown a lot of women that there's a third personality—'myself, I, the woman.' I found that out so, so long ago, and I've found that not only are those three personalities available to me, but there are forty or fifty or a hundred others. There's something new every day, and I write from whatever feeling I'm getting within myself.

Buffy Sainte-Marie (1974) | 65

Figure 7. Buffy Sainte-Marie, ca. 1963. Photo: John Edwards Memorial Foundation, Southern Folklife Collection, UNC Wilson Library. Public domain.

"If I'm happy, that's what I share. If a song has come to me and brought me up, that's what I'll give to people. If a song is about things that I've seen, like 'Universal Soldier' or 'Now That the Buffalo's Gone,' I'll write that too. Those are really college student songs. They're not like 'Sweet Little Vera,' they can't reach everybody. A thirteen-year-old or someone who's mentally retarded can't know what 'Universal Soldier' is about. 'Sweet Little Vera' he can feel, it's emotional, it brings him up . . . because it's a feel-good song.

"My songs are collectively reflective of my entire personality, and I'm very varied. 'Until It's Time for You to Go' is nothing like 'Universal Soldier,' which is nothing like 'Sweet Little Vera,' which is nothing like 'Piney Wood Hills.' I'm not with one person all the time and I don't write one kind of song. If someone were to say they didn't think I should sing this or that because I sang something else that they liked better and they only think I should write one kind of song, it would just make me laugh."

I asked Buffy what she meant by a college student song.

"A college kind of song would be like 'My Country 'Tis of Thy People You're Dying,' you know, it's a condensation of Native American [American Indian] history. It's six minutes to make up for the total lack of candor and truth and information available to the American people about Indians. 'Universal Soldier,' 'Suffer the Little Children,' they're high-protein lectures is what they are. I wanted 'Universal Soldier' to do what it did. I wanted it to get people out of their classrooms and onto their feet. But certain things I have to say are pitched at too high a level to bring any lasting benefit to as many people as I would like to bring it to. If I have something of myself that gets me off, that's brought me through hard times, and that refreshes and nourishes me, what good does it do if I'm not smart enough to get it to the people? And I don't mean only the people who are like me, I mean all the people. That's communication. There's no sense being a closet genius. It doesn't do me any good to keep the medicine in the bottle."

What other types of songs does she write?

"I have more love songs than anything else I think. I have fifty or sixty love songs I haven't recorded. There are intellectual songs, there are rock 'n' roll songs, and then there's another kind of song like 'Starboy,' which is really kind of intimate poetry. The only artist I know who does this kind of song in about the same way is Joni Mitchell—she does that real well. There are light kind of storytelling songs, like 'Poor Man's Daughter,' and there are country songs. I write a lot of songs in Cree that I only sing to Indian people. But 'Native North American Child,' 'Generation,' and 'He's an Indian Cowboy at the Rodeo' have been giant hits everywhere except in America. America is not ready yet to look at the American Indian except as a victim. That's the only way anyone here wants to see him.

"I never write the same song twice, but some songs go in generations. 'Moratorium' is not 'Universal Soldier' but it's like 'son of.' I mean, five years later 'Universal Soldier' is still true, but it hasn't said enough and I have to write another song because that's what's in my head.

"I also write what I call healing songs. I guess they're on the same level as religious songs, but they're not gospel kind of religious songs; they're the kind of song you'd sing to a person who really needed them. They're medicine songs. Some of them are in French, some in Cree, some in English, some in Hawaiian. Some don't have words at all, only sounds;

they're in Human. I haven't recorded them, but I have sung them in a lot of instances.

"Let me tell you something about American audiences. They mostly want to hear things that sound like they've heard them before. In other parts of the world that's not necessarily so. My songs are always at least two years ahead of their time. For two years I was criticized for writing 'Universal Soldier.' For two years I couldn't sing 'Now That the Buffalo's Gone' on television. Two years after I'd written it they finally let me sing it. Everybody wanted to be an Indian, right? But they wouldn't let me sing 'My Country 'Tis of Thy People You're Dying' because it was too strong. Two years went by, now that's all they want me to sing.

"I wrote 'Until It's Time for You to Go' and the folkies called me a sellout. I wore sparkles on my clothes and tight satiny dresses and high heels because that's the way I felt and it was the wrong way to feel at the Newport Folk Festival because it wasn't what Joanie and Bobby were wearing. I mean, for me music is ninety-nine percent of my life. I've sold out everything else. I've sold out my heart. I've sold out my head. I've sold out my body. I've sold out everything from my health to any lover I've ever had. When it's time to get on that airplane that's it. It's partly because I'm drawn as a performer and partly because I'm pushed by the music. I love being a performer. I think it's a noble profession."

Buffy explained her attitude about which songs she chooses to perform in public.

"I'm both an artist and a professional. The artist in me has great respect for the professional side. I have lots of songs I don't sing to other people. It's not a matter of commercialism so much as communication. Communication is my art. What I choose of my songs to get across to the people is conditioned by two things: it's usually the middle ground between one, where I'm at; and two, where whoever I want to reach is at . . . 'cause it doesn't do enough good to put out an entire album of songs that only four people in the world are going to understand. The songs I select to perform are determined by what I want to do that night, but for the most part now, in 1974, I'm trying to fill in a gap that has had to do with who I am in relation to the crowd that used to come and see me in the Village. Due to circumstances beyond my control people have not been exposed to all the feelings that I want to share, let alone all the ideas that I have, that my head sent me in terms of songs that I'm willing to share and able to share on a lot of different levels. I feel I have an obligation to an audience, and I don't sing just for college students or just to Indians or just for women or just for rock 'n' roll lovers. I know for a fact that because the audience reaches me, I'm going to reach them. It's an interaction between me and my life and between me and the audience."

Buffy was not always a performer, although she always played music. Until she got to college she was extremely shy.

"While I was in college my shyness kind of melted day by day through getting to know a lot of people. I wasn't in the high school situation of a small community; I went to a huge school, University of Massachusetts, and I was with new people all the time. I felt I didn't have to be any one special way.

"So I used to just sing in the dorm, just my own songs, for one or two friends. And I found that they really were feeling exceptionally good by the time I finished singing. I really began developing it as a kind of healing art for my friends. I never thought I'd wind up in the razzle-dazzle of show business.

"This songwriting stuff was just the same thing that was going on when I was supposed to be studying my math in high school. Or when I was supposed to be saying the right thing at the right time in the girls' lavatory. I mean, I thought I was crazy for a long time. I was just miserable in high school because I always had this music in my head and I didn't *want* to go to school. I just wanted to stay home and play the piano, even if I could only play in one key, even if I couldn't read music and flunked music class all the time.

"So I was finally able, within my own personality, to share what was already going on in my head. I didn't write songs in order to please people, but I began exhibiting what I was already digging to do, and able to do, for myself. I began sharing the music with other people."

Those who have followed Buffy from album to album might be surprised to learn who her first influence was.

"The first musician who really flashed me was Elvis Presley. It was for personality, it was for sex, it was because of music, it was because of chord changes. I mean, there was never a boy like that in my home town! That got me moving and I mean it, and it's affected me all through my travels and my performances."

The last thing we talked about was Buffy's ensemble.

"Let me tell you something about being a writer and having a band at your disposal. It could be devastating unless you have very generous musicians. As a writer it enables me to be like five writers at once. In

Buffy Sainte-Marie (1974) | 69

other words, when I go in to record a song, it's not only the words and the melody that makes it me, it's the whole arrangement.

"I'll play the song once on the piano and the piano player will watch what I do, then he'll play the same kind of runs that I do. Then I'll play it on guitar and the same thing happens. So there's me playing the piano and me playing the guitar and I'm also free to sing. The drummer will put down my licks. The bass player will look at the patterns that I'm doing. And then when we're playing it all together they'll add their own creativity and skill to the song, but basing the arrangement on my ideas. It will take probably a half an hour to record the song. It's lightning fast and it's always fresh, but it takes an extraordinary combination of musicians to build the song without destroying it.

"It's a new high every time. I can't tell you how thrilling the whole song receiving-writing-performing process is. If a song comes into my head, it's a high. The first time you play it on guitar it's another high, a different high. Then I play it on piano. Then you play it for someone for the first time and you see it react on them. It's like an entire growing up process. You learn that you have a body, then you learn that you can feel your body, then you learn you can do incredible things by feeling your body. Then you learn you can give your body to somebody else and let them feel it. It's the same thing. I can give a song to the musicians and I can feel what each person does with each song each night, how they change it, how they manipulate it.

"I'm a professional performer but not a professional songwriter. Composing is just a question of allowing the music to come to me and accepting the music. You don't get to judge the music that comes into your head (or I know I don't!). I don't judge it; I just accept it and then I filter it for an audience. It's the performer in me that filters it for an audience. I'm not going to sing something for somebody that I think is just going to bore them. As a performer I'd feel like a robber if I did that. But as a writer, I just write whatever comes into my head.

"The only thing wrong with traveling around and being on the run is there's just not enough music on the road. Instead of doing interviews like this I'd much rather, excuse me, be back at my place playing the piano and rehearsing with the band. I'd rather be doing that than anything else in the world."

Before retiring in 2023, Buffy Sainte-Marie continued to tour and record, with her last album being Medicine Songs *(2017). A controversy over her alleged Cree Indian background emerged after a documentary claimed she was born to an Italian American family in the US. Many in the Native American community were sorely disappointed by this news, while others vehemently defended her version of events.*

Paul McCartney (1990)

In 1990, I joined a group of my fellow scribes to assemble around a round-table to question the bass-playing Beatle. As arguably the most musical of his more verbal cohorts, McCartney expressed no need to explain or defend himself against the critics who charge him with failing to live up to his potential in the aftermath of the Fab Four. As the twelve of us who gathered to grill him during a press conference late last year in New York found out, even if he can't, or won't, explain himself, he does sometimes reveal quite a bit—unintentionally.

"My style?" he responded to a question of mine. "I never think about stuff like that. I never had any lessons. I made it all up by myself, so I really don't know what style I have. My dad gave me a trumpet when I was a kid, because trumpets were all the rage back then. My dad had been a trumpet player and I wanted to follow him, but then I got a guitar when I was about fifteen, because I wanted to sing and I figured you couldn't sing with this big brass thing stuck in your mouth. And the way we learned was just through the guys. Someone would say, 'Let's go to this guy's house. He knows B7,' and we'd all go on the bus. It was like the Holy Grail. We'd go to his house saying, 'Come on, man,' and he'd sing a C major triad and I'd take it down and spend hours practicing. I couldn't tell you anything about music. If you showed me 'Yesterday' on a sheet, I wouldn't know what it was. It's just not the way I do it. I don't connect the little black dots to music. It's like Morse Code to me. So, it's difficult for me to tell you what style I have. I'm just into music. I'm into a lot of different styles."

While this answer seems, on its own terms, substantial enough, it's wise not to ask him to delve into his relationship with the bass any further. "I'm hopeless," he said. "I don't know a thing about it. This young American guy came up to me in a record shop and he said, 'I like your playing, man, what kind of strings do you use?' I said, 'Well, these kind of long, shiny ones.' I mean, I know it sounds daft, but that's about it. I actually don't know what strings I use. I'm not one of these guys who says, 'I use a DC380 with a rack-mount.' I mean, I like quality, but the guys have to help me out with all that stuff."

When I ask him what he finds the most enjoyable aspect of songwriting, his answer is also typically vague.

"Making magic," he said. "I sit down and there's nothing there; it's like a blank page when you're writing, and if you're lucky, half an hour later, it's like these fingers have visited you and it's a song and you think, I have to do it. It all comes out at once. It was always hard work, but it's probably a little harder now, because when you've been doing it as long as I have, you've explored so many avenues." Then, almost as an afterthought, he throws this in.

Figure 8. Paul McCartney, 2021. Photo: Raphael Pour-Hashemi, Wikimedia Commons, CC BY 2.0.

"I've got a real great project going on at the moment, with a New York City guy named Carl Davis who lives in England. He's an orchestra conductor and the Liverpool Philharmonic Orchestra has commissioned me and him to write a thing for two years' time for the orchestra and chorus, and for the cathedral choir. It's ironic, because I failed the audition for the cathedral choir. This is the biggest cathedral in England, so I'm working on this so-called serious piece of orchestral music, which will be over an hour long. It's basically about me growing up in Liverpool. We're in the fourth movement now. We just keep meeting. He's very much my idea of a New York kind of guy. I say to him when we meet, 'How are you, Carl?' And he says, 'Fragile. A little neurotic. Terrible.' And I say, 'Come on, let's go write a song.' And then we get down to writing something. He'll suggest something and I'll say, 'That does it for me.' He's the opposite of me. He likes to write everything down. I like to hear it all. He writes it all down."

(The work was completed in 1991 and released as *Paul McCartney's Liverpool Oratorio*. Carl Davis passed away in 2023. The critical reaction was mixed. A review in *The New York Times* described the work as "a richly melodic, lavishly orchestrated piece about the loss and reclamation of innocence, love and faith . . . (with) an exquisite soprano aria and a five-minute violin meditation that suggests Mr. McCartney could be a superb concerto composer." While *The Guardian* said that "the work, while attractive, was simplistic, overlong and, given its aspirations, insubstantial.")

It sounds like this could have been just the kind of yin and yang that moved the great Lennon and McCartney all those years ago. But unlike Ringo, Paul will not admit to hearing John talking to him onstage. "I've heard Ringo say that, but I actually don't experience that. I loved John. I think about him a lot, but I never get the feeling he's watching." Writing a song is another matter. "I will kind of talk to him mentally, and just sort of think, 'No, he wouldn't do that.' When I was writing 'Hey Jude, the movement you need is on your shoulder,' I said, I'll be changing that, and he said, 'Don't, that's the best line in it.' I definitely would have dumped that line. So, yeah, I sometimes mentally refer to him."

One of his favorite memories of collaboration centers around the song "You Know My Name, Look Up the Number." Said Paul, "It doesn't mean anything, but it means a lot to me. I remember how many years it took to make it. I remember John coming in, just saying, 'I've got this great song, man.' I said, how's it go? He said, 'You know my name, look up the number. You! You know my name, look up the number.' We were laughing. We laughed a lot, man. It was great. That's why I like it. We said, 'We've got to finish it now that we've started. We couldn't figure out how to finish a song whose only words were, 'You know my name, look up the number.' "

He continued along the same misty trail. "Occasionally I do look back and just think, 'My God! What happened? Did I dream it?' Bloody hell. I sat down and wrote out around thirty-five songs for the tour that I thought were big songs—a lot of which we're not doing. And the interesting thing is that quite a few of them I or the Beatles never played onstage, things like 'Sergeant Pepper.' I never got a chance to play that onstage, because we'd finished touring by the time that came out.

"Obviously, with me, the disadvantage of having done so much and having become this venerable figure, you attract a lot of criticism, because people want everything to be as good as *Abbey Road*. I certainly like Elvis Presley's career before he joined the army. I don't really like anything after that. A lot of people love his stuff after the army, and people are like that with me. They would like to have seen me stay at the sort of Beatles height forever, but it's not that easy."

Easier to deal with are the critics who second-guess his every musical move. He came under fire, for instance, for doing "Ebony and Ivory." "The bottom line is," he sharply responded, "the song was a hit. I got to work with Stevie Wonder, and that's more than most people do in a lifetime, right there. I thought 'Say Say Say' was great. Michael Jackson is a very buzzy person to work with. I don't think they were the greatest lyrics I've ever written, but I think it's a good track. It's got some good playing on it. So, by this time, I don't analyze me. I'm just lucky to be alive and still doing it."

∾

Paul McCartney continues to record and perform, having released ten solo albums since 1990.

Keith Richards (1985)

Like a politician on the podium, whistle-stopping across the boondocks on a flatbed, Keith Richards has his share of timeless bromides, comfortable answers his tongue slips into after years in the public eye. In the midst of a searing query, or a deft, seven-tiered multiple choice essay question, you can pick them off like sand fleas.

"My first job is to turn the band on."

"When we go into the studio we spend the first few hours just playing the Buddy Holly songbook."

"I have a good feeling about this new album . . ."

"People haven't covered our songs too much, but I take that as a compliment. You don't really hear versions of 'Heartbreak Hotel' either. What it means is that your version is pretty much seen as the ultimate."

"More than half the people running record companies are just executives, guys who can sell a whole lot of baked beans. To them a record is just another unit. They couldn't care less about music."

The story about waking up in the middle of the night with the riff for "Satisfaction" is a chestnut, as is his well-documented affinity for the acoustic guitar. "I firmly believe that there ain't a good guitarist around who just plays electric guitar. You can do a lot of tricks on the electric, but as much as I love to play it, a guitarist can keep his chops up only if he plays acoustic. There's no tricks like sustain. It keeps your wrists and fingers strong. You can't fake it with feedback. You just have to play the thing."

Perhaps his opinion of heavy metal has also made the rounds. "I hate heavy metal," he said. "It just bores me to tears. It sounds like this plane we have in England, with fifteen engines on each wing. It was designed for fantasy. When they built it, it did a great job of charging down the runway, but it never took off."

Certainly you don't think his attitude about the new album, *Dirty Work*, is a freshly minted burst of enthusiasm, prodded out of him by the reporter's perspicacity or intuition. "Instead of working old formulas here," I noted about the title cut, "it looks like you're adding a few new ones. It could be the sound for the Stones in the nineties." I was falling right into his trap, I sensed, buttering him up with an easy one, but how could I resist? He was such a friendly, elfin sort of guy, smiling at me like a rock 'n' roll Dudley Moore.

"My favorite theme at the moment is that after all these years, rather than just marking time, the Rolling Stones are in the unique position of seeing if we can get this thing to grow with us. Rock 'n' roll is just about the same age as we are, so nobody's really had the chance to take it this far, not as a band anyway. All of the kings are dead: Elvis, Buddy, Otis Redding. Maybe the only one who can play a guitar in pretty much the same form as what rock 'n' roll is based on, and make it grow up and mature in an interesting way, is Muddy Waters. So for the Stones one of the most interesting things is to see how rock 'n' roll grows up, and see if we can grow it up with us."

So how do you pierce this polished exterior? How do you mine new territory on the much-plowed fields of Rolling Stone history, myth, and nuance? The answer proved simple, as obvious as the glimmer in Keith's eyes. So, fans of their rabble-rousing exploits, look elsewhere. Strings and picks fanatics, turn the page. For herein rhythm-cruncher supreme turns orator, nasty scourge of the earth becomes sage, as Keith agrees to expound at length on one of his most overlooked yet favorite subjects: songwriting. With a catalog of million-sellers as vast as it is unrelenting, surely the Stones' output ranks up there with the best that solid rock has produced. No need to give these monsters names, because for twenty years we've welcomed them into our kitchens and bedrooms and hot rods, one after another, chiseled gems of the form, consistently on the mark, lyrically compelling, absolutely rock 'n' roll.

"The hardest thing to write is a really good original rock 'n' roll song," Keith said, "because the form is musically very limited. So much depends on the feel and the enthusiasm of the playing. The song is almost an equal partner to the performance. Then there's that indefinable thing that makes rock 'n' roll what is it, that thing that somehow gets in there and nobody knows how."

As a songwriter, Keith Richards is first and foremost a guitarist. "To me songs come out of being a musician, playing. I cannot write to poetry, rhymed couplets and things like that. I can write a song out of a chord sequence, a riff, and eventually come up with lyrics to fit onto it, but the other way around, no way. The important thing to me is to sit down with an instrument. You might spend three, four hours going through the Buddy Holly songbook and then out of nowhere there'll be a little crash, and there it goes. All it takes is a split second. It might be an accident, a mistake that sets you off. It's a matter of sitting down and playing, more than with any definite intention to write. All you've got to do is be receptive and recognize it when it happens, because it can come from the weirdest angles. Rarely do I write a song totally by myself. Even if I actually do write it by myself, I always like to have someone around playing along with me, going, yeah, yeah. I'm a band man, a group man. I can't sit there alone in a room and say, it's songwriting time, ding ding ding."

In a sense, Keith views the songwriting experience as somewhat metaphysical, although he'd be the last to put such a label on it. "I never

Figure 9. Keith Richards, 2022. Photo: Raph_PH, Wikimedia Commons, Creative CC BY 2.0.

78 | They're Playing My Song

think I have to put anything down. I never care if I have it on tape or if the tape runs out and the song disappears, cause they all come back eventually. I've written songs and lost them and found them ten years later. Once it's there, it's there. It's just a matter of how long it takes before it comes back out again. I find the more I play, the more I'm into it, the songs pour out. I don't have a problem with being nonprolific. That's all psychosomatic. Music isn't something to think about, at least initially. Eventually it's got to cover the spectrum, but especially with rock 'n' roll, first it has to touch you somewhere else. It could be the groin; it could be the heart; it could be the guts; it could be the toes. It'll get to the brain eventually. The last thing I'm thinking about is the brain. You do enough thinking about everything else."

In the studio, he relies on the rest of the Stones for valued collaboration. "When we're doing an album I come in with a handful of riffs and some songs. One or two will be fairly well defined. Others, it would be, this could be dynamite for the Stones, but I have to wait until I get the Stones all together in the studio to find out. I can't take it any farther by myself as a song or a structure or an idea until I've got their input. On 'Dirty Work,' for instance, we had the hook. The bridge didn't come until we were in the studio trying out various ways of breaking it up in the middle, trying to find something that wouldn't be too obvious. I decided, let's just go Jamaican and turn the beat, and suddenly everybody looks around and says Yeah. And that's the way a song is made. It's in the studio that you get those final things that give it something extra."

Songs can also die a death under the caustic glances of his bandmates. "If there's no kiss of life; if everybody walks off to the toilet, then you know you've got to drop that one and go on to something else," he said. "But when you just sort of pick up your guitar when the studio is virtually empty, people are telling jokes in the back room or playing dominoes and then within two or three minutes they drift back, pick up their instruments, and begin whacking away, you know they're into it.

"What a songwriter loves more than anything is a sequence that comes with a hook. Once you get that, you try to expand it. You've got a hook and the first verse, you start to think of the second verse, how to expand the idea. Or do you want to turn it around? Do you want to leave it ambiguous or do you really want to make a certain point? Bobby Womack and Don Covay have been writing songs even longer than I have. Ronnie Wood has a great tape of them writing songs together one night and it's ten minutes of chords and the first verse and then this incredible conversation of 'Yeah, but she's gonna . . . or, is she gonna be the one with him or is he gonna?' And there's a whole soap opera going on. It's like writing a movie script. 'Well, he wouldn't do that because he's got to come back and that's why you're saying . . .'"

Keith works differently with Mick than he does with Ronnie. "When Ron and I sit down together to play we're two guitarists. Whereas with Mick and I there's maybe more of an idea in our heads that what we're after is a song at the end of what we're doing. When Mick comes in with a song, usually he's got it worked out pretty much. He may need a bridge to be written or a different beat or to turn it around a little bit. Over our whole period, maybe fifty percent of the time he writes the lyrics and I write the melody. But that's a far, far too simplistic explanation. We write in every conceivable combination of ways. It's really an incredibly elastic arrangement, especially when you're writing with a partner for a band, a specific unit, rather than just writing a song to see who you could sell it to. Some songs hang out for years before we feel happy with them and resurrect them and finish them off. Others, in two takes they've come and gone and you've got to relearn it off your own record to play it later. It happened so quickly you've forgotten how it went. In a way, I'm like a guitar maker. Some songs are almost at the end; others are hanging there waiting for that special coat of paint. You can't find the right color for them right now. Lots of times you think you've written four different songs and you take them to the studio and you realize they're just variations on one song."

These days the Stones have a lot of luxury in the recording studio, the ultimate luxury of using it as a rehearsal hall and sounding board. "When we go into the studio we have to knock the rust off," said Keith. "Nobody ever stops making music, but when you go back in to make an album, the first two months are spent just getting chops and sound together."

In the early days there were different forces moving the industry. In order to even quality for an album deal, a band had to make its mark in the singles world. Like the Beatles, the Animals, the Who, the Kinks, and the Dave Clark Five, the Rolling Stones needed to become past masters of the 45, that three-minute art form made heavenly with the perfect combination of hook and crook.

"I remember after 'Satisfaction' got to number one—bang bang at the door. Where's the follow up? I mean every twelve weeks you had to have another one ready. The minute you put out a single, you had to start working your butt off on the next one, and the bigger the hit, the more pressure there was on the follow-up. But it was an incredibly good school for songwriting in that you couldn't piss around for months and months agonizing about the deeper meaning of this or that. No matter what you were doing, like touring and recording, you had to make damn sure you didn't let up on the writing. It made you want to search around and listen for ideas. It made you very aware of what was going on around you, because you were looking for a song. It might come in a coffee shop, or it might come on the street, or in a cab. You get a heightened awareness. You listen to what people say. You might hear a phrase at a bus stop. Instead of accepting life, you start to observe it. You become an outsider rather than a participant. You're listening for it every moment, and anything could be a song, and if you don't have one, you're up the creek without a paddle."

For instance, "Ruby Tuesday": "I saw this picture in some fashion magazine that a chick had lying around her apartment. It was this great photograph of a great chick—she's probably a housewife now, with fifteen kids. It was an ad for jewelry—rubies. Also, it happened to be Tuesday. So she became Ruby Tuesday. I was just lucky it was Tuesday I guess."

In the sixties, the Beatles played "I Want to Hold Your Hand" to the Stones' "Under My Thumb," the essential and elemental rock and roll struggle for good and evil in the minds and hearts of men and women. The Beatles came to be known as the world's greatest songwriters, the Stones as the world's greatest band. Off to the side of the fray, lighting matches, the world's greatest lyricist, Bob Dylan, lifted the stakes even higher.

"I'd say that Lennon definitely felt a strong urge not so much to compete with Dylan," Keith surmised, "but Bob did spur him to realize he could dig deeper. Mick and I felt that too, although maybe we didn't feel it as strongly as John. The differences between John and Paul were always greater than between Mick and myself." Keith cited "Symphony for the Devil" as the Stones' most Dylanesque song. But his description revealed how he himself influenced Jagger as much as Dylan. "Mick wrote it almost as a Dylan song," Keith said, "but it ended up a rock 'n' roll Samba."

But with songs like "Sympathy for the Devil," "Street Fighting Man," "Gimme Shelter," "Stray Cat Blues," and so many others, the Stones broadened their bad boy reputation into a decidedly warped young manhood. None of this was lost on the Glimmer Twins, as they concocted the image for greatest benefit.

"You use every available tool in the kit," said Keith. "To a certain extent you play on your image. Oh, that's the general perception? And I'd just come up with a line or a song and lean on it, push it, go for it.

You get a general feel for what people want to hear from you and when you're good at providing it and they like it—oh, you want more? Here's more. When you first strap on your guitar you just want to play it like so and so. Then suddenly you're up there and the spotlight is on and you become aware of the pressures. You have to try and gauge your perception of what you're doing. Nobody writes a song or makes a record to put it in a back drawer."

So although the Beatles and Dylan have catalogs that have long been ensconced in the bosom of pop literature, here's a vote for the collected works of the Stones as belonging right up there on that sacred mount.

"I don't write songs as a diary. None of them are autobiographical," said Keith, "but in some sense, they're a reaction to certain emotions. Some of the best songs, some of the happiest ditties in the world come out because you're feeling exactly the opposite. Sometimes you write to counteract that feeling. I was feeling anything but happy when I wrote 'Happy.' I wrote 'Happy' to make sure there was a world like that, a feeling like that.

"I work best when the sun goes down. I've eaten, had a few drinks, and I've got some good buddies around. I love sitting around with an acoustic guitar and whacking out songs with friends and family. Somehow they never sound as good as they do that first night on the living room couch.

Keith Richards and the Rolling Stones keep rolling. Their most recent album, Hackney Diamonds, *their first album of original material in eighteen years, came out in 2023.*

Pete Townshend (1974)

Pete Townshend has always represented rock 'n' roll at its best: emotional, intuitive, energetic. Although somewhat overshadowed in reputation by his illustrious contemporaries Keith Richards and Mick Jagger, John Lennon and Paul McCartney, Townshend's songs are first-rate classics of the era, and his longer works will go down as the most ambitious use of the form to date.

Townshend's success in America is largely due to his rock opera *Tommy*, the story of a deaf, dumb, and blind pinball wizard who rises to legend hood—and *Quadrophenia*—based in part on autobiographical vignettes of the four members of the Who, and also an epitaph for the Mod era in England.

The interview with Townshend took place in Los Angeles, where the group was preparing for an evening show. Although I was the tenth and last interview of the day, Pete was still accommodating and pleasant. The topic of songwriting was something he'd rarely discussed at such length in an interview and he was quite interested in pursuing it.

"At age twelve or thirteen I wanted to get a guitar. My friend got his father to make him a guitar. Not a musical instrument, just sort of a prop so he could stand in front of the mirror and pose. It had piano strings and no frets. I was actually able to play it in some way. This guy's father used to say to me, 'Listen, if you can get any music at all out of this thing, you'd probably make a good guitar player so why don't you get a proper guitar.' So, that Christmas my grandmother got me this cheap guitar and I struggled away on it for about a year. Then I got a banjo and struggled away on that. Finally, I got a good guitar. It was a slow transition.

"Another reason I played guitar initially is that I really did feel at the time it was going to be the only way I was ever going to get laid—to have a guitar and be in a group. One day some girl would sort of spot me and fall in love with me because I was a genius guitar player. I figured there was absolutely no point in me going out with the guys, and going through the whole thing 'down at the club' because I wasn't confident enough, firstly, and not good-looking enough, which affects the first. So I felt that a couple of years stuck in a bedroom learning the guitar wouldn't do me any harm at all. While the other kids were out dancing, I was learning the guitar."

Townshend described the scene "down at the club."

"The youth club dances were often run by the churches or guilds. You'd go down to the club and sit around and maybe ask some girl to jive, and all the girls seemed to be about five years older than the guys. You wore a suit and that kind of scene. In fact, it was at one of those dances that I used to go to—it was run by the Congregational Church, so it got the subtitle, The Congo Club—that I first appeared onstage, with John Entwistle playing trumpet and me playing banjo in a trad jazz group. We used to play Dixieland stuff like 'Marching Through Georgia,' 'Farewell Blues,' and all that kind of stuff. And we stood there, with about five people in the room, and I really blushed. It was the only time ever in my whole life that I've been nervous on a stage.

"What really changed things for me was going to art college. I couldn't believe all those rules: that you had to be good-looking and smartly dressed, that you had to be intelligent, that you always had to have something to say and you had to be big and strong; none of those unwritten rules applied in art college. Incredibly beautiful women would talk to you without needing to see your credentials. It took me about a year to get over that.

"I remember the first really crushing romance I had. It still brings tears to my eyes thinking about the lost romance that could have been in art college with an amazing woman, all just because I wasn't really prepared for it. Art college was where I really grew up. I had been going to a silly boys' school, with silly girls running around, and all the childish games people play. And I walked into this thing where all that counted was what really mattered. It was pretty staggering.

"In *Quadrophenia* I wrote a song that didn't get included about this girl at school and how I blew the relationship because I lied a lot. She was going out with a jazz musician and I was just like on the sidelines and I used to talk to her. I never thought there'd be a relationship, but I used to like being in her presence and we used to sit next to each other,

Figure 10. Pete Townshend, 2013. Photo: Ross, Wikimedia Commons, CC BY 2.0.

work, talk, and eat together and that sort of thing. That was as far as it got. At the end of the day the jazz musician would come and pick her up and take her home.

"So I started to expand a bit on my musical capabilities in order to perhaps bring myself into line with this other guy. Like, 'Well, I'm in a band and I play really well. I've got a number of guitars. I've worked with all kinds of people, all sorts of bands. I've got four or five different color jackets.' And we used to talk about jazz because my father was a legitimate player, so I knew a little bit, but I didn't really know quite what I was talking about.

"The final boob was when her old man left her and she was shattered by it because he was older and she was very young, and she turned to me for emotional support, and apart from me not being able to recognize it or being able to handle it . . . I got into a conversation about Charlie Parker and said that I'd met him in a club and shook hands with him.

Pete Townshend (1974) | 85

It was a tragic thing that I remember to this day. Because it was then she knew it was just not going to work. And what was tragic about it, looking back on it, was that she knew I was in the way of myself, that I really couldn't handle it.

"So I wrote a pretty song, which we actually got to the point of laying down, called 'We Close Tonight.' The last verse of it is 'I got three red jackets and a Fender Jazz and I play guitar in a mainstream band,' and the last line of the thing is 'You could come see us, but we close tonight.' But the song seemed out of place in *Quadrophenia*. It seemed too much like a cameo stuck in to lighten what was essentially a sad story."

From there we moved into a discussion of his two major works.

"I tend to think in trains of thought for maybe up to two years. I'll start to write a song and I won't really know what it's got to do with, then two years later I'll look back on it and then I'll know why I wrote it. It might have some kind of catch thing that fits in with all the others. I know when I put *Tommy* together I drew on all kinds of sources that came from earlier on that just fit. And even in *Quadrophenia* there's quite a lot of material from earlier that just fit. Every time I wrote I was writing about that kind of thing—adolescence or spiritual desperation. Also, last year, prior to the recording, I really did go through a strange frame of mind. I did start to get a little bit desperate again, in an adolescent sense, that feeble clutching at some sort of sense of identity. 'I'm One' was written in a genuine melancholic state.

"Then in order to draw all the loose ends together I have to sit down and do it. I have a studio in my house where I finish things off and organize music. I have to shut myself up in this room and work. I start to build up to it in a way that it becomes sort of inevitable.

"What I do is force myself to do it by announcing the thing up front. I talked about *Tommy* at incredible length to Jann Wenner in a long, long article in *Rolling Stone* before I'd even finished writing it. I said so much that I just had to get it done. It's really good to do it that way, give somebody an idea to gauge your own enthusiasm. You can work it out by seeing how well you can sell it to somebody else. And if you sell it really well, you know that you're behind it. If you sell it to fifty people and you're still really up about it, then you know you're onto something that's going to get done.

"I had a lot of people say I shouldn't touch the opera form, and my argument then was that I wasn't really touching opera at all. 'Rock opera' was a Kit Lambert phrase, a managerial term.

"But it's such a peculiar working process. Often I pretend to everybody that I know what I'm doing when a lot of the time I really don't. That's why *Tommy* doesn't have a properly conceived ending, because it was never properly conceived in front. It was allowed to happen in a spontaneous way, sort like a Buster Keaton two-reeler, rather than being scripted in front and made to happen. And if you didn't have an ending, you didn't really care about it. You just had everybody walk off into the sunset. *Tommy* came out too soon. The last part was very rushed. There's so much I would change, but we had to stop working on it. We were sick of it. The last part of it was very rushed."

From there we segued into *Quadrophenia*.

"I first had the idea for *Quadrophenia* somewhere in Europe. No, maybe it was actually the last time we were in America on tour. In any case, it was about this time two years ago. Anything big that has happened to me has happened around November. I fell in love in November. I got stoned on pot first in November. I had my first acid trip in November.

"Symbolically the rain in *Quadrophenia* is a blessing, like the thunder and the sea," Townshend said. "They're all heavily symbolic in a structural sense and in an impressionistic sense. It's all that garbage in the mix. That kind of thing we did just to impressionistically set things up so that the music seemed harsher and shoved itself out more rather than just a series of songs that had to be listened to as cameos. And the rock in the ocean, the fact that it's in the ocean, like the island, is all fairly symbolic. I was very conscious of that kind of an idea. The rock being most likely the Who, you know, something you could swim out from, but you had to come back to it. And the ocean is like everything . . . universal in a mystical sense.

"I first wrote 'Drowned' years ago, a short while after finishing *Tommy*. I'd written it as a kind of tribute to Meher Baba, this spiritual master I follow. He said something like 'God is the ocean and individuals are like drops of water. They think they're separate, but once they're in the ocean, they know they're an ocean, but so long as they're a drop of water, they think they're a drop of water.'

"I was thinking about that when we started to play and then it started to rain outside. Then it started to thunder outside. We were about halfway through the number and even in the recording studio we could feel the fucking explosions going on outside. Chris Stainton, who had come down to play piano on the track, was banging away in the piano booth, which was in a completely separate room. We finished the number

Pete Townshend (1974) | 87

off and I could hear the piano deteriorating in quality, cause by then it had really started to pour. Chris ended up shouting at us from the piano room, which was full of water. He opens the door and all the water comes rushing out. I look up and the walls are streaming with water pouring into the studio. Everywhere water. I had six feet to cover from the door of the studio into the street into the house and as I ran across from there to there I was completely drenched and it was great. I just thought it was great, that sound of the rain. Ever since then we've got this thing in the band that if it rains, it's gonna be a good night."

Townshend has said that *Quadrophenia* is about, at least in part, the separate personalities of the four members of the Who, merged into one central figure. "The liner notes are a little strained because they're put together around the album itself. It's a little bit of character building to let you know just how uneducated the character was, but also the fact that he was all right beside that. I found it quite hard to write. That's why I went heavy on a sort of *Catcher in the Rye* thing to get it across.

"I hope I've gotten that type of thing out of my system, because up to now I've written the same sort of thing, even in *Tommy*, where I tried to write something that was a fantasy, it seemed to have a lot of familiar threads running through it, like family problems, the street social problems, like the bullying cousin Kevin, and the druggy things. I don't think up to now I've really been able to break loose from that sort of thing. But I'm really starting to get bored with adolescence and writing about it. It's starting to become a sort of semi-senile middle-aged attitude toward adolescence. I don't feel at all ill at ease where I am. I don't feel I'm suffering from maturity. Actually, I'm quoting myself there. 'Suffering from maturity.' I was doing this interview in *Melody Maker* where I said that. One of the best things I ever said. I think a lot of people walk around acting like adults. It's got nothing to do with morality or dignity. I mean, you can be free or you can act stupidly, but you can still be dignified. So I tried to make *Quadrophenia* feel like the last Who album of that type."

From shy college kid, Townshend has morphed into something of a social butterfly. "There was a time when Jimi Hendrix was in the country when I became part of a kind of jet set with Eric Clapton, Hendrix, John Lennon, and Paul McCartney. Ringo and George were around quite a lot too. I think it was around the time we were about to be managed by Brian Epstein. Kit Lambert and Brian Epstein were very respectful of one another and very similar in a way, and they were going to form a partnership to manage us. And through that we got to see a lot of the

Beatles. John was always incredibly funny and Paul was always a little bit embarrassed because he was never very sure of himself. He used to start off conversations with 'Don't treat me like somebody big or anything. I know you think I'm great and I know you're good, and you know I'm good . . .' And this would go on for about five minutes, and then John would come in and say, 'Hello, want a sandwich?' I still see Ringo quite a lot. He was good friends with Keith Moon. I see George fleetingly. I get invited to Paul's a lot but we never seem to end up going."

Before that, Townshend and the Who were always much more attuned to the street concerns of their peers in England than either the Stones or the Beatles. Most of his songs were based on the exploits and misadventures of his crowd—the Mods—and the pressures that affected their daily lives in the early sixties, leading to "My Generation."

"I really believed I was going to be dead. There was a huge atomic crisis through the Cuban missile thing. I remember in England going to school one day knowing the world was going to be blown to bits. In college, a lot of people were walking around like normal and occasionally one person would say what are we doing all this for? Everybody was so resigned to it. They knew there was going to be an atomic war. No one looked like they were going to back down. That was the kind of consciousness at the time. A lot of people have forgotten about it, but I remember the feeling and it lasted for a number of years, when everybody was living 'in the shadow of the bomb' but they were totally resigned to it.

"I was in the Ban the Bomb movement in England for a little while, but the thing that bowled me over was LSD. It wiped me out. I stopped working and got very obsessed with it. I really did believe it was something enormous and important and I was also involved with some of the sentiments surrounding it, the whole peace and love thing.

"During that period I can only remember three songs I wrote. Just pre my first acid trip I wrote 'Relax,' which ended up on an album, then 'Pictures of Lily,' which was released as a single. The other one I don't think anything happened with. Afterwards, I wrote some very weird songs. I wrote 'Faith in Something Bigger,' 'Happy Jack,' and what became the 'Underture' to *Tommy*, and 'Welcome' from *Tommy*. This is way before I had the idea for *Tommy*."

Townshend claimed he was influenced as a writer more by the Stones than Bob Dylan, or certainly the Beatles. "I was influenced a lot by the Stones. I've always felt Mick Jagger to be much older. He's two years older than me, but he feels a lot older. I liked almost everything they did. I also liked a lot of the Beatles stuff but I was never influenced that much by it. I mean, musically they just seemed to have such a peculiar method of working. Also, a lot of it was melodic in a way that although it sounded great when they did it, when you tried to find out what it was that made it tick and react to it musically, it was sort of like Italian love songs. How can you be influenced by that? Ray Davies is one of my favorite writers. His stuff is a bit heavily nostalgia, but I really like it. I was quite keen on Elton John, although I didn't entirely realize at the time that it was a two-man show. That sort of weakened it a bit for me. Joni Mitchell I really like; then again I don't always listen to the words. What gets me is the sound. But she writes so personally and I sort of shy away from that a little bit. But I'm deeply in love with her."

Townshend spoke about his earliest songwriting success. "Almost from the first time I put pen to paper I was a successful writer. 'Can't Explain' got into the British charts. It was kind of a lift off the feeling the Kinks had in 'You Really Got Me.' I suppose in a way it's a moon and June song. But later I thought, no, it's got nothing to do with love at all. It's got to do with a whole lot of other things.

"So then I discovered I had this ability to just sit down and scribble things out and think I was writing consciously, but the real meaning was coming from somewhere else that I had no control over. I suppose I was surprised by how observant I was without being conscious of it.

" 'Anyway, Anyhow, Anywhere' was the second song I wrote. It was modified a bit by Roger Daltrey, so that's why he shares a credit with me. Those two songs I wrote while I was living in complete squalor, getting stoned every night, and listening to Jimmy Reed records. Those were just three words I wrote on a piece of paper. You know, you used to do that when you were stoned out of your head. You look at it the next day and say, what the fuck was I talking about? Those three words were what I wrote to describe the way Charlie Parker plays. So that became the title of our next single, which was required the statutory two weeks after the release of the first one. I knocked out the song and it was much more of a conscious thing. I already looked back at 'Can't Explain' and started to think, yeah, this one's going to be about a punk kid.

"About a year after I started writing, Kit Lambert started announcing to everyone that he thought I was a genius. I mean, I produced a fantastic amount of demos. I holed up in my flat with two tape machines, writing consistently. Kit often used to fantasize about doing something on a grand scale even then. It was his idea to do the mini opera on 'A Quick

One' ('Happy Jack' in the states). It was him pushing me to do grander things. Kit Lambert was telling me I was a great writer and I believed him because I wanted to believe him.

"There were other people I respected who liked our music. Jagger really liked it and said so. The Beatles really liked 'A Quick One.' Paul McCartney was saying that they were in the recording studio—at that time they would have been recording *Sgt. Pepper*—and they heard that album and really liked it and he said they were doing something similar and that was affecting what they were doing, which I thought was very nice.

"Funnily enough, I did write a couple of songs early in the band's career, even before Keith Moon joined us. Then I laid off writing for about two years and we started getting into rhythm and blues. Then the Stones came on the scene and they sort of affirmed that we were all right with rhythm and blues, so we got even more into it. And then when we went for a recording audition with EMI they said they liked the band but they felt we needed original material. Actually, EMI could very well have said, they'll make a good R&B band 'cause a little bit later a lot of R&B bands did get recording contracts, like John Mayall and Georgie Fame, just on the strength of their covering other R&B material. It might never have occurred to me to write. It was more EMI's idea. Actually I'm deeply indebted to them."

෨

Townshend has remained prolific throughout his career, penning over one hundred songs for the Who and a hundred more for his solo albums. As a consummate literary man, he's written novels and short stories, articles and essays, and developed several more concept albums, culminating with the publication of his 544-page memoir, Who I Am. *In the meantime,* Tommy *himself refuses to die, revived on Broadway in a new production in 2024.*

John Sebastian (1974)

"The heaviest influence on my songwriting was approval. The fourth or fifth song I wrote was 'Do You Believe in Magic' and the band loved that one. So this tremendous thing started. It was totally one of those great surprises."I think in a way the Spoonful started off being sort of a jug band and country music–influenced rock 'n' roll band searching for material among the various archives of great songs, and in the meantime, I kept coming up with them. One time it would be a song; one time it would be an improvement on an old song. One time it would be 'Gee, this is a great melody, but they're never gonna buy "Colored man at the end of de war,"' those strange lyrics that some of those old jug band tunes used to have. So that's when I started actually thinking of writing songs on purpose and putting time into it. And since I never wrote more than, say, ten songs that didn't appear on a Spoonful album, you can judge my output totally by the Spoonful output.

"Whatever patterns that songwriters have, you can pretty much eliminate in my case. I've done everything from write a song in ten minutes to write two verses of a song and then five years later finally come up with a third verse. And all extremes in the middle. Many of the idea elements of the songs happened with me and Zolly throwing around a subject. Zol never liked to do anything like songwriting, so it would usually be an idea or an outgrowth of a conversation that I would then sit with and mull over by myself and try to come up with a structure. Then I'd sing it to somebody in the group who'd say, 'Gee, that's good, but did you forget the part when we were laughing about such and such?' And I'd say, 'Okay, we'll get to that in the third verse.' That kind of thing.

"My only standard was that I wanted to like the song, and I don't like very much. Also, I don't write music, so if I could remember it and like it, that was it."

Sounds simple, doesn't it? But when you can turn out a magnificent string of rock 'n' roll pearls like Sebastian did during the midsixties, you can afford to be simple.

"I can say with no vanity that it was just heavenly to listen back to those early songs. The reason is, you haven't done it, it's not all you. It's, you know, modern miracles, combined with an awful lot of good chemistry that has to happen in the studio. Moments—you have to get a series of them. Magic moments that you did not plan, that you couldn't train for . . . that just happen. All of those things that have been thrown aside in the last couple of years as far as methods that guys adopt to go into the studio, those things all contribute.

"A 45 is special. I mean it's three minutes of heaven. It's got to be an opiate. I never intentionally tried to write a hit, but some of them, maybe three-quarters of the way through, I'd start to go . . . Hmmmm, and I could smell it. And listening back to the playback of something like 'You Didn't Have to Be So Nice,' the first couple of times, after we put the vocal parts on and the drum fills . . . it was, my God . . . something else!"

Figure 11. John Sebastian, 2015. Photo: James Brooks, Wikimedia Commons, CC BY 2.0.

I asked him then if, during that time, he'd ever wanted to write something longer and possibly more personal than the small miracles he'd been creating.

"My writing was as personal as I wanted to get at the time. You see, I wasn't aspiring toward anything but what I was doing. I really wanted to be in *rock 'n' roll* and I wanted to write *rock 'n' roll* songs. If anything I was pooh-poohing people who were trying to put art into rock. At that time I was going, 'Bullshit! That's really bullshit.' I still feel the same way, absolutely . . . except that my own horizons have expanded [*laughing*] to include a few more things.

"For instance, a song I spent a lot of time on recently is 'The Face of Appalachia,' about a young guy, thoughts occurring to a young guy growing up in New York City listening to country music. I knew very early on that it was never going to be a single, but it was nonetheless something that I wanted so much to get out and to have it done right, that I cut it five times before I was satisfied."

John finally did make the step out of the three-minute rock n' roll mold in a song called "The Four of Us," which occupied an entire side on an album entitled, aptly, *The Four of Us*. Covering approximately fifteen verses and three thousand miles, the song is an autobiographical tale of a cross-country journey, written as it happened, week by week, verse by verse.

"That song was actually the outgrowth of Catherine and me, and for me it's very much of a personal love song. It was never intended as a million-seller; I merely wanted, once again, to please myself . . . and the three other people on the trip. I also wanted to write something that was longer than three minutes, so I was very happy about what was coming out in that sense. During that particular trip I was writing all of the songs contained on the album. I wrote 'Lashes Larue' in there and 'I Don't Want Nobody Else.' 'The Four of Us' was just one of the songs . . . and it kept growing."

Although many people may not be aware of it, John Sebastian was one of the first of the generation's rock 'n' roll writers to make the great leap to Broadway, writing the words and music for a show starring Dustin Hoffman, entitled *Jimmy Shine*. John entered into the situation wanting to "put a rose on Broadway," but the way he described it, things were not so rosy.

"I told them I was writing songs for them. I had written half the songs already. Just by coincidence they fit in. I wrote one or two for the show, custom made, and they were so awful they were great. I mean what was funny about them was that they were making a slight parody of the desperation the lyricist always shows in plays. Very often you can see that lyricist up at three a.m. saying 'Christ, it's going into rehearsal tomorrow; I've got to have this done!' so that the words are just silly, you know? I wrote a tune for the show called "There's a Future in Fish, Mr. Shine," which was my show tune. It was sung by the guy who used to play one of the uncles on the Molly Goldberg radio show.

"You see, they weren't sure whether to consider me important or not, because they weren't sure whether they wanted a musical. They wanted to have music in it, but they didn't want to spend the money to have music in it. So they were telling me, 'This isn't a musical, this is only a show with songs in it.' Okay, I got it. Then I'd say, 'All right guys, you don't have to give me an orchestra or anything, all I need is a four-piece band.' And they'd say, 'How about a three-piece band?'

"I mean, they didn't know where to put me. It was a bunch of people who were trying desperately to adjust to this new thing. They said, 'Hair made it; maybe we should pay attention to him.' It was so strange, and in a lot of ways I came to have such little regard for the whole style, the way the thing was being put together, that it gave me more confidence. You know, actors and actresses and directors relate to each other every bit as crazily as musicians. It's weird if you're not somehow initiated.

"Here's another thing they did. I had a song in there that they cut in half. The guy they assigned to me to teach the song to could not sing. Hence they said, 'Okay, we'll cut the song in half and he'll sing half on his entrance and half on his exit.' So I said, 'Okay guys, I'm just going to go ahead and make the record my way and make a recording of it.' The song is 'She's a Lady.' It's a nice song; it has impact onstage. It stops a show or two now and then in my shows. So I knew the song was valuable and I also knew that none of the people there saw the value, forget musical, the dramatic value of the song. So it was at that point that I, you know, became discouraged by the people around me."

Would he ever venture near Broadway again?

"Absolutely! I'm sure that something marvelous could be done on Broadway that could make everybody so much money that it would be fantastic. I would love to do it, but with somebody who had an idea or two."

As far as musical influences, "Chuck Berry's gotta be among my top three influences, but that's a cliché by now, to say you were influenced by Chuck Berry. I also liked the blues writers, like Arthur Crudup. I mean, whether or not it's the same musical format for eighteen verses, some of those verses were killers. I don't know if I was consciously interested in lyrics, but I do know all the words I've ever heard in a song. I have a photographic memory for words. Another thing I dug was being able to understand the lyrics . . . and on a lot of the records I was listening to, the lyrics were not readily understandable, so I would go to great lengths sometimes in slowing records down in order to get the words. Whether I was consciously saying, 'This is great writing,' or 'I'll be a great writer someday,' or anything like that, it was nonetheless making an imprint."

I asked him if songwriters talk shop this way when they get together.

"I do it with a couple of guys, pretty much the ones whose lyrics I like. For instance, with Randy Newman, within the first ten minutes of talking to him we were talking about dry periods and he's so eloquent on the subject, and so hilarious. I love that guy. He's real cynical about songwriting, but Jesus Christ, he is so touching as a writer. And I never felt more sympathy when we were talking about dry periods than I did from him.

"The dry period I had wasn't in terms of not writing, it was just that I wasn't writing anything good. And my impulse when I'm not writing good things is not to release anything, which has not been the particular style of a lot of characters in the last couple of years. But now that I have a handful of songs I can't say I know any more about them than I would about any other batch.

"I've got a song called 'Friends Again,' a song called 'Stories We Could Tell,' that's a reminiscing song that I wrote for the Everly Brothers but sort of pertains to me and Catherine. But I couldn't tell you that I was changing directions or staying in the same place, because I always find out after the fact.

"Like I said, I've been writing when I was miserable; I've written when I was happy. I've written when I was unhappy in love; I've written when I was happy in love. I've written on the road, off the road; in a studio, not in a studio. So that even in the search, I couldn't really find a system."

Sebastian did, however, have a few definite statements to make about the process itself.

"As time goes on you start to like writing more and you start to become more conscious of it. I started wanting to write more and simultaneously to not write as much. In other words, there is a natural outburst that happens when somebody goes into songwriting in their late teenage years the way I did. I hadn't done it before; I hadn't intended to do it. It was a wonderful thing that came falling out of the sky, so it was a very spontaneous, easy, and thoughtless process, not anything I worried about or particularly enjoyed going after. But I'd say that from then on I started to enjoy it more and to not have quite so much of a flood, which is only natural, because you write a given song about a given subject and that's one subject you can't ever touch again.

"It's not hard to write now, although it is harder than it was during my eighteenth year when I had never tried it before, when I knew something about rock 'n' roll that nobody else knew, or so it seemed. Now so much is just common knowledge; so much of the stuff that I've produced has already been copied by a second generation that it's hard to go into the same area that you've already touched and find much in the way of vegetation growing."

$\sim$

After his comeback single "Welcome Back" hit the top of the charts in 1976, Sebastian has continued to release rootsy albums, including John Sebastian and Arlen Roth Explore the Spoonful Songbook *(2011).*

Jimmy Webb (1989)

"Glen Campbell had heard 'By the Time I Get to Phoenix' on an album by Johnny Rivers," Jimmy Webb told me. "Before that it had been recorded by Tony Martin. And before that, when I was working with Jobete Publishing at Motown, I had originally written the song for a Paul Peterson album. So, it had really been around the game board."

Since Campbell's hit version, the song has traveled a path around the game board even more circuitous than the narrator's vehicular journey, one that Webb himself has admitted would be impossible to actually drive, among them an eighteen-minute pit stop on Isaac Hayes's *Hot Buttered Soul*. According to some estimates, it is among the most covered songs of the twentieth century.

"The first time I met Glen we had already had two top ten singles and we were working on another project together, where I had been hired to arrange and do some score charts and he was the guitarist. I'll never forget the first thing he said to me. He said, 'Why don't you get a haircut?' We were sort of philosophically on opposite sides of the line, at least politically, but what started out as kind of shaky, developed into a wonderful friendship. We've been working together for twenty years.

"As far as my songwriting process, I seem to have most of my problems at the beginning, when I'm trying to decide what actual shape the song is going to have. I would think that painters have the same difficulty when they're first laying out a work; the composition of the work is important and the shape of it. The tone of it is very important, and it takes a long time to work that out.

"Once you see how it's going to go, then it's a race for the finish line, and that's the way it is with me. If I can get through the first verse, then I know the shape of the second verse. So all I have to do is fill in the second verse, which is harder than it sounds, because—just as a completely unfair rule of thumb—songs in general tend to open stronger than they finish. So you have to discipline yourself to work as hard on the second half of the song as you worked on the first half of the song, and not give in to that impulse to just fill in the blanks. I've probably been guilty of that when I was younger, and when I was in a hurry just trying to get finished. But Joni Mitchell and I were very close friends for a while and I've watched her work and I've seen her notebooks. I've seen how many times she rewrites something; how completely meticulous she is. If there's a possibility she could go back and make just one line better, you'll turn over the page and see where she's recopied the song and changed things. Paul Simon also does a lot of rewriting and does a lot of free association on legal pads, where he opens up the idea that a song could go in any direction, rather than be obsessively controlling about which way it's actually going to go. Stephen Sondheim works that way as well—free associations on a page, where every idea is given entrance and then they're honed away until the very best ones remain.

Figure 12. Jimmy Webb, 2016. Photo: Tore Sætre, Wikimedia Commons, CC BY-SA 4.0.

"Lyrics have to come first and I've never said that to anyone. But I think that lyrics have to come first. Or at least the central idea and intent of the song has to come first. You have to know what you're going to say. That's when it's great to have a good title, because if you have a good title, you have a tremendous clue about what you want to say. It's great to go off with some great melody or some great chord change, but talking about pure songwriting, you've got to know what you're writing about.

"There are two kinds of discipline involved with writing every day. There's the discipline to get up in the morning and go to work and work on something for five or six hours. And then there's a reverse discipline to leave it. I don't play the piano at home, even though I might be tempted to worry a tune some more. And since composers are obsessive by nature, it's tough. You have to say I'm not going to look at that until tomorrow. I know from playing tennis, sometimes I play my best after I've been away from the game for a couple of weeks. It's about letting yourself breathe a little bit. Plus, I have five kids, so when I get home they have a way of blowing everything else out of my head, whether I like it or not. I used to be quite a lot more obsessive about what I did, but then when I listen to the old stuff, I sometimes see where I could have stood back a little bit and been a little more objective about what I was doing. In retrospect, if I were going to rewrite something, I'd probably rewrite 'MacArthur Park,' because I feel that maybe it wasn't my best work.

"Working on Broadway, I've learned a lot about making things clear. Because on Broadway everything has to be clear and it has to relate to the book. If the person singing the songs wouldn't sing those words, you're in big trouble. You're in trouble if it doesn't resonate with the character. On Broadway, the music serves the book, serves the scenario. It can never become more important, for a second. But it's good discipline. It teaches you to work with other people and it teaches you to put across an idea that isn't totally selfish, that isn't totally your own. You have to be of service to the idea."

As opposed to his friend Barry Mann, Webb has had some success as a solo performer. "There's a built-in resistance in our particular business to someone trying to do too many things. Anytime you try to do something different you'll hear someone say: 'What makes you think you can score a film? What makes you think you can write a Broadway musical?' Or if I want to be an artist and sell records, and if I sing in tune and I have a way of putting my songs across that's unique and original and interesting, I have every reason to think I should be able to do that.

100 | They're Playing My Song

"I remember when I was at Dunhill Records, working with Thelma Houston and Richard Harris, there was a young writer there named P. F. Sloan, who wrote a lot of hits with Steve Barri. He's one of the first writers I ever knew who wanted to cut his own album, and he ran into such resistance over wanting to do his own records, you would have thought he had committed some kind of heinous crime. That's actually what inspired me to write the song 'P. F. Sloan,' because I didn't like what happened to his record."

In Webb's case, the song has since become one of his signature numbers.

❧

Unanimously elected president of the Songwriters Hall of Fame in 2011, Webb has recently worked in the soundtrack area. As a performer he's released seven albums since 1993. As a writer he's written two celebrated books, Tunesmith: The Art of Songwriting *(1998) and* The Cake and the Rain: A Memoir *(2017).*

Frank Zappa (1974)

Combining a Theater-of-the-Absurd sensibility, sharp-edged satiric humor, and a hair-trigger threshold of outrage, Frank Zappa's odes to teenage life, set in a fifties backbeat, are classics of the snide put-down.

Always in the vanguard of modern music, Zappa was the first (and is still perhaps the only) musician to bring a classical orientation to the form, producing pieces that certainly might be thought of as symphonic rhythm and blues.

With his group, the Mothers of Invention, in the summer of 1967 (the infamous Summer of Love), Frank Zappa brought a wicked and spontaneous theatricality to the rock stage at the Garrick Theatre, similar to what the Fugs were doing a few blocks down the street.

Since then Zappa has extended his vision further into the realms of classical music, rock, jazz, and R&B. He has also become involved with films (*200 Motels*).

Known for his hostility to reporters, Zappa was nonetheless quite cordial in our meeting at the Golden Gate Motel in Brooklyn, overlooking scenic Sheepshead Bay.

"I didn't start listening to music until I was about fifteen years old because my parents weren't too fond of it, and we didn't have a radio or a record player or anything. I think the first music that I heard that I liked was Arab music and I don't know where I ever ran into it, but I heard it someplace and that got me off right away. Then I heard a song called 'I' by the Velvets on the Red Robin label and 'Gee' and 'Sh-boom,' 'Riot in Cell Block Number Nine,' and 'Annie Had a Baby.' By accident I heard those things and they knocked me out.

"I didn't start writing songs per se until I was about twenty years old, twenty-one maybe, because all my compositions prior to that time had been orchestral or chamber music. I think the basic idea of being a composer is if you're going to be true to yourself and write what you like, you write what you like without worrying whether it's going to be academically suitable or whether it's going to make any mark in history or not. My basic drive for writing anything down is I want to hear it.

"The very first tunes that I wrote were fifties doo wop. 'Memories of El Monte' and stuff like that. It's always been my contention that the music that was happening during the fifties has been one of the finest things that ever happened to American music and I loved it. I could sit down and write a hundred more of the 1950s-type song right now and enjoy every minute of it. I think my writing is as influenced, however, by country blues as it is by 1950s stuff. I've always been fond of Muddy Waters, Lightning Slim, Howling Wolf, and those guys.

"At the time I was living in a part of town called Echo Park [Los Angeles], which was a Mexican, Japanese, Filipino, Black neighborhood, and I lived in a little two-room place, grubby little place on the side of a hill, 1819 Bellevue Avenue. In that house I wrote 'Brain Police,' 'Oh No, I Don't Believe It,' 'Hungry Freaks,' 'Bowtie Daddy,' and five or six others. A lot of the songs off the first album [*Freak Out*] had already been written for two or three years before the album came out. And a lot of songs wouldn't come out until the third or fourth album.

"About fifty percent of the songs were concerned with the events of 1965. Los Angeles, at that time, in the kiddie community that I was hanging out in, they were all getting into acid very heavily and you had people seeing God in colors and flaking out all over the place. You had plenty of that and meanwhile there was all that racial tension building up in Watts.

"I was up to San Francisco once or twice, but I wasn't interested or influenced by the scene there. Basically I thought what was happening in San Francisco in that early stage was . . . well, I'll tell you what I saw when I went there. Whereas in LA you had people freaking out—that is, making their own clothes, dressing however they wanted to dress, wearing their hair out, that is, being as weird as they wanted to be in public and everybody going in separate directions—I got to San Francisco and found everybody dressed up in 1890s garb, all pretty specific codified dress. It was like an extension of high school, where one type of shoe is the 'in' shoe, belt-in-the-back peggers, or something like that. It was in the same sort of vein, but it was the costume of the 1890s. It was cute, but it wasn't as evolved as what was going on in LA. In San Francisco they had a 'more rustic than thou' approach."

Frank Zappa (1974) | 103

Figure 13. Frank Zappa, 1970. Photo: Noord-Hollands Archief / Fotopersbureau De Boer, Wikimedia Commons, CC0 1.0.

From there Zappa and the Mothers moved on to New York in the summer of 1967.

"There wasn't too much going on in the Village that interested me. The people who came to see us at the Garrick mostly had short hair; they came from middle-class white, Jewish environments, mostly suburban. They came to see our show because we were something weird that was on that street and we were a sort of specialized recreational facility.

"The reason they were shocked in those days was that they hadn't seen or heard anything that came close to what we were doing. Now, after so many groups imitating various aspects of what we did, they've seen it from other sources. Take, for instance, Alice Cooper. Basically what they're doing is a cosmeticized version of the same thing we were doing in 1967. He's taken the obvious showmanship aspects without doing the difficult musical things. By simplifying the music to the point where you don't have to worry about it too much and, doing it with a lot of lights and a lot of props, you can put together a show that can have wider appeal."

Eventually, our discussion shifted to his feelings about lyric writing.

"I think that by the time I put a lyric down on a piece of paper and go through all the drudgery of setting it to a musical format and rehearsing it and so forth . . . that they're all reasonably successful in saying what they were intended to say. There's plenty more that could be said, but there are mechanical obstacles in the way of getting that out to an audience. I think there are lots of things that I'd love to be able to express to people in lyrics, but being sort of a rational person I sit down and figure out, do those people really want to know, and is it worth the trouble to write it out, rehearse it, perform it night after night, record it just to express my point of view on a subject when it's none of my business to inform somebody else about it in the first place.

"Basically what people want to hear in a song is I love you, you love me; I'm okay you're okay; the leaves turn brown, they fell off the trees; the wind was blowing, it got cold, it rained, it stopped raining; you went away, my heart broke, you came back and my heart was okay. I think basically that is deep down what everybody wants to hear—it's been proven by numbers.

"So you start to think about the performer's role as an entertainer, and that the audience is paying money to come there and see you do something that will basically gratify them. And I have a conflict where I believe that people are entitled to get off as much as they can, and I think entertainers ought to do just that; however, I don't merely want to go out there and bullshit my way through a show. I want some substance too, so I have to mix it up a little bit and do some of the things that people wish to have done before their very eyes onstage, and at the same time keep myself from going crazy by writing down some of the things I want to hear.

"Usually after I finish writing a song, that's it. It doesn't belong to me anymore. When I'm working on a song, it takes weeks and weeks to finish and the orchestra stuff takes even longer than that. It's like working on the construction of an airplane. One week you're a riveter, or you're putting the wiring in, or something like that. It's just a job you do and then you go on to the next step, which is learning how to perform it or teaching it to somebody else. I feel that all the material I've written, as far as my own appreciation of it, goes through a cycle where, especially if it's something I'm going to record, where you work on it so much that by the time you finish it you can't stand it anymore. You know, you just get saturated with it. When you get to hear it played right for the first couple of times, that's the get-off. After that I don't like it again until it's

Frank Zappa (1974) | 105

a few years old and it's been recorded and I'll pick up the record and I'll say: 'That's hip.'

"'Brain Police' was a phenomenon because I was just sitting in the kitchen at the Bellevue Avenue house and I was working on 'Oh No, I Don't Believe It,' which didn't have lyrics at the time . . . and I heard, it was just like there was somebody standing over my shoulder telling me those lyrics and it was really weird. I looked around . . . I mean, it wasn't like 'hey Frank, listen to this . . .' but it was there. So I just wrote it down and figured the proper setting for it."

I remarked that Zappa seemed to be drifting away from the kind of social protest that characterized his early albums.

"I haven't become less conscious, it's just that I don't feel a driving need to write songs that are so obvious to everybody. We have one in the show now that's obvious to everybody, with some Richard Nixon jive in it. But I'd rather write 'Penguin in Bondage.' My experiences have changed, they're getting less specific in certain ways, more specific in others.

"It used to be that I would write specific things about obvious social phenomena that a large number of people could identify with because they had seen it in action. But that's less specific in terms of my own personal experience. You know, I could observe something happen that may or may not have happened to me personally, and I could still write about it. These days such weird things have happened to me as a person that I'd rather put some of those down and do it that way. That's why I have songs like 'Penguin in Bondage' and 'Montana.' I write about the things that are part of my personal experience."

"Montana," which is, in part, about a man who dreams of raising dental floss on a ranch in Montana, started out this way: "I got up one day, looked at a box of dental floss and said, Hmmmm. I assumed that nobody had done the same thing and I felt it was my duty as an observer of floss to express my relationship to the package. So I went downstairs and I sat at the typewriter and I wrote a song about it. I've never been to Montana, but I understand there's only 450,000 people in the whole state. It has a lot of things going for it, plenty of space for the production of dental floss . . . and the idea of traveling along the empty wasteland with a very short horse and a very large tweezer, grabbing the dental floss sprout as it pooches up from the bush . . . grabbing it with your tweezers and towing it all the way back to the bunkhouse . . . would be something good to imagine."

I asked how extensively he revised.

"Sometimes I show the lyrics to my wife, or after a while I'll get her to read them to me so I can see what the sounds are like, because part of the texts are put together phonetically as well as what the information is supposed to be. I change lyrics all the time. A lot of them get changed by accident. Somebody will read them wrong, and it'll sound so funny I'll leave it wrong.

"I've always hated poetry quite a bit. I really hate it. The whole idea of it just makes me gag. And usually people who produce it—I don't like to make sociological generalizations, but that's not something I readily identify with . . . the suffering and the pumping on the chest with the closed fist, bowing of the head . . . leaves falling off the trees, the wind coming up and all that shit. I hate it.

"I don't like books. I very seldom read. My wife and I have a joke because she likes to read. I say there's two things wrong with the world today, one of them is the writers and the other is the readers. The main thing wrong with writers is that they're dealing with something that is almost obsolete, but they don't know it yet—which is language. Language as a by-product of the technological growth of civilization has . . . well, think of what's happened to the English language as a result of advertising sloganism. The meanings of words have been corrupted to the point where, from some semanticists' point of view, how can you convey an accurate piece of information with this language?

"I'm not saying writers should be replaced. I feel sorry for them. They have a problem similar to people who write music. It's just as hard to write an accurate musical concept down on a piece of paper because of the new techniques on all instruments.

"The other problem is that I'm not much of a singer and most of the vocal stuff we put out I've had to give to other people to sing if I wanted to get a listenable performance out of it . . . consequently, if they don't say the things with the right inflections, it changes the meaning.

"There's just bunches of problems in getting the true meaning across. The only guy who's really got it made is a painter. All he's got to worry about is whether his colors are going to fade or whether his canvas is properly stretched because there's no middleman. He does it and that's it. He doesn't have to send it through a bunch of other processors.

"I think, ideally, the way it should be is you could use words for amusement purposes only, because the spoken word, the sound of

Frank Zappa (1974) | 107

words . . . strikes me as funny, because of the differences in people's noise-producing mechanisms. But as far as the information communicated in the words, it would be better if people could communicate telepathically.

"Actually, that's all a bunch of crap. Who needs to worry about all that technical stuff? I'm telling you, folks, I just don't read very much. I don't like books too much. I don't like poetry at all. And that's it."

Picking up an earlier thread, I asked Zappa if he didn't think it was the artist's responsibility to educate those who know less than he does. He didn't.

"It's hard for people to imagine that somebody else knows something they don't know. And suppose you actually do know something that somebody else doesn't know and you want to tell them about it, well, you've got a problem, because, first of all, they don't want to know; and if it's you saying: 'If you knew this you might be better off,' then you have to sit there and say to yourself, do I really want to tell them that, will it make them feel better, will it do them any good if they know? I realistically look at it this way. It doesn't work. I think that it's quite possible that what I have to say is useful only to very few people and I should not bust my ass to make it available to a large number of people, because, first of all, they can't use it; second of all, they probably don't need it; and third of all, I know they don't want it. So, kiss it off and boogie!"

Why then, I continued, would an artist keep making records?

"I think in contemporary America most artists try to make records so that they can eat."

But, didn't you ever have something you said get through to someone else in a positive way, I asked.

"Yes."

And how did you feel?

"All I knew was that I was tired."

෴

Nothing if not prolific, Zappa has created a catalog that includes forty-three albums released before his death in 1994, and sixty-five more after it, most recently the 2024 release of Whisky a Go-Go, 1968.

108 | They're Playing My Song

Laura Nyro (1984)

One of the most enigmatic and evocative and emotionally intense song-writers ever to have songs on the top ten, Laura always followed her feelings, often to her own detriment. At Monterey in 1966 she may have been marked as one of the outcasts, but so were Simon and Garfunkel. "We thought at the time that it was the cultural revolution," said Paul Simon in an interview I did for *Saturday Review*, "or even the Revolution that everybody was talking about. We thought it was really going to come into effect and that Simon and Garfunkel were going to be artifacts of the New York–eastern-early-sixties days, which could no longer continue because we didn't understand about things like the ecology." "I think I searched," Nyro told me, "and I think I traveled far to find something that was very close. People who are going to find their own convictions will all have to go through a certain number of obstacles. I don't think I'm different from other people who are searching . . . to be happy, really."

Nyro described her songs as simple and basic, "although sometimes you'd never know it. It's a musical starting point and you could stay with it or take it to the ends of the earth, because as beautiful as simplicity is, it can become a tradition that stands in the way of exploration. I started off in music with simplicity and then moved into abstraction and some uncharted waters with the exploration of it. Some people would say I went off the deep end. I wanted to learn more, and I took freedoms with the principles of composition. I used these dark chord structures, suspended chords, advanced dissonances (advanced for rock), rhythms leading to other rhythms within the same song. My jazz background put certain inflections into my songwriting and singing. Throw in all the poetry I'd read since I was a kid and just being a woman, and that's what made my songs complex and emotionally rich.

"When I was very young, I remember sitting at a piano and hearing the notes and the chords ring out in the air and I knew there was something special in that sound, some kind of freedom. As a kid, I listened to the fifties songs of urban romance: 'The Wind' by the Diablos, 'Oh What a Night' by the Dells, 'Happy Happy Birthday Baby' by the Tune Weavers. The first two 45s I bought were 'Bye Bye Love' by the Everly Brothers and 'Mr. Lee' by the Bobbettes. A year or two later my favorite songs were by Curtis Mayfield and the Impressions. By the age of fifteen I was seriously listening to John Coltrane and jazz singers like Billie Holiday, Sarah Vaughan, and Nina Simone. I remember one spring afternoon at [the High School of] Music and Art. The weather was lovely, and me and my friends were sitting outside looking at a newspaper picture of the Beatles arriving in America. We were listening to 'I Want to Hold Your Hand' and I felt this thunderbolt in my heart.

"I don't think you should categorize yourself as an artist. You should allow yourself to grow. Growth is the nature of the creative process. You have to accept it, respect it, and move on. The thing that's important to me is to express life as I see it. That's my priority. There've been many changes over the years as I saw life differently from age eighteen and age twenty-five. You have to remember; I was still a teenager when I made my first record and the world around me started changing at the speed of lightning just because I'd written some provocative songs. The sixties started spinning into a whirlwind and outside of some recognition for my music I felt like I was living inside a hurricane. My rhythm of life was more of a free-spirited one and then it changed. I kind of felt like I was losing the rhythm of my youth. So many things were happening at the same time. This is how I experienced it. So I started slowly moving out of that scene so I could experience other things in life without a bunch of people breathing down my neck. When I turned thirty, my love songs changed from romantic notions to a deeper taste of life. My mother died right before I wrote the songs for *Nested*. My child was born right before I wrote *Mother's Spiritual*.

"The last few years have been so musically abundant that I felt like the Goddess of Creativity. But who knows? Next year I may only write one song, because that kind of songwriting is cyclical, seasonal; it's the culmination of a deeper experience. It's like nature, it takes time to seed and then it blooms.

"*Mother's Spiritual* was a wonderful idea that flew through my head in a minute and then took years to manifest because the relationships and responsibilities that were inspiring the music were also pulling me away from it in terms of time. Since I was recording while I was writing, it actually took me two and a half years to complete the fourteen songs. Most of the songs I wrote at night. I would just wake up in the middle of the night. I had a young baby and that's when I found the space to write. I didn't work with a tape recorder. I would write my ideas down. I have love songs written upside down on matchbook covers. I'd write on my hand if there was no paper. Sometimes I might hear a particular instrument; like when I wrote 'Melody in the Sky' I heard gypsy violins.

"Once I'm writing I'm very disciplined. I'm there for the music. When I'm writing music, there's a certain magic from the music underlying life. It's like you're living at a deeper current. It's a very complete feeling. You're taking care of everyday things, but you're living at the edge of a song."

Laura Nyro recorded one more album—Walk the Dog and Light the Light—before her death in 1997. Angel in the Dark, recorded in 1994-1995, came out in 2001. She was inducted into the Rock and Roll Hall of Fame in 2012.

Paul Simon (1976, 1985)

While Bob Dylan stands alone as the central songwriting figure of the sixties, the one who woke this sleeping giant of a generation determined not to go silent, none of the other poet laureates of the era addressed themselves to all of us middle-class cowboys as directly as Paul Simon. We were the ones who rode through the sixties on Schwinns rather than Harleys, who grew our hair then cut it, moved through dope and the draft into and out of meaningful relationships while at the same time proving to be too brainy (or repressed) to follow the freak-out route of the kids in San Francisco.

At first exercises in English composition, Paul Simon's early works nevertheless reflected the position of most young white middle-class Americans at the turning point of the sixties. Especially if you were of the segment of the generation whose experiences tended more toward the Volkswagen than the Harley, the Saturday-night date as opposed to shacking up, the ski-weekend trip rather than the acid trip, Simon's troublesome miniatures struck much closer to home than Dylan's frenetically eloquent dissertations. At the same time, they were meatier by far than Lennon and McCartney's adolescent trifles.

Here you were, still in school and somewhat alienated and repressed ("The Sound of Silence"), trying to explain yourself to women ("The Dangling Conversation"), or to yourself if they wouldn't listen ("I Am a Rock"). But even though your head weighed approximately twice as much as the rest of you, sometimes, unaccountably, you felt good ("The 59th Street Bridge Song"). So, if Lennon and McCartney were still essentially foreigners, and if Dylan had leaped one too many synapses to reside in the perpetual ozone of the stoned poet, Paul Simon lived closer to Ozone Park, Queens, New York. Actually, right across the 59th Street Bridge from it, on the Upper East Side of Manhattan, a short jog from Gracie Mansion.

"It was a neighborhood largely unaffected by the youth culture," he told me when I interviewed him at his monumental apartment, a city kid's dream, with picture windows that encompassed all the ball fields of Central Park. The maid had just served us tuna fish sandwiches for lunch. "Simon and Garfunkel never drifted into the pop hierarchy like John Phillips (of the Mamas and the Papas). We didn't know how to do that. We were fairly isolated from other musicians and mostly stayed together. I wasn't involved in anything. I was just by myself. I was crazy most of the time, high, and relatively depressed throughout those years."

He never had the hair for the sixties; it was too thin and curled a little at the ends when he let it grow past his ears for the photograph on the cover of Simon and Garfunkel's soundtrack album for *The Graduate* (1968). Definitely he was on the wrong side of the mind-body split that separated college graduates from street people, dope from acid, folkies from rockers. Whatever the sixties' lust for parsley, sage, rosemary, and THC distracted in his bloodstream, Simon managed to evince a portrait of control, the straight-arrow, house-plan image that had haunted him for years. "We took drugs, we just didn't sleep in teepees," he said. "We were quiet about it. I never wanted to be busted in Des Moines, you know? So, we just played it straight, and it made life a lot easier and safer. I didn't believe the hippie thing, anyway, that laid-back, minimal-vocabulary California existence. I didn't believe all the smiles. I thought there was a lot of vindictiveness behind them."

If it seems his hard-won fame had been dissipated by a classic case of New York City neurosis, the middle-class blues, Simon was quick to amend that impression. "It was really a good run," he said. "We got knocked, but the overwhelming majority of people treated us with great affection. We had far more success than we ever anticipated. If I felt at a certain time that I wasn't getting enough credit for writing the songs, I don't feel that way now. In the middle of things, you can get competitive or petty. I know there were a lot of demands on me, pressure to put out records, self-induced pressure to write when it was difficult, drug stuff clouding up my brain, tensions between myself and Artie as our careers grew. There were times when it seemed pretty miserable. But looking back on it, it wasn't miserable at all."

Certainly the hits kept coming, although songs like "At the Zoo" and "Fakin' It" were among his most insubstantial works. But *The Graduate* revived Simon's profile, opening up the duo to hip mass appeal. Coming out a month later, *Bookends* revived his and Garfunkel's career and show-cased what was Simon's best song to date, "America," recounting the story of a very specific all-American malaise, as experienced by a generation of thumb-struck children of Jack Kerouac. Nevertheless, Simon the writer wasn't entirely satisfied.

"For me the significant change occurred around 1969, after I wrote 'The Boxer,'" he said. "At that point I stopped smoking grass and I never went back. I told a friend of mine, a really good musician, that I had writer's block. And he said, 'When are you going to stop playing this folkie stuff, all the time the same G to C chords? You could be a really good songwriter, but you don't know enough, you don't have enough tools. Forget about having hits—go learn your ax.' So, I started to study guitar, classical guitar, and I started to study theory. I began listening to other kinds of music—gospel, Jamaican ska, Antonio Carlos Jobim. Gospel music was very easy for me to feel at home with because it sounded like the early fifties rock and roll I grew up with.

"Bridge over Troubled Water" was a gospel-influenced song. As Simon recalled, it was partially written in the recording studio, at Art Garfunkel's urging. "I wrote a third verse, which doesn't really fit in as well as the other two, and we decided to throw in the kitchen sink on it." It became their biggest hit.

"Paradoxically, *Bridge over Troubled Water* (the album and the single) was our most intense success, but it was the end of Simon and Garfunkel. As the relationship was disintegrating, the album was selling ten million copies. And by the time I decided I was going to go out on my own—you can imagine how difficult it was telling the record company there wasn't going to be any follow-up to an album that sold ten million. But for me it really saved my ass, because I don't think we could have followed it up. And it allowed me to just naturally drop down a couple of rungs on the ladder, because there was less attention. I could go and learn what I had to learn again about writing and singing and making records. I was able to step back into the shadows for a while."

The years in the shadows have been fruitful ones for Simon. Combining further study with a less frenetic performing pace, he's produced three fine albums, *Paul Simon, There Goes Rhymin' Simon*, and *Still Crazy After All These Years*—each one revealing a variety of influences, each one musically rich as well as emotionally complex. In the meantime, his miraculously consistent singles output has continued virtually unabated. From "Kodachrome" to "Mother and Child Reunion" to "American Tune" to "My Little Town" to "Fifty Ways to Leave Your Lover," Simon tells us as much as we need to know about the ten years he's been out there on the edge of his sensibility. Not only is he producing songs of quality, but

114 | They're Playing My Song

he's reminding us who we are as he sadly reflects on the past, slyly flirts with affairs and fears (but secretly hopes) he may someday let go.

"I write about the past a lot, my childhood, and the last couple of years—my marriage. Not intentionally. I didn't set out to write about the disintegration of a marriage. It's just that that was what was happening at the time. I guess I have an easier time expressing myself in a song than in real life. It's a structure that works for me. I can say things in a song that I would never say otherwise. It's a way of telling the truth, but again, not intentionally. It just turns out that way."

Simon neatly summed up his early success. "What separated us from the rest of the folkies, and a fact that was completely ignored, was that we had experience in the recording studio. I had been writing rock 'n' roll songs since the age of fifteen—they were all flops, but we knew about the studio, we knew about sounds, textures, voices, overdubbing. We really came out of the rock and roll of the fifties, although the music we were singing was the folk/rock of the early sixties. But I think that's why we had hits."

Apart from Artie, Simon learned a lot in those days from a fellow Queens College student, Carol Klein (aka Carole King). "Carole would play piano and drums and sing. I would play guitar and bass. The game was to make a demo at demo prices and then try to sell it to a record company. Maybe you'd wind up investing three hundred dollars, but if you did something really good, you could get as much as a thousand for it. I never wanted to be in groups, I was only after the seven hundred dollar profit.

He's also, for the most part, gotten past any complaints he may have had about the critics who analyze his words and neglect his music. "I mean, if you're saying something with music and words—if you're saying one thing with words and the opposite with music and you're creating a sense of irony—that's lost. Or if the idea of the song is a musical idea, how to write a song in 7/4 time and make it feel natural, let's say, it's beyond them. I've never heard anyone say, now that was a clever way of doing 7/4 time. Instead, most critics are basically analyzing words. It's English Lit all over again.

"Nevertheless, today I'm functioning on a value system that is relatively well defined in my head, and it doesn't matter what somebody says about my work. I feel I know how far away I am from what I could potentially be. It's nice to be praised, but my eye is on a place farther down the line. It will require more work and either I'll get there or I won't. Check back in ten years and see if I've done anything."

Figure 14. Paul Simon, 2007. Photo: jurvetson, Wikimedia Commons, CC BY 2.0.

"Graceland"

When I spoke to Paul Simon in 1986, he was journeying further into the depths of his youth and his soul, to the roots of the doo-wop he grew up with, on *Graceland*, recorded with South African musicians, a move that some regarded as politically incorrect. But Simon stated he found he had more in common with South African musicians than American accountants. The songs on the album, like "You Can Call Me Al," "The Boy in the Bubble," "Diamonds on the Soles of Her Shoes," and the poignant inner journey "Graceland" have nothing at all to do with politics. "Part of the impulse to write is to have a catharsis," he said.

By the summer of the year, he was fully immersed in the project. "As the writing continues you can get into a little pocket where things are coming easily. You find yourself with this inexplicable flow of images, ideas, thoughts that are interesting. You also have to have a very low level of critical faculty operating. The opposite is when you experience periods where nothing comes because the critical faculties get heightened, and you won't allow a line to come out without criticizing it. You have to loosen up on yourself to allow things to come. I found that reading different books from people who were writing in the mood that I was writing was helpful. When I was writing "Crazy Love" I was reading Chris Durang. When I was writing "Under African Skies" I was reading Yeats. With "Graceland" I was probably reading Raymond Carver. Actually, I did read a book called *Elvis and Gladys*, but I don't think it affected me."

What probably affected his writing more than anything was that he was writing from prerecorded rhythm tracks. "I had a cassette player that had an automatic memory, and I'd just keep playing it over and over, thousands and thousands of plays," he said. "I didn't have a guitar. All I needed was the tracks. A lot of writers write backwards from the tracks, particularly writers who are writing groove records and dance records. They find the groove, then they write the song. I've done it before but never for an entire album. All the elements that became mainstays of this album, juxtaposing music from one culture against music of another, recording with musicians from another musical culture, writing backwards from track to song, I had done in little bits and pieces in the past. So it wasn't a new move for me. The only thing that was new about it was the proportions. The other thing that was new is that I found it didn't really inhibit what I was writing lyrically. In fact, I think it helped. There was a certain assumption at first that what I could say lyrically and melodically would be severely limited by what was already on tape, but it didn't take long to see that it wasn't a disadvantage at all. I refused to compromise in any way on what I wanted to say."

～

Paul Simon has continued to record and write new songs over the past decades. His latest album is Seven Psalms *(2023).*

Jerry Garcia (1984) and Robert Hunter / Grateful Dead (1974)

"Hunter is much more prolific than I am," said Jerry Garcia, "so the most typical way we work is that he'll give me his output, which is just like lots of lyrics of various sorts. I go through those and a few of them will stick with me in little phrases, which find their way into a melody just by hanging around in my mind. But we've also done the thing of actually flogging it, where we get together and sit around a piano with nothing in mind and nothing worked out and build from the ground up. Everyone once in a while I get a song with the phrasing and everything, except lyrics. I have a sense of where I want the vowels to be and so on. Sometimes Hunter will give me a piece that has eight or nine verses but I'll only like two of them. And I'll say, we need a stronger verse plus a bridge that I want shaped like this and he'll take it back. It's reciprocal too, where I'm developing something and then he'll feed me something and I will in turn update an idea.

"One song that had dozens and dozens of versions evolving over a four-year period of continuous working on it and changing it from the original concept was 'Rueben and Cherise,' which is totally unrecognizable from the initial concept and melody I had. I had just a little simple-minded Calypso melody and Hunter came up with a lyric to it that was sort of the groundwork, a story about a musician and a train that evolved into something that was about New Orleans. But it went through countless incarnations, none of them quite satisfying, but the lyrics got better and better until finally they were getting to be really beautiful."

Robert Hunter

"As far as writing, there's three kinds of songs I mainly do: the ones I work hard at, the ones that pop out of my head finished, and then the jigsaw puzzles, where I carve lyrics to slip into prearranged holes in someone else's changes [collaboration]. These are three different crafts—each of them has its own requisite talents, its rules and rewards. I am not so rewarded by the popular success of a tune as by whether I continue to think it's good. I'm not a hit writer. I don't know if I could be as I've scarcely tried. I try to give my work some endurance characteristics, aware that this is not what the market requires at the moment, but confidently expecting that what I do of value will emerge in retrospect. I keep to myself and don't have many associations with the rock world; I fear it the way I fear Fame, Cocaine, Getting Rich, and Leading Others. Their destructive potential as a rule outweighs their gratifying aspects. I find a great deal of satisfaction in my writing, in the pleasant interplay of creative forces, and I spend a lot of my time with guitar, pencil, and cassette machine.

"Songwriting as an art requires all the traditional artistic attitudes and disciplines: dedication, emulation of good models, patience, and resignation to the amount of acclaim allotted you (always seeming too small) as well as natural aptitude. Also needed is an unruly ego with which to do battle, so that your life is not empty of psychic battles and exploits—the raw material of mistakes. Without mistakes we don't learn *better*, and learning nothing better, have nothing to teach. Having nothing to teach we approach crafts empty-handed, with nothing to assert but identity, a questionable proposition to begin with.

"A lyricist intent on exploring the heights and depths of his medium, who attempts to fathom its potential, must soon realize that he is walking a thin line between humility and colossal egotism. Making assured, positive statements to the world is a pretty presumptuous thing to do, especially if you know it will be heard. Though it must be done with caution, too much caution stiffens the art. Before that point is reached you must finally go ahead and trust instincts and hope they are pure. Many of us will be remembered as colossal asses, and some recalled with gratitude and pleasure. What is written only to sell records, it is my expectation, will tend more to putting the perpetrator in the former category. Unless it's done with grace, of course, for I must grudgingly admit that pop is a craft in itself, though as much aligned with politics and demagogical savvy as with music.

Jerry Garcia (1984) and Robert Hunter / Grateful Dead (1974)

"It was only in the last year or so that my work came under critical fire. For the first six years of my writing career my work was largely ignored or relegated to the rubbish heap of psychedelia, an attitude which brought me as close to throwing up my hands and quitting the work as I have ever come. Now I'm seeing the first direct references to my work. Being largely ignored has been as good for me as it has at times been frustrating. Now I am glad it developed that way: my work has had the opportunity to develop almost privately.

"To anyone contemplating entering this profession, I would extend my sincerest discouragement. It is a fiercely competitive field, a ladder with no bottom rungs and only a few top ones. Financially, you must learn to live in a state of imminent disaster. If money comes, it comes in a bomb, and when the smoke clears all that is left is taxes. This is by way of countering the myth that a songwriter's life is a laid-back Aeolian paradise. But then, when you get all that other stuff together and are still alive, it's a breeze. What isn't?

"I've lately gotten into recording my own works and, by the time this little essay is seen, shall either be enjoying some success from this endeavor or nursing my wounds. I'm into this not because of dissatisfaction

Figure 15. Grateful Dead at the Warfield Theatre in San Francisco, October 9, 1980. Photo: Chris Stone (gratefulphoto.com), Wikimedia Commons, CC BY 2.0.

with the interpretations of my friends, far from that, but because I am rather prolific, seeing that I put a great deal of time into what I do. This also affords me the luxury of more personal statements, as only I must be answerable for their content.

"I'm living in London right now. I try not to drink or smoke as it messes with my creative frequencies, but so far have had only token successes. I am an extremist who epitomizes temperance as the crowning virtue and cannot by my nature ever quite achieve it. I live around the corner from the Victoria and Albert Museum, which I try to visit daily as a break in output to take some input.

"Everything is grist for the creative mill; anything which was done with grace, precision, and some consideration of the artist's place in the scheme of things. I choose especially, possibly perversely, things which have no great interest for me and try to develop an interest, as I feel that the areas of my ignorance are characterized by subjective antipathy. I spent several days, for example, studying examples of pre-Reformation alabaster ecclesiastical decor. I studied it precisely because it was *not* interesting to me. I find, by exercising my facilities in such a way, that my appreciation for what *does* naturally interest me is greatly heightened.

"When I admire a poet, I like to read his works into my cassette machine, then listen back, hoping to influence my work with internal music not necessarily my own. But it is my own when the work is finished, because I refuse to incorporate blocks of ideas while realizing the necessity of influence. In other words, I'm at a point in my career where I feel that I am faced with two alternatives: assimilate or perish.

"I don't see why work in the popular vein must be plebeian or obvious; with a bit of conscious effort it seems that all the available influences might be brought to bear, none more important than the others, but all crucial. It is my firm conviction that no medium is more apt to cover the territory, while remaining accessible, than the art of songwriting.

"The Dead are the personification of my values in popular art. We began as traditional musicians, working in Old-time and Bluegrass music, were influenced by Phil Lesh to spread out and improvise a little, but never beyond capacity, and eventually, year by year, invented our own conception of the whole of the music native and accessible to us until it became something entirely itself. We never took day-to-day popular music as our guide any more than we rejected it, and I feel that we have evolved a form of music which is not only unique, but which gives each of us the ultimate creative liberty possible, short of license.

Jerry Garcia (1984) and Robert Hunter / Grateful Dead (1974) | 121

"If this should sound like blowing my own horn, I must add that I don't play or sing in the band but only write lyrics and never cease to be overwhelmed and entirely gratified at the context in which my words occur.

"'Truckin'' was written over a long period of time. I wrote it in different situations. I wrote it while I was on the road with the band trying to capture the flavor of all that. I provided many more verses than needed, some of them angering the real people who were named in them."

Still, what remained had its chilling aspects, revealing a scene dominated by drugs, unexpected encounters with the police, and death. Recorded for *American Beauty*, work on the album coincided with the death of Phil Lesh's father and Jerry Garcia's mother, and it concluded just before the deaths from overdoses of Jimi Hendrix and Janis Joplin. As the scene in San Francisco continued to deteriorate, the national success of "Truckin'" seemed to act as a life raft, rescuing the band from a sinking ship.

The interview with Robert Hunter took place entirely through the mail, with Hunter providing me with a ten-page letter. A second letter followed up my request for more information. Before his death in 2019, he released twelve studio albums (including one spoken-word).

Jerry Garcia's catalog contained more than a hundred albums, solo, acoustic, with the Grateful Dead, the Jerry Garcia Band, Merle Saunders, David Grisman, the New Riders of the Purple Sage, Old and in the Way, and many others. He passed away in 1995.

Valerie Simpson (2009)

In Detroit, songwriter-producers Norman Whitfield and Barrett Strong were perhaps the most in touch with the zeitgeist of 1969, as evidenced by their work for the Temptations, including "Cloud Nine," "Run Away Child, Running Wild," and "Ball of Confusion." In 1970 they'd write the anthemic "War" for Edwin Starr, followed up by the even more explicit "Stop the War Now." But Diana Ross had become socially conscious, too, with 1968's Holland-Dozier-Holland–influenced "Love Child" and 1969's "I'm Living in Shame." By the end of '69 she'd be singing "Someday, We'll Be Together" as her farewell to the Supremes before launching her solo career in Hollywood with "Reach Out and Touch (Somebody's Hand)," written especially for her by the gifted team of Nickolas Ashford and Valerie Simpson. Ashford and Simpson had scored the plum of all plum Motown staff assignments, to write and produce an entire album for the magisterial Diana, after Gordy rejected the work of the previous producer, the accomplished LA vet Bones Howe.

"It was a coup for us," said Valerie, "because most people only got to contribute a song or two to an album, so for him to give us a whole important project was one of the biggest things we did as a production team. Creatively, he left it all in our hands. Once he gave you power he let you do it. He didn't hear it until it was all done." At which point the professor had a minor quibble with their slow-building, Isaac Hayes–influenced, extended version of the 1967 Marvin and Tammi hit "Ain't No Mountain High Enough," which Diana introduced with a sexy monologue. "Berry thought we had gotten it wrong with all that talking in the front," Valerie said. "He thought the build was too slow and he encouraged us to change it around, put the big part in the front. We told him no, we wouldn't do it. Then he told us he wouldn't release it as a single."

But after "Reach Out and Touch (Somebody's Hand)" peaked at number twenty, disc jockeys started playing "Ain't No Mountain High Enough" from the album. Having little choice, Berry revisited his previous decision, with a nod to his producer's original wisdom. The song reached number one six weeks later. "That was kind of nice," Valerie admirably understated.

By then, the rule book of decorum was basically out the window in polite society, let alone impolite rock society. About the only place it was still posted on the wall of the cafeteria for all the employees to read was at the Motown commissary.

"The manner of grooming a group certainly helped prepare them for what they were going to encounter in the outside world; Motown was strong about that," said Valerie from her vantage point as a staffer based in New York City. "But nobody has control over anybody when they close the door. It really comes down to the values you're raised on and how crazy fame makes you. Some succumbed to demons and that's going to happen in all genres of music. The tremendous exhilaration an audience can give you can push you into places that are not real and it's like, can you come back to reality and find your footing?"

That year Motown scored a total of fourteen top ten singles and the label showed no outward signs of losing its mojo. "We were such an insulated world," Valerie recalled. "Motown had its own scene, its own clubs. Everybody was doing well, at the height of their popularity. Everywhere people went they were treated like royalty. So, you were part of a very special inner circle. The average person in Detroit, working for Ford, might have been going through a very different thing."

Like the town's resident automakers, however, Berry maintained an assembly-line approach. "Everyone had a cubicle, so you could almost literally hear the music coming out of everyone else's room," said Valerie. "We all worked with an ear to the door, listening for what everybody else was doing, just to make sure your stuff sounded stronger. You were always amidst creativity; it was like going to college." And Berry Gordy was the cool but demanding professor whose class was always filled to capacity, even if he was stingy with the A's.

"We were really lucky because in the first batch of songs we sent in was 'Ain't No Mountain High Enough,' which was recorded by Marvin Gaye and Tammi Terrell," said Valerie. "So we got music on the street right away. After 'Your Precious Love,' when it came time for the third single, we kind of realized we had sent them great demos and they were

124 | They're Playing My Song

Figure 16. Nickolas Ashford and Valerie Simpson, 2000. Photo: Kingkongphoto and www.celebrity-photos.com, Wikimedia Commons, CC BY 2.0.

pretty much following them, so maybe we should produce as well. That's when we asked for a production deal."

But Berry always believed his writers should be well schooled in the fine art of competition. Said Valerie, "He decided we should cut 'Ain't Nothing Like the Real Thing,' and Johnny Bristol and Harvey Fuqua should cut it as well, and whichever version came out the strongest would be released. We were lucky again that ours turned out stronger. And that's how we started off as producers, thanks to the indulgence of Marvin and Tammi, since they had to pay for both songs."

Adding to the pressure during that particular production were a couple of unannounced visitors to the studio, Smokey Robinson and Norman Whitfield. "They were standing in the control room watching us," said Valerie, "so it made us a little nervous, but it was also reassuring, like whoa, this must be important here. We gotta get this right." That they did. "Once it was determined you could write a good song and produce it well, we had total creative freedom."

Marvin and Tammi remained their biggest clients until Tammi's death in 1970 from a brain tumor. "When she got sick, I was always doing the demos anyway," said Valerie. "I would sing with Marvin and then we'd bring her in and we'd kind of put together a vocal and doctor it up a bit. That's been perceived as I did the singing, but basically it was her singing and it was just doctored."

Marvin Gaye was a particular favorite of Valerie's. "The studio was a place where he was totally free of whatever demons he might have been dealing with on the outside. We got to see him at his happiest," she recalled. "He was always my favorite artist, because his gift was so tremendous, his sensibility as to how to bring out a lyric. In duets, he excelled at making the other singer better. He didn't have a lot of ego, where he tried to outshine anyone."

In 1970, reeling from Terrell's death, Gaye was on the brink of retirement. Shortly after the murders at Kent State, he went into the studio with a heartfelt message song he helped Al Cleveland and the Four Tops' Renaldo Benson write, called "What's Going On." He thought he might give it to the Originals, the group he was producing, whose "The Bells" had just peaked on the pop charts at number twelve. Then he decided he wanted to do it himself. Just one thing stood in his way: Berry Gordy, who didn't think the track's antiwar sentiments conformed to Marvin's sexy image. Marvin threatened to leave the label if Gordy didn't let him release it. Gordy threatened to let him. A legendary impasse ensued.

"He was the most charming man," Valerie said of Berry. "He could talk you into anything. Even if you didn't agree with him, he was still charming."

But Marvin Gaye was equally staunch in defending his passions no matter how charming his antagonist; he eventually prevailed in his standoff with Gordy, releasing "What's Going On" eight months after it was finished. On the *Detroit Metro Times* list of the 100 Greatest Detroit Songs, it ranks number one.

∽

Valerie Simpson released a solo album, Dinosaurs Are Coming Back Again, *in 2012.*

Lou Reed (1974)

When Lou Reed arrived in Greenwich Village in '67, the neighborhood had been engaged in a mini civil war. The Village west of Fifth Avenue had tradition on its side, some notable watering holes, the Vanguard for jazz, and the coffeehouse scene, with Folk City, the Night Owl, the Café Wha, the Bitter End, the Garrick, the Au Go Go, and the Gaslight. But the East End had those marvelous slum apartments, perfect for dropout living, had the Summer of Love in its backyard, rock flow, the Balloon Farm, and the legendary Fillmore East. St. Mark's Place was giving Bleecker Street a run for the hippie dollar. There was more than mecca at stake here, more than a territorial skirmish for possession of those sultry girls in tight dungarees, weekend runaways to decadence. There was a philosophical debate raging too, a war of lifestyles. It was like the difference between folk/rock and heavy metal, between grass and heroin. In the West Village, you still held on to your day job, got stoned every night after work. Acid was a risk worth taking, every once in a while, for the world it revealed. Primary to your lifestyle was control, discipline in your craft. For years, you might plod along, revising.

Once past Fifth Avenue, everyone *freaked out*. No one did acid over there because they *believed* in it, only because it happened to be a good kick at an orgy. Minds were blown and busted routinely out on the edge where hippie genii spewed speed raps into microphones, issued verbatim transcripts as works of art, and were rewarded with the keys to the vault as they slouched through the ozone.

So, if you were a Western Yankee, the Rebel Eastsider was an object of envy and ridicule. You longed for a taste of such liberation—to really go psycho for a month or two—but knew the price was way too high—spontaneous art was fine, but let's see them do that again for posterity.

Meanwhile, those on the other side of the divide held the Yankees in the same ambiguous contempt, whining for your Establishment praise and approval, while at the same time calling you gutless or worse, conventional.

With their image of leather lips and contemporary cool—so chic and vague and dispirited—their melancholy songs of addiction and despair, led by Reed scowling in sunglasses, the Velvet Underground started at the Café Bizarre, off MacDougal Street, a tourist trap, where they didn't even have hawkers. Then came Andy Warhol and soundtracks at the new Cinematheque. When they opened at the Balloon Farm, a converted dancehall above the Dom, later to be known as the Electric Circus, all the freaks in the neighborhood made the place the number one local hangout. The group did "Heroin" and "I'm Waiting for My Man"—songs of another culture, the new age, written in blood, accompanied by a grinding, atonal backbeat.

"At one point you seemed to be into describing a certain kind of scene," I said to Reed, "and making it very real for people who knew about it, but didn't really know about it."

"Especially for people who didn't know about it at all," Reed chimed in.

"Well, people might have heard of the East Village, but that's as far as it went."

"Yeah, but I brought a little taste of—" Catching himself, he held back. "Ah, maybe that's pretentious. It's just I wrote about what I knew about."

"What would you call it, the Lower East Side experience?"

"It was a show by and for freaks, of which there turned out to be many more than anyone had suspected, who finally had a place to go where they wouldn't be hassled and where they could have a good time."

"Did it surprise you that this crowd was out there?"

"Well, you see, Andy had a week at the new Cinematheque when he could put on whatever he wanted, and what he wanted to put on was us . . . with films and stuff. And the people who showed up—everybody just looked at everybody else and said, 'Wow, there are a lot of us.' So, we knew they were there."

One of the few musicians in the rock community of 1967 who could have foreseen the fatal unraveling of the love and LSD agenda floated at Monterey (aside from Bob Dylan, who had his own problems with invading hordes in Woodstock), Reed's jaded worldview was in a different universe from that of the Flower Power brigade. Even as far back as 1964, when he was briefly employed as a staff songwriter at Pickwick Records, Reed displayed the kind of sarcastic, if not self-destructive streak that would

128 | They're Playing My Song

both fuel and plague his career by attempting to pawn off an early draft of "Heroin" as suitable fodder for the teen market bopping to the Shangri-las.

Like his East Village crony, Tuli Kupferberg of the Fugs, Reed was college educated, majoring in English at Syracuse University, where his mentor was the poet Delmore Schwartz, author of, among many others, "What Curious Dresses All Men Wear." While his work had been published in serious poetry journals, Reed preferred rock magazines "because that's the people I want to read the stuff, not the people who read the Harvard *Advocate*," he said.

Like most of his lyrics in those days, "Heroin" was written quickly. "The lyric part of it comes in one clump," he said of his working method. "I like to leave the lyrics for the very last possible minute and then just sit down and zap, go through them. Just take each song and put a lyric to it, put it away. Take the next song, put a lyric to it, put it away. Do the next

Figure 17. Lou Reed, 2003. Photo: Man Alive!, Wikimedia Commons, CC BY 2.0.

song. And just not even look at them. I look at them later to check, 'cause I know the basic thing is perfect, for me. Sometimes one or two words have to be changed. The real danger is that maybe I'll be tired . . . and my handwriting is so bad I won't be able to read the whole damn thing!"

Although many listeners assumed the song was in favor of heroin use, comparing the feeling of the high to being Jesus's son, most of the lyrics are harrowing in their description of the narrator as being "better off dead," married to heroin, and trying to "nullify" his life. Years later, after too many fans approached Reed and the band with tales of shooting up, they cut back on performing the song as he started to question his songwriting approach.

Talking about his album *Berlin* was another highlight moment of our conversation. "*Berlin* needed a lyrical approach that was direct," he said about his 1973 album. "There could be no mistaking it, no head games. You didn't have to be high to figure out what was happening, or be super hip or anything. It was to-the-point, whereas some of my other albums and songs had puns or double entendres. In other words, the difference would be, in 'Heroin' I wrote, 'It makes me feel like Jesus' son.' Now if the *Berlin* guy had said that, he'd say, 'I take heroin.' That's the difference. Like in 'Heroin' I say, 'I wish I was born a thousand years ago.' The guy on *Berlin* would say, 'I don't dig it here.' You can go through the whole album and he's consistently saying these very short, straight, to-the-point, unmissable things."

Also unmissable in the early days of the Velvet Underground was Reed's atonal opposition to the flowing good feelings of folk/rock and acid/rock (interrupted by the occasional well-intentioned protest song). "Ralph Gleason, the dean of American reviewers, wrote in a review, I'll never forget it; he said the whole love thing going on in San Francisco has been partially sabotaged by the influx of this trash from New York, representing everything they had cured," he said. "Let's say we were a little bit sarcastic about the love thing, which we were right about, because look what happened. We knew that in the first place. They thought acid was going to solve everything. You take acid and you'll solve the problems of the universe. And we just said that's not the way it is and you're kidding yourselves. And they hated us."

Lou's idea of great writing moved him to talk about Dorothy Parker. "Now if she wrote a song, that would be something else, because she was right on target. I mean, just a little short story about a guy and his wife, where he's reading the newspaper and she's setting the table and they've

130 | They're Playing My Song

got nothing to talk about. That story's unbelievable, so painful sometimes you just have to put her away or she'll drive you through the wall."

I asked him if any songs had ever affected him that way.

" 'Mother' by John Lennon. That was a song that had realism. That's about the only one I can think of on that level. When I first heard it, I didn't even know it was him. I just said, 'Who the fuck is that? I don't believe that.' Because the lyrics to that are real. He wasn't kidding around. He got right down to it, as down as you can get. I like that in a song."

"Do you think you'll get any further down in your songs?"

"I think I've gone as deep as I want to go for my own mental health. If I got any deeper, I'd wind up disappearing."

Lou Reed continued recording until his death in 2013. He was inducted into the Rock and Roll Hall of Fame in 2014.

Tim Rice (1974)

"Jesus Christ, Superstar"

First Tom Sankey brought *The Golden Screw* to off-off Broadway. Then, summarizing rapidly, Al Carmines applied his lyric touch to the outrageous *Home Movies* and *Promenade* of Rosalyn Drexler at the Judson Theatre in Greenwich Village; after being inspired by Megan Terry's *Viet Rock*, actor-writers James Rado and Gerome Ragni got cab fare uptown from Joseph Papp and put "Rock Theater" on Broadway with *Hair!* Following in the wake of that enormous breakthrough came some epic bashes, chief among them being *Godspell* by Stephen Schwartz and *Jesus Christ, Superstar* by Tim Rice and Andrew Lloyd Webber. *Superstar*, the record album, the play, the movie, the original cast album, the soundtrack, "I Don't Know How to Love Him" by Yvonne Elliman, the semi-hit single of the title by Murray Head—has been a huge moneymaker, as has *Godspell*—the movie, the play, and "Day by Day"—to say nothing of those out of the Rado and Ragni songbag—"Hair!," by the Cowsills; "Easy to Be Hard," by Three Dog Night; "Age of Aquarius," by the Fifth Dimension; "Starshine," by Oliver; and "Frank Mills." And we are still awaiting Ken Russell's filmed spectacle of Peter Townshend's *Tommy*, which has been everything from opera to ballet to rock concerto.

On the other hand, whatever happened to Tom Sankey?

The interview with Tim Rice took place at the Plaza Hotel in New York City, where Tim was staying on a brief visit to those shores. "We had the tune first every time. Occasionally I might say 'I've got a fantastic title,' but very rarely. On the bigger projects like *Superstar* I would first provide a framework, a kind of a plot. I'd say, for example, 'This song is going to be a violent song. It's got to say a, b, and c; therefore, we need a certain kind of tune.' Andrew would then write a melody knowing what sort of tune was needed and then I'd put words to it after that. In the case of *Superstar*, obviously, we both discussed the framework, too. "So he'd play a tune for me, and I'd pick it up. If I couldn't pick it up quickly, obviously, it wasn't a good tune. I'd tape it on a recorder if I happened to have one on me, or if not, I'd just have it in my skull. Often I'll write down just nonsense words like 'I want you in the bath' or 'I need you on the floor,' anything just to remember the rhythm. "I have written lyrics without actually knowing the tune. Once or twice in an emergency Andrew has rung up or written to me and said, 'Just write lyrics to I love you my baby I need you,' and I would then write something that's completely different, but it would scan. Later he would show me how the melody goes.

"Usually I've got the tune in my head. I can play piano well enough so that if Andrew gives me the chords I can play the tune. Lyric writing for me is a nine to five office thing. You have to sit down and wade through it, like a crossword puzzle. You get a nice high, I suppose, if you write something good, but it's more like solving a puzzle. You simply get the feeling of 'Yeah, that's it!' But you have to work hard at it. I don't walk down the street and get inspired. The number one thing to make me like a song is a good tune. I don't care if it's corny, or if it's rock, it just has to have a bit of a melody. That's why I like people like John Fogerty, who I think is one of the great rock writers. In addition to the excitement and whatever else he has, he writes beautiful tunes.

"I don't think I could write lyrics like Paul Simon's particularly well. He's a brilliant lyricist, but I tend to think more theatrically. I think that the kind of lyrics I write are in one sense more old-fashioned. They're more in the style of the traditional theater, and they tend to be more specific whereas Paul Simon and Dylan, of course, write more often in abstract. They use a lot of imagery, which is great, but that's not really my sort of song. I do better with the more factual stuff. I can write a fairly amusing point number. I never could have written 'Proud Mary' or 'Mr. Tambourine Man,' although I'd have loved to.

"I do follow the theater quite a lot now. I usually find if I come to New York for four or five days, I'll see four or five plays. [Although in town for only two nights, Mr. Rice managed to see *Jumpers* and *Over Here.*] I always did follow the theater quite a lot for an average bloke, compared with the other people at school, and the way I follow the record industry is phenomenal. I could name you every artist on the Hot Hundred. But I don't have a fanatical interest in the theater. Andrew was the one with the

Tim Rice (1974) | 133

burning ambition to write for the theater. I just did it because it seemed like a good idea at the time."

Rice and Andrew Lloyd Webber met in 1965. Both had been trying to break through in the pop market, Rice as a singer, Webber as a composer. "On the side, Andrew was working on a show. He said, 'I've got backing for a musical if I can come up with a lyricist,' and I said I'd have a go. And although the musical came to nothing, we discovered that we could work well as a team. So it was as a result of Andrew that I found myself trying to be a lyricist, whereas I'd been trying to be a pop singer."

Their first effort concerned Dr. Barnardo, an East End figure of the Victorian Age. "It was a bit like *Oliver*, except it wasn't as good. It had some good things, and I think anybody listening would have said those lads are quite promising."

Later on they got their next assignment. "We were then asked by a schoolmaster friend of ours to write anything we liked, just a fifteen or twenty-minute piece, for his kids at school for the end-of-the-term concert. It was a great comedown, because we'd had all those visions of a fantastic show on Broadway and in the West End of London, and now we were writing something for eight- to ten-year-old kids. There was no money in it, but we thought we'd do it. The schoolmaster said that if it went well, he might get a publishing company interested and perhaps it would become something that schools would use. So we did it on spec, for nothing. It was called *Joseph and the Amazing Technicolor Dreamcoat*. We chose a Bible story purposely because we wanted something that would appeal to teachers, so that they might buy it for their kids. And we made it funny because we wanted the kids to be amused. So it was a big success at this concert and the publishers who'd been asked along by the school said they loved it and would like to publish it. So we made it into a half-hour piece, expanded from the original twenty minutes, and they printed it up in a book and we made fifty pounds each and it did very well.

"For a couple of years before *Superstar* we were earning a small amount of money from *Joseph*, and of course, since *Superstar*, *Joseph* has boomed. We expanded it to ninety minutes, and it has now been quite a big hit in England as a professional show."

About six months after finishing *Joseph*, the songwriting team of Webber and Rice felt it was time to begin work on something new.

"For a long time I'd had a great interest in Judas Iscariot, who I thought was a fascinating character. Even before I met Andrew I thought it would be great to write a play about Judas in which Jesus is only a minor character. Or tell the story with Jesus as a major character, but tell it from Judas's point of view. If you study the Bible, which I have as a result of writing *Superstar*, you'll find that the character of Judas Iscariot is non-existent. He doesn't really have any motives. He doesn't say anything, and he's only mentioned a couple of times. The Gospels were written sometime later, and it was convenient and easy to make Judas one hundred percent bad, a figure of evil, the exact opposite of Christ. It was obviously helpful to the story, also, to have it blamed on one guy. But I couldn't believe that this was plausible. These are not colossally original thoughts, but I still had this idea about trying to do a thing from Judas's point of view.

"After the success of *Joseph* one realized that one could mix modern music and the Bible. So we thought, let's have a go at writing a play on Judas.

"Well, it was obviously a heavy undertaking and we still at that point had had no commercial success. One little thing in schools wasn't going to make people fork out fifty thousand pounds to produce a show. So we decided to do it via record. We were producing a few of our own songs at that point and I had worked at EMI, so we had some connections in the record world. So it was for economic reasons that we were forced to try to get somebody to back a record, when we really wanted to write a show.

"After being turned down by several people, we got MCA records in London interested, but they said it would be too expensive to do the whole LP. They said they'd put out a single, 'And if that goes, it will justify spending all that money for an album. It will prove there's a market for it.'

"This was late summer of 1969. We just had an outline, the framework, which was a lot of work, but there were only a few tunes and a few ideas. We hadn't thought in terms of a single, but we thought the actual song 'Superstar' would be possible. So we went away and polished it up and took it back to them.

"As soon as the single was finished, even though we didn't know whether it was going to be a hit or not, we went away and began writing the rest of the album, because we felt that we wanted to do it regardless. This was around Christmas 1969. In about three or four months we'd done eighty percent of it. Meanwhile the single, by Murray Head, began taking off. It was a small hit in the US and a big hit in Brazil and Belgium and Australia.

"On English sales alone, the project would have been killed, but the worldwide sales were big enough for MCA to say go ahead. By about

Tim Rice (1974) | 135

February of 1970 . . . we'd written most of the work . . . and we then had the colossal job of actually getting people to sing on the album. That almost took longer than writing it. It was like a military operation.

"In October it was released in England and America and it sunk in England. It was an immediate total flop. No one wanted to know about it. It got very good reviews, but it didn't get any airplay. But we'd been booked to come to the States, because MCA liked what it had been given. So we thought at least we'll get one trip out of it. But when we got here, at the airport we were met by a great army of press and everything, and we suddenly realized it was going to be a big hit here.

"Ironically, the whole thing really was not what we'd aimed for, because we were still really trying to write for the theater, and this album was a kind of demonstration record."

After *Superstar*, "Our output has declined colossally, largely because we've been so busy running around the world doing an awful lot of work connected with it, but not actually creative work. Of course, since *Superstar* we've expanded *Joseph* to twice as long as it was. An awful lot of pop songs we'd written, the tunes have gone into the new bits of *Joseph* with new lyrics. Andrew has done a film score and I'm doing some broadcasting. I have a show every week on English radio as a disc jockey, playing oldies. So we've been quite busy, but we definitely got a bit off the rails in terms of output.

"Which I don't think matters. First, it takes a long time to get over the shell shock of something like *Superstar*, and second we don't really want to hurry into something else. Take Lionel Bart who wrote *Oliver*; he's a great writer, he's written an awful lot of pop hits in England, but he did come out with a lot of stuff very quickly after *Oliver*, and each one didn't do quite so well as the one before. I don't know how he worked, but I often think if he'd waited three or four years and put all his best things into one, it might have worked out better. So we can afford to wait, but I do think that about now is the time to do something else."

Among other works, Sir Tim Rice has contributed lyrics to Evita, Aida, Aladdin, The Lion King, *and* Beauty and the Beast.

Melvin Van Peebles (1974)

To many, Chuck Berry is rock 'n' roll. But his lyrics spoke of a universal teenage rather than a specifically ethnic experience. In the early sixties Eddie Holland (of the Holland-Dozier-Holland Motown combine) started churning out machine-like hits for such groups as the Supremes and the Four Tops. Smokey Robinson brought the process a step further, adding lushness and a touch of poetry. And David Porter (with Isaac Hayes) provided stiff top forty competition from Memphis via Otis Redding and Sam and Dave. But still, aside from the performance, most of these songs could have been interpreted, identified with, even written by songwriters of any number of colors, creeds, and national origins.

In the late sixties Sly Stone represented the freak-out of Black lyricism, while Bill Withers and Gamble and Huff brought things back on course—in line with the rest of pop history. In the seventies, Curtis Mayfield injected a wordy prose into the rather sparsely populated field of Black social protest (along with Whitfield and Strong of the Temptations).

Of all the Black songwriters working today, the one who perhaps most truly seems to be operating within the structure of a Black voice, telling of a specifically Black experience, is playwright, filmmaker, novelist, composer Melvin Van Peebles. Author of two Broadway musicals (which between them collected nine Tony Award nominations), a movie script or three, eight books, and songs for six albums, Van Peebles has come up against a variety of reactions to his singularly unique style of writing and singing. Not all of which have been hostile. And although his songs have yet to gain top forty acceptance, his artistry, in certain elite, tasteful circles, continues to impress.

Van Peebles expressed surprise when I asked him to be included in this collection. Nevertheless, he agreed to the interview if I could be at his New York office within the hour. I was there in fifteen minutes.

"I can't read or write music. I can't even play piano. I prefer to get a lyrical idea, or a story that I want to tell and then write it down. The idea usually comes first and then I sit down and find the music that goes directly along with it. The form, fast or slow, evolves afterward. And the chords come after that. Sometimes it will all come out fast. Usually I will have the form, then change words here and there a great many times.

"Right now I'm writing a play, I'm writing a novel, and I'm writing a film script. I find each stage of writing a different experience and each type of writing also. Songs are a gas to work on because you can hold them in one concept, and you can see where you're at, whereas with a novel you may have done fifty pages and you'll do another fifty pages and you're nowhere near knowing. Sometimes with a novel I'll do the overall concept of it and then fill in, sometimes I don't know what's going to be on the next page myself.

"Lyrics usually come as a spin-off. Because I do a lot of very heavy, long writing, the music is a spin-off. It's not a release, but, having the discipline say, of running the ten miles, all the time doing marathons, having to go around the stadium once is easy. And since you only have to go around once, I spend an exorbitant amount of time on the lyrics . . . even though they may seem as though they just fell off. Sometimes I'll be writing one thing and stop to work on a song.

I asked him if he often got ideas for songs from certain lines of prose.

"I don't work from that end of the stick. I work from the other end of the stick. I'll write something and I'll say, gee, this is a film or a poem or this or that. I'll write a feeling, or analyze or conceptualize, and then it dictates in itself the form that it's going to take."

I wondered what sort of feelings seemed to translate successfully into songs.

"Unfortunately it's very difficult for me to answer that, because I do not have the commercial success in songwriting as I do in the other things, so I don't think it warrants me giving an answer because I'm probably not adhering to some part of that form that I must, to make them work. They are succeeding, no doubt about it, but on a very limited basis. This enters into my mind only as a fervent hope that the songs will someday work. But if I change to make them work and if they become less than they were, then they're not working. I won't do it. I won't change them to make them less and end up being just what it was that I was coming away from."

What were his early feelings about rock 'n' roll?

Figure 18. Melvin Van Peebles, 2008. Photo: David Shankbone, Wikimedia Commons, CC BY-SA 3.0.

"Well, I'd heard it, but I'd already heard the original from where it was stolen. And the music where it was stolen from in most cases had more validity. I grew up listening to Jimmy Rushing and the daddies of the Howling Wolves and the granddaddies of the Little Richards. I heard Dinah Washington before she had strings—which was cool too—but I knew her before. You see, all that changed with the advent of 'Blueberry Hill' by Fats Domino, because they used to have Black records that were only shooting for that small, narrow margin, and when the universality came in, the larger money, growing up with the parallel cultures, the music branched out into those things and as it branched out the songs became bleached and homogenized and so forth, hoping for a shot at that market too.

Probably one of the first historical examples that I can remember is Leadbelly, years and years and years ago, doing 'Goodnight Irene, I'll

Get You in My Dreams,' which became 'Goodnight Irene, I'll See You in My Dreams.' Well, that type of thing happened, and something goes with each one of those chippings away.

"I've been very illiterate in my taste. Now let me explain what I mean by that. When I started in films I didn't know the names of directors. I'd just go 'Hmmm, yeah, well I dug that flick,' and so forth, and didn't ever realize the line that followed through. As far as I was concerned I was one hundred percent consumer. I mean, when I heard a single, half the time I didn't know who was doing it, but I danced to everything. Also, quite interesting, I was influenced by the singers on the South Side of Chicago.

"You know, sometimes I'll get onstage and people will still look at my voice and so forth, but I'm not the least bit intimidated because the voices I remember hearing in my childhood sounded a great deal like I do—my first musical reality, you dig? Of course, there were other styles of singing too. Today it's all going toward one style of singing. And Blind Smokey, Reverend Skippy, these voices didn't have musicality, but that wasn't where that was headed from. And because of the programming of these things, many of the kids in the audience have not even heard those old voices. Now the Rolling Stones and the Beatles went back and heard these people and were able to branch out from there. Perhaps one of the difficulties with my music is that it doesn't explain itself well. Or maybe people are very provincial."

I wanted to know how he got involved with songs.

"I got into songs sideways, through the music that I needed for my films. When I did my first short film I needed music and I couldn't afford to pay anyone, so I had a kazoo and I hummed my soundtrack. That was 1957. I got into it parallel with my other activities. Then, in 1967 or 1968, when I came back to the States from Europe (I'd been gone for six and a half years) I was surprised to find that Black music, lyrics-wise anyway, didn't really mirror any of the everyday aspirations, problems, or lifestyles that were going on. I mean, I felt the lyrics, especially in Black music, had almost become just a phonetic accompaniment to the music; whereas you had guys, such as Dylan or Kristofferson, dealing with words, and even pop tunes had more significance—you no longer had the Leadbellys or Blind Lemon Jeffersons.

"I think it's partly the form that can't handle it. The form that Black music has now put itself into, the gradual limitation of one idea itself—baby don't go—and nothing else. I mean, you get the first idea and you get the beat and then you know if you're gonna shuffle or do the slop or the

140 | They're Playing My Song

bump or whatever, and that's it. It's a vicious circle. It's attention span, also. You train people's attention span to one thing, in a very limited way, and they're much more easily controlled too.

"Now what I feel, in words, is that you can work with a thing that's indigenous to where it's coming from. It doesn't mean that it's exclusive to where it's coming from, but it's indigenous. So I conceived the idea of giving a voice—this is before Agnew was around—to the silent minority. That's what I tried to do in my original songs. Each song was meant to encompass a lifestyle, a personality, a character. What I had hoped was that the sketches, my renditions, would be taken by mainstream artists and be performed in a more normal format. But it's never happened. That's probably been the most disappointing aspect of the whole musical part of my career. There's a lot of Black groups out there, and none of them have ever chosen to do the tunes.

"It would be different if I felt that the tunes they've been doing had any significance, and I'm not talking about even necessarily revolutionary significance. You take most of the songs and look at the words without the music, and you're shocked with the intellectual level. They have one idea and a good punch line, which is cool, but that's as far as it goes.

"There are exceptions continually that break the rule, but I'm talking in general. There are some things the O'Jays have been doing—'Don't Call Me Brother' and like that. Fine. Terrific. Maybe it's moving a little. A lot of times I'll get notes that say, 'Baby I dig this stuff; it's inspired me,' and so forth.

"What happened in *Don't Play Us Cheap* was that the music was for a specific show and for singers, real singers in the classical or pop classical sense of the word. So it was arranged differently. Now people will say, 'Gee Mel, why don't you do it like that? Why don't you do tunes like that?' Well, the other tunes were like that, or at least that's how I heard it in my head. And I was all ready to say, if the Temptations asked me for one of the tunes, if they asked me to take a tune and arrange it in that format, I'd be more than happy to.

"I think there's just a general embarrassment on the part of the listener because I work in the vernacular. Not the bullshit vernacular of 'hey man,' but real vernacular, which doesn't seem as real to people . . . because it's too real."

I asked about working habits.

"I've got discipline, but because of the diversity of the work I do not have a particular discipline for music. If I had, tomorrow, a play where

Melvin Van Peebles (1974) | 141

the music had to be done at a certain time, then whatever discipline was required, I'd sit down and do it. I have an overall discipline, the same kind of discipline that I could bring to an editing table for twenty hours . . . or doing four sets a night.

"There are certain places for me where I establish a sense of work. So you come into that room and you have that sense of work there. I like small, quiet rooms, preferably uncluttered. Overall conceptualization occurs late at night or in the wee hours. The rest of it whenever I can."

I asked if writing came easily.

"I hate it! You can tell I'm working now because the room is very clean. I've cleaned up the room. I've vacuumed. I've read the paper, sharpened four hundred pencils."

We concluded by talking about the satisfaction to be derived from songwriting as a craft and art.

"The revelation I hope my songs bring to people about themselves, about the human condition, that's the joy. I had a very good experience recently at a prison. The prisoners really dug my songs. They were not intimidated by them. I started to do 'Lily Done the Zampoogi' and the prisoners all started clapping. They said, 'We got a prisoner here who does that.' So we brought him up there onstage and it blew his mind. He had a band and everything. That's what it's about. And those guys became the family that now have done the play *Short Eyes*.

"It's very interesting that the kids who dig my work—mostly because I'm sort of a listening artist rather than a pop artist—are kids who had a theatrical background or a protest song background. By the way, isn't it interesting with all the protest songs that no Black protest songs came out, or protest singers. I mean, there are two or three songs, but no real Black protest singer ever rose out of that."

I asked Melvin Van Peebles why he thought that should be the case.

"Well, I can let you draw your own conclusions on that."

A true renaissance man, Melvin Van Peebles continued writing books, musicals, plays, and music until his death in 2021. In the meantime, artists like Kendrick Lamar, Nas, and Gil Scott Heron have picked up the gauntlet he laid down.

Don McLean (2020)

"American Pie"

To most casual listeners and purists alike, "American Pie" was a massive hit record. At 8 minutes, 33 seconds, it was a second coming of "Like a Rolling Stone," a long and winding anthem for its generation. A metaphorical tapestry of familiar characters and events held aloft by a killer chorus and an unstoppable arrangement. The ultimate FM album cut that unexpectedly went to number one on the singles chart in six weeks, along with the album that contained it. The song was added to the National Registry in the Library of Congress, alongside "Over the Rainbow," "Hound Dog," and "In the Midnight Hour." The original lyrics were auctioned off in 2015 for a cool million.

For Don McLean, however, it was a crucible of fire. An unnecessary rite of passage. The sword of Damocles hanging over his head at every performance. A cruel joke from the Gods who grant you wishes you never wished for.

"Life always holds strange and quirky twists of fate that you can never predict or think will happen," Don McLean told me back in 1973. "There can always be something sliding up behind you that makes you blind. 'American Pie' completely disrupted my entire value system."

A middle-class Catholic boy from the suburbs, Don McLean took the same cries of "Judas" (probably from the same purists who directed them at Bob Dylan), for daring to have a hit record, more to heart than most. "In effect my next album, *Don McLean*, is an effort to try and show the same audience that made that song, what it felt like from my end," he said in that 1973 interview. "*Rolling Stone* magazine just tore me to shreds and the very same things they said about me, I'm saying about myself in that album."

Even today, nearly fifty years later, having been the words and the voice behind twenty albums and six top forty songs (ten on the Adult Contemporary chart), with a new album called *Still Playing Favorites* due out (containing ancient and creaky country, blues, rock, and folk odes like "Tell Old Bill," "Backwater Blues," and "Six White Horses," i.e., the furthest thing from top forty fodder), McLean wanted to make sure his audience knew one thing about him above all else, "I'm not a one-hit wonder.

"I set very high standards for myself, maybe too high. I always wanted every song I wrote for an album to be different. I think I was heavily influenced by that because of the Beatles and, before that, the Weavers. In my own unschooled kind of way, that's what I was after. So I spent ten years collecting songs for my first album, which came out in 1969. I kept adding songs to it because I was in the midst of this period, when I was on the Hudson River sloop, where a lot of singers were around and a lot of information was coming into my head. That album was turned down by lots of record companies, as many as there were out there. Finally, I met a great guy named Alan Livingston who signed the Beatles, the Kingston Trio, the Beach Boys. He loved me and he was my savior. He was my white knight.

"I spent six or eight months promoting *Tapestry*. I was on the road all the time, doing one-nighters and meeting with independent promo men. All the while, my record company was going under. I already had another album almost done. In fact, if you take 'American Pie' away and you add 'Aftermath' and 'Mother Nature,' which were two songs that were supposed to be on the album but had to be dropped because 'American Pie' was so long, you could have put out the album that way. Actually, that might've been a good idea to put that album out and save 'American Pie' for the third album, which would've come at a time when I had established myself. Of course, I didn't know that then.

"The record company [Mediarts] going out of business was very daunting, but I said I still had to finish the new album. I wanted something long about America and different and really rock and roll, old fashioned rock and roll. That was my goal. I said to hell with it. I'm going to keep working on songs. I came up with the whole first part of that song out of nowhere. All the way up to 'the day the music died.' It came out of my mouth in one go and onto the tape recorder. I was living in Cold Spring, New York. I looked at the lyric and I said, wow, what is that? I had always

144 | They're Playing My Song

been so interested in Buddy Holly. I loved his music. When that whole crash happened, it was a real ache in my heart. So, I ended up bringing back all those memories of 1959 and the things that happened later.

"The chorus didn't come to me until about three months later. My memory of this may not be accurate anymore because it's so long ago, but it seems like it all occurred in a three-month period. After I had that first thing, I was thinking I've got to come up with the chorus. I remember thinking that, one day in front of the Butterfield pharmacy in Cold Spring, which is on the Hudson River, across from West Point. I used to go to Butterfield's a lot. There was a wine store next to it as well. So, I came up with the chorus walking into the damn store. I said, I've got to write this down. I ran home. It was several miles away.

"Now that I had the chorus I knew what I wanted to do. I wanted to speed up the verses and tell the story, but what was the story going to be? Well, I couldn't figure that out. And then it just came to me and because, as I've said a million times before, I figured out that politics and music influence each other, I decided I was going to make a song that went forward and toward it. I wasn't sure what type of an ending it would be, whether it'd be a happy ending, or an apocalyptic thing. You know, a lot of pretty happy people tried to be like Bob Dylan and be always miserable but I couldn't do that, because I'm not that kind of a person. But, nonetheless, the song led to the ending, which was almost quiet, you know, the Gods from the Bible even jumped on the train and went to California, which of course is a garden of sin.

"As I was writing it, I didn't show the song to anyone. That's not how I work. At that time, I had begun an association with Pete Seeger, through my love of the Weavers, going back to 1961. The sixties were very exciting for me. Meeting people you only dreamed about. It was the most fun of any time in my life. Nothing has been even close to that since 1970. I was signed with William Morris. I was on the road with Ten Wheel Drive, the James Gang, Steppenwolf. Blood, Sweat and Tears took me everywhere and treated me really nicely. One day when I was home, Pete asked me if I wanted to sing at a festival in Nyack. And I said sure. I think it was at one of festivals that I sang 'American Pie' for the first time. And it did not get a great response, you know, because it went on and on.

"Meanwhile, United Artists had bought Mediarts. And they were putting a lot of money into turning UA into a better label. So, I went from thinking I'm out of the business to all of a sudden this thing went bang, and it all changed. Somebody there heard the song and immediately cut all the slow parts out and made it chorus and two verses and chorus over and over at the end and put it on the radio. And I went to number one, just like a rocket. I didn't know what was happening. I didn't listen to the radio and I didn't care. But suddenly William Morris was telling me, you're getting bookings in major theaters now, and college concerts in big halls. And it ruined my career because I was immediately branded as a sellout.

"In the next five years, I played all over the world four or five times as well as doing one hundred one-nighters in the United States. I played Carnegie Hall, but I didn't do too well there at first. Everything was on my shoulders. I am a strong person, but a lot came down at once. You had this number one record. Now you've got to start working and proving yourself. It's a hard job. Most people don't realize how hard it is. It's a grueling schedule and you have to be nice all the time. You have to succeed onstage all the time and you have to make recordings that are very good all the time, otherwise you're done.

"I got advice at the time from all of the Weavers. They were very

Figure 19. Don McLean, 2013. Photo: SolarScott, Wikimedia Commons, CC BY 2.0.

helpful. Fred Hellerman was a good friend of mine. Eric Darling became a good friend of mine. I was right there with Eric in 1962, even though I was still in high school, when he had the hit 'Walk Right In.' I would hear what it was like to have a number one record. He'd be busy every weekend, playing these big shows, but he was very humble. He wasn't a braggart or anything. He stayed in the same rent-controlled apartment around Columbus Circle.

"I wasn't so humble. I always loved cars. The first thing I bought with my royalties was a Mercedes-Benz 450 SEL. The biggest one they made, electric blue with Palomino leather seats. And that was the best damn car I ever owned, except for the BMW that I have now. Well, that threw the Weavers into a tailspin, because that was a message that I am not on your team. I am not the next folk-singing embodiment of an ideal. I'm an American boy and I want that Mercedes Benz.

"I never bought a Chevy. I don't know why. I guess I thought they should have given me one."

❧

The latest of Don McLean's twenty-two studio albums, American Boys, *was released in 2024.*

Neil Smith / Alice Cooper (2012)

"I'm Eighteen"

The missing link between the protopunk of the Stooges, the glitter rock of Bowie, and the arena rock that would dominate the seventies, the band Alice Cooper had been discovered in the sixties by Frank Zappa and were greatly influenced by his onstage theatrics. By 1970 they'd split from Zappa and relocated to the Midwest. According to drummer Neil Smith, guitarist Michael Bruce came up with the idea for "I'm Eighteen" on a Farfisa organ while the band was living in a house in Cincinnati.

"At first it was almost like a Pink Floyd kind of thing," he said. "The intro was a melodic, haunting tune that built and built. Since we wrote everything for the stage, it wound up being an eight-minute song. We wanted to work with a producer who had a track record of hits, so we focused on Jack Richardson from Nimbus 9 in Toronto, who had worked with the Guess Who. Jack hated us. Didn't want anything to do with us. We still had the reputation of biting the heads off of chickens and drinking blood and all that, so people in the music business thought we were insane. But there was a new man in their stable, a young guy, younger than us, named Bob Ezrin. Jack sent Bob Ezrin down to Max's Kansas City in New York in September 1970. Bob came down and loved the band, and the song he loved the most was a song he thought was called 'I'm Edgy.'

"In the fall of 1970 we started working on the preproduction of this four-song demo for Warner Brothers and the lead song was 'I'm Eighteen.' It was a song about growing up in the sixties, with lines in it like you could go to war but you couldn't vote. We had no idea it would become an anthem; we were just thinking it would be a cool song. Bob's job as a producer and arranger was to cut five minutes out of it. We worked on that song for weeks and weeks and we finally chopped it down to three minutes.

"We were very hungry for a hit single. We had specifically targeted Nimbus 9 because of their ability to make hit records, so we were very willing to do whatever had to be done. I had joined the band in 1967. We were going into our third year together. We had two albums out that didn't slam up the charts. We were playing every night onstage. We knew how to get a crowd excited. We were like a pot ready to boil over. But the heat wasn't hot enough yet. We always worked with a total group effort, everybody collaborating, everybody making suggestions. But Bob became like the sixth member of the band. He was the one person who had the final word.

"Warner Brothers signed the band on the basis of the song and released it late in 1970. By the time the album came out around the holidays, the single had been out for two months and we were getting airplay on CKLW, the big station in Windsor, Ontario, right across the bay from Detroit. Its signal went across the lake into Cleveland. Glen and I were both from Ohio and Alice was from Detroit, so when that song broke, it was really great that it was in that part of the country. They were the first ones on it. Ultimately, we were the opposite of Pink Floyd, a band that crossed our path many times in the early days. Pink Floyd was huge on the West Coast and huge on the East Coast, but they couldn't break the heartland for a long time. We were huge in the heartland but we couldn't break New York City radio, and we couldn't break top forty LA radio. If you look at the charts for those years, it's all soft rock. The harder songs were mainly funk. The real heavy rock and roll stuff had a problem. I remember when it started climbing up the chart in January, it went right along with 'My Sweet Lord' by George Harrison.

"The first show we did was the Detroit Auto Show. It was the big teen event of the year. It was the very first time we played a song where the crowd went crazy. That's what we were trying for the whole time. We wanted to be the Beatles. We wanted to be the Stones. We wanted to take what was Alice Cooper and still make it commercial. We had the real dark side of the band, but we had to figure out a way to make a hit record and keep our identity and believe me, we couldn't figure it out until we started working with Bob Ezrin. He was the one who could see it. When he first went back to Nimbus 9 and talked to Jack Richardson, Bob told him: 'It's not the sixties anymore; there's a whole new wave of music coming. We can be ahead of the curve, but if we pass on this band, it'll just wash right over us.'

Neil Smith / Alice Cooper (2012) | 149

"So that's how he became our biggest fan and cheerleader. I can't underestimate the impact of what Bob did. Once Bob got involved that was the missing part of the puzzle that we were looking for and it took three albums to find him. For a lot of bands it never happens, but once we had our foot in the door we just kicked it down and all hell broke loose. Once we had the basic guidelines of what Alice Cooper was about we could work on writing our singles and we could still have 'I Love the Dead' and 'Sick Things' and 'Dead Babies.' 'No More Mr. Nice Guy' is a good combination between the dark side and the commercial side. Bob produced every one of our albums.

"The royalties on 'I'm Eighteen' took their natural course, because the band stopped playing in 1975, when Alice went solo. He's always been on tour since then, but his career was sort of waning in the early eighties. And then things went to CDs, and the technology started to change, and everybody replaced their record collections with CD collections, so the royalties started shooting up in the late eighties. When we were inducted into the Rock and Roll Hall of Fame in 2011, there was another spike. Alice is out there playing all the time and that certainly doesn't hurt the classic songs, since the majority of the songs he plays are the songs that made the band famous.

"But even back as far as 'I'm Eighteen,' our relationship with Warner Brothers was a continual battle and Alice Cooper was always a risky situation. According to our manager at Alive Enterprises, Shep Gordon, every time we did something all the way to the band's last album, they considered it a fluke. That was one of the things that was always frustrating for us. Four decades later the records are still selling worldwide and we're still making royalties, and 'I'm Eighteen' and 'School's Out' are the two lead songs in our catalog. To this day there are people when their children turn eighteen, that song is around. It's become a perennial for generations that followed. It just shows you that Warner Brothers had no idea what they were doing.

Neil Smith has been involved with commercial real estate since the early eighties, but he's continued to keep up with his chops as a drummer in several metal bands.

Steven Tyler / Aerosmith (1985, 1987)

"Dream On" and "Walk This Way"

With its slowly building whisper to a scream format, "Dream On" was the early prototype for the "arena ballad," soon to be a staple of every hard rock or arena rock band's repertoire for the next twenty years. Add in its memorably repeatable title and you have one of the genre's defining gems and the cornerstone of Aerosmith's lengthy career. Significantly, it was among the first songs Steven Tyler ever wrote.

"It was written four or five years before the group even started," he said. "I wrote it on an upright piano in my parents' living room at Trowrico Lodge, in New Hampshire. My father was a classical musician. When I was a child in the Bronx, he had a piano in the apartment and he would literally practice four hours a day. That's what I grew up with. I don't play guitar or piano very well, but it seems to me as though it's easier to write on instruments I can't play too well. You don't have that many choices, but if you're well versed and have a good ear, you tend to jump on something that's really pretty and work with it, as opposed to going to a million different changes and chords and augmented and diminished and so on. So, it's very easy for me to write on piano, where I'm limited, although the piano is a limitless instrument. I play in the keys of C, F, F minor. If somebody plays some chords I'll go, stop, and sing a melody over it. It's as easy as that. It comes natural to me. If you can get the melody line out of the way, you can start working on other things.

"Never in a million years did I think I'd take it to guitar. All the bands I'd been in were the kinds of bands where everyone would always be practicing but never get anything clear when it came to writing songs. Then I saw this band in New Hampshire that was the makings of

Aerosmith. It was Joe Perry, Tom Hamilton, Pudge Scott. They played at this place called the Barn, where I used to play. They were horrible, but the way they did 'Rattlesnake Shake' was something else. Joe was really into Alvin Lee. And I went, if I can get this groove with this guy and start writing songs . . . Then I met Joe on the front lawn of Trowrico Lodge. Joe pulls up in his little MG. I was mowing the lawn. I said, 'Listen, maybe someday we'll have a band together.' I'll never forget saying that to him. It's in the trees. They heard it. It's still there. When I transposed 'Dream On' to guitar, Joe played the right fingers and Brad played the left hand on guitar. Sitting there working it out on guitar and piano I got a little melodramatic. The song was so good it brought a tear to my eye."

After being mired in a midcareer slump, the 1986 revival of Aerosmith's "Walk This Way," by rap group Run-DMC, brought the group to a crossroads.

Figure 20. Steven Tyler, 2018. Photo: Gage Skidmore, Wikimedia Commons, CC BY-SA 3.0.

"We were down to whether we thought we could even write again," Tyler said. "I mean, that question came up. 'Are you going to be able to write without drugs? But don't you realize you gotta get off drugs or you're not going to have a band? I mean those questions came up. The snake that was eating its own tail. Everything was a paradox, and we had to settle on one thing and that was that we were going to give up drugs and play like we owned the world and wanted it back again.

"We went into the studio with Rick Rubin right after the 'Walk This Way' video. And Joe and I were just up against a wall, a flat black cement wall. We couldn't come up with jack. We listened to what we put down the next day and it was so bad. But I heard this parable about this guy who lived in a cave and a big tree grew in front of it. He had this tiny hatchet and for years he thought, I'll never get out of here, not with this thing. But someone told him, just tiny swipes, a little bit at a time, and eventually the tree comes down. Well, he did that and in a month's time, that huge tree was chopped down. So I looked at that with Joe Perry and we went into the studio, and we just rehearsed every day for five hours, Joe on guitar and me on drums, with a little tape recorder, and we did that for two or three months and that's how we came up with *Permanent Vacation* and *Pump* as well.

"When I get home, and get my Korg hooked up, I get into my own little world and everything I've accumulated over the past year starts flowing. I like to get down with 99% of the lyrics and work it up until the thing shines. Then I drop it and forget it. Go into the studio a month later and go, 'Whoa, wow!' That's a major league get-off. You can feel the sparks from the tape from that magic moment. Then you spend three weeks mixing it and adding the instruments and you go, 'This is it. The album's finished.' Then, a month or two later, the record's been released, and you play the songs live, in a huge hall, and you hear that song like a monster and you get goose pimples like crazy."

***

After the release of Pump, *Aerosmith hit a career mother lode, with six more studio albums, two of which (*Get a Grip, *1993) and* Nine Lives, *1997) hit number one on the album charts. In 2024, due to Tyler's ongoing vocal problems, the band announced it was retiring from performing.*

Linda Creed (1974)

While Memphis briefly grabbed the title as the capital of Soul in the late sixties, in the early seventies Philadelphia came to prominence with its own brand of "Philly Soul," dominated by producers Kenny Gamble and Leon Huff and writers Thom Bell and Linda Creed. Influenced by the songwriting style of Smokey Robinson, the Philadelphia-born Creed was an outcast not only as a white girl in a predominantly Black high school but also as a music freak. "My friends didn't quite understand me," she told me. "I mean, they would like a song, but I got into the *bass line*! From the moment I got into music, and particularly R&B, people laughed. At school they were listening to WDAS and WHAT. Where I lived I had trouble getting those stations, but I would listen through the static for hours. Then I branched off into jazz and going to jazz festivals. I became very Black-oriented, because to know something you have to experience everything and only through that experience can you know what you're talking about. So, I was scorned all the way through. But Smokey's lyrics were spellbinding. I loved them. He said things simply, but it carried over into your emotions.

"It makes me feel good when a deejay will say listen to the lyrics on this one. It makes me want to do better. I can definitely see my growth pattern from my first six songs, which were written over a number of years—I didn't write that much in the beginning because Tommy was doing a lot of outside productions. My lyrics are a lot more complicated, a bit wiser. The more of myself I've discovered, the more it's in my songs. The early songs were very corny. Even though I still write love songs, I think they have more depth than they did back then, only because I had never experienced love.

"I started writing songs in 1969. Originally I was a singer and Tommy Bell tried to help me, but I was unsuccessful. Then Tommy suggested I get a job as a secretary at Gamble=Huff. I figured as long as I'm around music, I don't care. Then one day he said, Creed, have you ever tried writing lyrics. I told him I'd written poems but never thought of them as lyrics. So we tried it. We sat down and wrote 'Free Girl' and that was it. Ever since then we've been writing together." Although she started out as a poet, the songwriting form both contained and satisfied her creative urges. "I would never go home, say, and knock out forty lyrics and bring them in. We'd always write for a particular artist. There was no excess."

Epitomizing this attitude, one of their biggest hits, "Betcha by Golly Wow," which reached number two on the R&B charts in 1972, was originally released on Bell by Connie Stevens ("Sixteen Reasons") in 1970 as a midtempo pop ballad called "Keep Growing Strong." Changing little but the title (which was already a significant part of the existing lyric), they next gave it to the Stylistics as a follow-up to their top ten hit, "You Are Everything," also written by Bell and Creed. It was their biggest hit until "You Make Me Feel Brand New" in 1974.

"I wrote 'You Make Me Feel Brand New' when I was engaged," Creed said. "I was so happy while I was writing that song. Each line I was jumping up and down saying, 'I love it!' I'm basically a happy person, but before I got married I was writing sad tunes. My lyric writing changed completely when I got married. For some reason, it made me very creative. I guess it's because my husband inspires me.

"I love what I do and I love writing, but I'm the kind of person who's always looking for a new challenge and since lyric writing has become kind of easy, now I have to find something else. Presently I'm working on my own material for a solo album. But I will not perform. I would just like to do the album for my own satisfaction. I work with performers every day and I see what happens to them. It's a very rough life. I was on the road, performing, when I tried to make it as a singer. Now I'm very happy at home. I'd like to be a mother someday. I want to have an equal balance between my business and my home life."

∽

Creed did some of her best writing while diagnosed with breast cancer, including "The Greatest Love of All" with Michael Masser for the film bio of Muhammad Ali, The Greatest. A hit in 1977 for George Benson, it was covered by Whitney Houston and released as the fifth single from her debut album in 1986. Creed's first and only number one hit peaked on May 17th, five weeks after she succumbed to breast cancer at the age of thirty-seven.

Donald Fagen / Steely Dan (1985)

At the keyboards, Donald Fagen was the smoky voice and songwriting coconspirator (with Walter Becker) on all of Steely Dan's classic hits, from "Reelin' in the Years" to "Rikki Don't Lose That Number" (Rikki Lee Jones, that is) to "Peg" and "Deacon Blues" and "Hey Nineteen." Carving perverse lyrics into cryptic and sardonic storylines, wound around a sampling from the literature of pop-rock-jazz-blues melodic constructions, the Dan's output also included some of rock's most memorably ragged character portraits, among them "Charlie Freak," "Rose Darling," "Kid Charlemagne," "Pearl of the Quarter," and Dr. Wu. Charting the inevitable comedown from a decade of street theater, Fagen and Becker swung from the chandeliers while the roof was caving in.

Now, removed from such turbulence and approaching his songwriting midlife alone, Fagen contemplates the glittering standard-strewn byways that led him to this juncture in a much more measured fashion. In the last thirty years he had produced but four albums, including the recent *Sunken Condos*. Befitting his reclusive reputation, Mr. Fagen agreed to this interview only if he could answer all questions in writing.

∽

"I don't think Walter and I were songwriters in the traditional sense, neither the Tin Pan Alley Broadway variety nor the 'staffer' type of the fifties and sixties.

"An attentive listening to our early attempts at normal genre-writing will certainly bear me out. It soon became more interesting to exploit and subvert traditional elements of popular songwriting and to combine this material with the jazz-based music we had grown up with. In college we were both intrigued by certain humorists of the late fifties and early sixties, such as John Barth, Joseph Heller, Kurt Vonnegut, Thomas Berger, Terry Southern, and Bruce Jay Friedman (I've since cooled on a lot of these writers). Walter read a couple of novels by Thomas Pynchon. We both thought the predicament in which popular music found itself in the middle sixties rather amusing too, and we tried to wring some humor out of the whole mess. We mixed TV-style commercial arranging clichés with Mersey beats, assigned nasty sounding, heavily amplified guitars to play Ravel-like chords, etc. The fairly standardized rock instrumentation of the original group added to the schizy effect. We never tried to compete with the fine songwriters of the era (Goffin and King, Lennon and McCartney). We were after a theatrical effect, the friction produced by the mix of music and lyrics—the irony."

Work Habits

"At this point I can't really remember who wrote this verse or that chorus, but the way it often worked out was like this: I would come up with a basic musical structure, perhaps a hook line and occasionally a story idea. Walter would listen to what I had and come up with some kind of narrative structure. We'd work on music and lyrics together, inventing characters, adding musical and verbal jokes, polishing the arrangements, and smoking Turkish cigarettes. Of course, the musicians would kick in with arranging ideas, bass lines, etc., when we got into the studio. Working without Walter was shocking to begin with. I got used to having somebody to bounce ideas off. It wasn't that difficult coming up with the music, because I basically used to come up with the musical material anyway. But the lyrics were quite difficult. I think I was lucky to be able to draw on my own background for some semiautobiographical songs.

"Lately I work mostly in the daytime, in a small sunny room. I own a few pieces of electronic gear, but I work at the piano, for the most part. I compose almost every day, usually five or six hours on the average. I also make time to play some standards and jazz tunes and maybe run some scales. I used to be a workaholic (what a terrible word that is)—up all night, running to the piano before breakfast, that sort of thing. Nowadays I sometimes stop to smell those proverbial roses. These days I listen to very little music. When I do, I play old jazz records, Ray Charles, Chicago blues, some French composers, and once in a while, with shutters drawn, I sneak a listen to my crackly copy of *Highway 61 Revisited*. A goal I have now is to one day write a really terrific song and hear it in a movie theater."

Studio Musicians

"When Walter and I decided we weren't cut out to be leaders of a touring band, we started looking for a more mature (some might say slicker) sound. Our original players went their separate ways and studio players were just the ticket. Because the cost of rehearsal time with studio players was (and is) high, we began to prepare fairly detailed charts before going into the studio, sometimes with the help of one of the musicians on the date. The players would run down the tune a few times and then we'd start recording. With luck we'd get an early take. More often we'd do quite a few. Solos were usually overdubbed and judged on flow and originality; however, a player with a nice touch could get by easily on blues alone. Larry Carlton played on quite a few of our records. He's a real virtuoso.

Figure 21. Donald Fagen, 2017. Photo: Raph_PH, Wikimedia Commons, CC BY 2.0.

In my opinion he can get around his instrument better than any studio guitarist. He's also quite a good blues player. He did the solos on 'Kid Charlemagne.' The middle solo he did in two takes and we used parts of both. The last solo was straight improvisation. Sometimes a player would come in and rip off a solo like that; other times, if they were playing something which we didn't think was stylistically consistent with the song, or if they were just having trouble getting any idea, we might suggest a stylistic or melodic idea to get them started."

Covers

"Because most of our tunes were written to be performed only by Steely Dan, they don't lend themselves very well to cover renditions. The lyrics are not the sort that would inspire singers to cover them. And most of the melodies are instrumental type lines, and not songs in the usual sense of the term. By that I mean that a real song, it seems to me, has a kind of melody which is, first of all, very easy to sing. It has a natural flow, usually in a stepwise motion, with consecutive notes, simple arpeggios, and so on. That's a quality a lot of the great songwriters had. You can sing the melody without any chordal background and it'll still sound good. The melody is not dependent on the harmony; it's just a really good melody. I think our songs were derived more instrumentally, more in the way—not to make a comparison in quality—Duke Ellington would write. I think his songs in fact don't work that well as songs. He wrote for the people in his band, the specific players. He wrote lines he thought they could play well. And although we weren't writing for instrumental performers—we were writing for my voice—I think our background, because it mostly comes out of arranging and jazz, made us lean toward melodies that had that kind of structure—they're more chordally situated.

"When I hear the occasional cover, I almost always experience what I've come to think of as the Bill Murray Effect—i.e., Buddy Greco doing 'Born to Be Wild.' "

Since the death of Walter Becker, his musical partner in Steely Dan, in 2001, Fagen has released four studio albums, but none since 2012.

Randy Newman (1974)

Slowly but surely, almost against his will, Randy Newman has become a legend in his own time—although not too many people know it, or his work. His legend is largely restricted to the hard-core aficionados and a soft corps of music-business heavies who admire him unashamedly and rerelease his notoriously poor-selling albums semiannually.

Although only one Randy Newman lyric ("Mama Told Me Not to Come," sung by Three Dog Night) has hit the top of the pops, his lyrics—variously droll, poignant, and grotesque—have won the hearts of performers like Judy Collins ("I Think It's Going to Rain Today"), Blood, Sweat and Tears ("Just One Smile"), Tracy Nelson ("God's Song"). A noted hard-worker, Newman once had to be virtually pushed onstage to perform his own songs. Now the reverse is true. And surely the prayers of the nation are with him in his battles against the Muse and the rigors of the easy life.

Borrowing a quote I once used to describe the late poet John Berryman, I'd have to call Randy Newman the songwriting equivalent of a "cryptic critic in clipped verse."

The interview with the morose, self-deprecating Mr. Newman took place between sets backstage at the Cambridge Performance Center in Cambridge, Massachusetts.

"A lot of the people I write about are insensitive or a little crazy in a different way than I'm crazy. I don't ever actually run into any of these people on the street. Maybe there's a part of me in there sometimes, in what I'm having this person say, and my attitude is reflected in how I have him say it. Or like in dreams, you could say this comes from here and means that. But it's never a situation where I'm living through these twerps that I write about. Still, they're more interesting to me than heroic characters. Way more interesting.

"You see, *I* don't interest me, writing about me. I couldn't name you any song where I was writing about me. I mean there's a whole world of people and there's no reason why a songwriter should be limited any more than a short story writer or a novelist. I hate songs like 'I've Got to Be Me.' That's an obvious example, but songs don't always have to be personalized.

"I've been trying to write something about a Southern industrial worker. I've had the idea for a long time. Stuff like that interests me, the average person, nothing startlingly dramatic. I read that they had figured out the average person in the country would be a forty-seven-year-old woman who's a machinist's wife outside of Dayton, Ohio. I wanted to do a song about her through this industrial worker character.

"At one point I was at this project fairly regularly and wrote a lot of songs real fast, but then I took a look at it and I didn't have a way to go dramatically. Parts were all right, but I think the songs were suffering because I was trying to fit them into a mold that couldn't hold them.

Figure 22. Randy Newman, 1975. Photo: Rob Bogaerts / Anefo, Wikimedia Commons, CC0 1.0.

Some of the songs were too obscure. Obscure to the point where people would say, 'How great, how obscure'; but even if they did, that's wrong. I really don't like to do that to people too much. I would resent it if a fucking song made me feel dumb. And I didn't want to use anything like liner notes to explain it. I wanted it all to be within the body of the work.

"For instance, there was this fairly long song in there called 'Kingfish.' Now, that's what Huey Long was called, but who the fuck knows that? I was kind of interested in Huey Long—his biography. Someone wanted to do *All the King's Men*, but I didn't want to do it. When I was real little, I lived in New Orleans. My father was in the army. My mother used to tell me about Huey Long.

"I still may do this concept. I do think a major work, a play or something, to make that try, would be more satisfying than getting hit after hit."

I asked Randy when he started writing songs.

"I was sixteen or seventeen. I was always going to be a musician. I never thought about being anything else. In fact, I never thought about it at all. My first songs were bad rock 'n' roll, typical Shirelles stuff. At the time I liked Carole King, Barry Mann, that type of writer. I liked the music better than the words, but it was a different time. When I started working for a publisher, my only concern was that the lyrics should be commercial. We may have said, 'What a great lyric!' but it was great because Little Peggy March could do it. A lot of people started out at the same company—Leon Russell, David Gates, Jackie DeShannon, P. J. Proby. Glen Campbell used to do the demos.

"I wrote love songs, whereas I'm not interested in doing that kind of song anymore. I think eventually I became too interested in words to put up with songs that said nothing, or in writing things that embarrassed me. At the time they embarrassed me, but I look back now, and I would not be proud of them.

"But it hasn't gotten easier for me to write; it's gotten harder. It was easier when I was writing for people—not that they'd do it, but I'd have someone in mind and then I'd write the song and file it away and wouldn't have to think about it anymore. When I have to think about writing for myself, it's a different matter—what I'd be willing to put in Tom Jones's mouth and what I'd be willing to put in mine.

"In fact about a year ago I said to myself, 'I'm going to write a song for Tom Jones.' I was kind of worried that I was slipping out of the mainstream, or any stream. I didn't give him the song, but I did write it, and

Randy Newman (1974) | 163

it made me feel pretty good for a while. It was a fairly representative Tom Jones song. Not a good one, just a representative one. I like being able to do things like that. Now all I have to do is be able to make songwriting seem less unpleasant, or I just won't write. It'll be all over. I'll have to go back to North Hollywood or play in a lounge somewhere."

Randy Newman's attitude on songwriting is known throughout the music business. Also known is his penchant for dramatic overstatement.

"Every time I've had to talk about this I've gone into a grim litany. I know I'm making it worse than it is, it can't be as bad as I think it is, but it depresses me just to think about it. For long periods of time I've been unwilling to do it, to be there all alone in a room. I don't mind if I'm all alone reading, but like when I'm walking into the room with the piano in it, my legs begin to get heavy and I feel a pressure. Recently I've overcome my guilt about it, which had always acted as a goad. Now I don't feel bad about not writing at all.

"I don't know what it would take to get me writing again. I mean, I've had financial disasters, owed the government money. I had an album deadline looming over me. It loomed and went right by. Maybe in a way what I wanted more than money, or sales, or fame was praise, and I kind of got it. Now it seems I'm worried that I won't get it again, but it probably isn't as important to me as it was.

"When I was twenty-one I ran a Thermo-Fax machine. I liked that. There's a great gratification that comes with having a nine to five job, in that you had to be at a certain place at a certain time and you could go home at a certain time. You didn't have to impose any discipline on yourself. I wish I could get into a set routine. I've made up schedules for myself since I was eight years old, but I haven't followed one of them. Tolstoy made those kinds of lists for seventy years and never kept them."

I asked him to remember a time when he was writing and from that recollection to piece together some thoughts on his working process.

"I've always worked the same way. I just sit there. Very rarely, maybe a couple of times, I've jumped out of bed with an inspiration. But usually it comes while I'm sitting at the piano. I hardly ever have the words first. A piece of a melody or a figure of some kind will be enough to get me going, and sometimes it'll be right there where you can see to the end of it. And sometimes it won't, and you'll change it and you'll go somewhere different than where you thought."

I asked him why his songs are generally so short.

"I guess I just say what I have to say and that's all I have to say about it and I'm done. There're a couple of songs that could have been

164 | They're Playing My Song

longer or more successful, like 'Beehive State'; I really couldn't think of anything there. I tried. But usually I'm just happy to be done. I can generally feel when they're finished. I've been wrong a few times, more than a few. I have urges to change them all the time. I would do it, but I know I could never get them right. There's ruin there if you start to do that. But I can't think of many of them where something musically or lyrically doesn't really bother me. Which is another deterrent from working. You bust your ass with a crazed kind of worrying about every little thing and seeing all these bad things about it two weeks later. It's a psychosis. It can't be as bad as I think it is. In performing them they all seem okay. It's only when I have to think about them . . .

"Performing is so easy, so immediately rewarding. Writing, although I know it's more important, is just rough. I had a talk with Nilsson once and I thought he was crazy. He said he didn't want to perform because he thought the audience would sway him unduly about songs, and he might get to thinking shit wasn't shit and that something that was shit was okay. Now I'm not convinced that he was totally crazy. Or it might be that performing is so easy and lucrative that I'm getting the gratification that I used to only get through writing, without all the grief.

"Actually, I could quit *both* and just do nothing at all. I'm capable of doing absolutely nothing for long periods of time without much remorse. But every once in a while, in the morning I'll wake up and say, 'Jesus Christ, what a waste. What a big talent I used to be, like a meteor across the sky.'"

Does he like any of his songs?

"I still like 'Davy the Fat Boy'; I always liked that. I kind of like 'Political Science,' but I didn't like it for a long time. I thought it was too close to a Tom Lehrer–type song, not that there's anything wrong with Tom Lehrer. I'm proud I wrote 'Sail Away.'

"In fact, the thing that did precipitate some of my writing was the Watts riots of 1965. I think that's the biggest thing that happened, the biggest shock to me, and the biggest inequity in this country. The way black people are treated in this country is obviously the worst thing to me. I always felt that the race situ-ation was worse here than anywhere.

"Other than that, I'm essentially apolitical. I don't think my views are of any interest. I never could buy the sincerity of all those people singing the peaced-out numbers, but I wouldn't quarrel with the sentiments."

At this point our conversation suddenly veered into a detailed reminiscence by Mr. Newman on the early days of rock 'n' roll.

"I remember the day I first heard of Elvis. Everyone was giggling and laughing at school saying, 'What's an Elvis Presley?' I think I was

Randy Newman (1974) | 165

in junior high. I liked some of his stuff. I liked 'Heartbreak Hotel' and I liked the narration in 'Are You Lonesome Tonight?'

"I never could dance too well, but I was in a club and all at school, and in a feeble way I was into it. I haven't seen anything recognizable in these films that are supposed to be so accurate. Some of *American Graffiti* maybe . . . but it was all more sullen and boring and small and vile. You know, barfing and stuff and making fun of old people. It wasn't any of that fairyland stuff that I've been seeing. It was social castes, where you ate your lunch, standing around looking tough . . . or whatever the fuck you were supposed to do.

"I went to my high school reunion. That was something! I remembered a lot of people. Jesus Christ, it was tremendous. A lot of people had been beaten down by life. Some of the girls who looked tremendous in those days didn't look tremendous anymore, and others had come on a bit. And I discovered that everybody was scared all the time socially, whereas I thought that people were really together. Talking to them I found out they weren't together. No one was.

"There were very few freaks. It was all very middle-of-the-road there, drinking and getting into trouble. Now, one guy, who was always going to be a farmer, freaked out in some way; it might have been acid. The least likely person you'd expect. He's a theater arts major. His brother had wanted to be a baseball player. Now he's selling sandals.

"It's a meaty topic, and nobody's done it right. Not the reunion business, but the whole way it was. I've thought about it for years. It was so seedy. You might have thought it was fun. I mean, at this reunion we talked about all the good times, how sick we were. But it was pretty grim and not for me alone. I was all right, you know, on the approved list. Although I never approved of the approved list.

"A little later on I was in a band. We were really terrible. It was a band started by this trumpet player. He had a trumpet with him all the time, but he never played. He organized the band. We had our first thing at some fraternity party. I think I was still in high school. We got up to play. It was the first time we were ever going to hear him. And he fell off the bandstand and that was it. I think he fell off on purpose."

❧

Randy Newman continued to put out solo albums but gained more fame for his soundtrack work in Toy Story *and many other films.*

John Prine (1974)

Going head to head in 1971 and '72 with Dylan-influenced folksy singer-songwriters, among them Paul Simon, Neil Young, Joni Mitchell, James Taylor, his mentor Kris Kristofferson, and his pal Steve Goodman, with Bruce Springsteen looming around the corner, the unassuming John Prine gained a foothold that would last a lifetime with his first album. His introductory work contained some of his most beloved and powerful and most covered songs: "Angel from Montgomery," "Paradise," "Sam Stone," "Hello in There," and his personal favorite, "Far from Me."

Fusing his country and western background with a rock beat and folk sensibilities, Prine's songs focused on life's little people and their poignant minidramas. But over the course of his career, some big stars were drawn to them, including Bette Midler, Bonnie Raitt, Johnny Cash, the Flying Burrito Brothers, REM, Joan Baez, the Everly Brothers, John Denver, John Fogerty, and Jackie DeShannon. Although he never had a hit single, "Angel from Montgomery" has been covered forty times, "Paradise" thirty-three, "Sam Stone" thirteen.

My interview with John Prine took place at a restaurant in New York City. The usually shy and taciturn ex-postman warmed easily to the subject at hand, becoming quite verbose . . . sometime around the third drink, when we started discussing the Dylan influence. "I first heard about Dylan when my brother told me the guy who wrote 'Blowin' in the Wind' sounded a lot like Jack Elliott. And I liked Jack Elliott a whole lot. I never did take Dylan's stuff word for word, though. I always liked the whole balance of it, the whole feeling of it. I never knew one song all the way through, but I liked it that way and wanted to keep it that way because I thought it was a nice way to take the songs. Particularly when a lot of people went real overboard, picking the vowels apart and everything."

Mood and feeling dominate the works of John Prine as well. "In general I'd say it's not subjects I'm trying to pinpoint, it's different moods," he told me. "I'm trying to find a situation that would fit the mood. I'm more interested in the framework. A lot of times I'll pick the form before I write the song, because otherwise you run out on too many tangents. If you happen to run out on a good tangent, fine . . . then you can start all over again with that."

This leads to free writing and free association. "A lot of stuff has come out of just writing a couple of pages and rambling on, going from one mood right into another. Then I put it away and, if I wait long enough, I pull it back out and the good lines stay there, and the others just fall right off the page. You can't tell the good lines from the bad lines right at first sometimes. It's a matter of editing. I happen to type at the same speed I edit, so a lot of times I can knock out stuff while I'm typing it. Once I had about three-quarters of a page that I got three songs out of. It was a stream of consciousness thing that didn't make any sense at all as it was. That's why I made it into three different songs. I do have a lot of stuff that's half finished. I've got a song that I've been working on for a year and a half. The first part of it came out in like three seconds, the first verse and chorus. I can't get any further than that and keep up with the original theme of it, so I have to keep going back to it until I get it right. I hate to stop when I start with an original idea, because it's really hard to pick up on it again. It's possible, but it's real difficult.

"A lot of times I'll find a good line that I just can't use in the thing I'm working on, and rather than try to beat it to death, I'll file it away and pick it up when it's fresh again. I've done that really often, gotten two songs out of one thing I've started on. Usually the best thing is a real, real strong line that's a strong image. Sometimes an entire song will pour right out after it, if it's real strong. In most of the ballad stuff I do I try to use a chorus like a needle and thread, to pull the song together. A lot of times I've written just with the idea of experimenting. Like with 'Donald and Lydia,' I had no idea what I was going to write about, but I knew how I was going to set the song up. I was going to set it up character by character."

This observation segued into a discussion of how he creates his characters. "The names mean a lot, like Loretta in 'Hello in There.' I wanted to pick a name that could be an old person's name, but I didn't want it to stick out so much. People go through phases one year where a lot of them will name their kids the same, so I was just thinking that it was very

Figure 23. John Prine, 2016. Photo: Yellowstone National Park, YPF/Matt Ludin. Public domain.

possible that the kind of person I had in mind could be called Loretta. And it's not so strange that it puts her in a complete time period. Any of the names I've ever put in a song I've spent a lot of time on. In 'Donald and Lydia' I was looking through a baby book, starting with Andrew down through Zeke. I was hollering them out like a mother calling her kids in for lunch. Take Rudy, from 'Hello in There.' We used to live in this three-room flat, and across the street there was this dog who would never come in and the dog's name was Rudy. And the lady used to come out at five o'clock every night and go 'Ru-dee! Ru-dee!' And I was sitting there writing and suddenly I go 'Rudy! Yeah! I got that.'"

While Prine didn't really start writing songs until he got into the army, he was developing his writerly skills much earlier than that. "In school the only thing I used to be able to do at all was when they gave me a free hand at writing dialogue," he said. "Writing nothing but dialogue. Everybody else, all these kids who were straight A students, would just bang their heads against the wall, and I'd just go, whoosh, and hand it in. The teacher would say, 'Who'd you buy this from?' because I was a horrible student otherwise.

"When I started to play guitar, I found that the easiest way for me to put a story down was as a song. My brother always used to hear my stuff because he taught me how to play guitar. He also taught himself how to play the fiddle, so I'd have to sit with him and play rhythm guitar. I'd sit with him for hours. If you've ever heard anybody teach himself how to play fiddle, it sounds horrible. But in return he'd listen to my songs. It was easier for me to write a song than to learn somebody else's. I'd never play them for anybody else. A lot of times I never wrote them down, but they were in ballad form. I'd just sing them until I got sick of them."

In the meantime, aside from his brother, his constant companion was the radio. "The people who made the biggest impression on me as lyricists were Hank Williams, Dylan, and Roger Miller, because he managed to write humorous songs that weren't novelty songs, and I hadn't heard anything like that. Then I didn't hear anything until Kris Kristofferson came along. I can remember my first contact with his stuff was an article where they had some of his lyrics. And these lyrics carried their own melody. He writes like he's got a meter built inside of him. I asked him once if he worried that much about meter and he said, 'I just throw in "oh Lord" if it doesn't balance out.' Jimmy Webb has written some real nice stuff. A lot of people in Nashville have excellent ears. They're Tin Pan Alley writers, but they're good at it. The Beatles wrote songs that flowed like Chuck Berry stuff and Buddy Holly stuff, which I'm sure they were very aware of when they wrote them. Of all the people I admired I never found anybody that I thought was saying exactly what I wanted to say, and that's why I wrote. But my first reaction was that I thought there must be something wrong with my songs, because they were a lot different from the stuff I'd heard. I thought if they're that much different, then why hasn't someone done them before?

"I wrote a couple of songs in the army, but still mostly humorous stuff. It was after I got out of the army that I started writing anything serious. I'd sing them at first for friends, and they were encouraging, but I always felt like I was imposing on them. I never thought of selling songs until about a year before I went on the stage."

When asked about his struggle to gain credibility as a writer, Prine had some strong opinions. "When you're an amateur and you're writing songs, everybody is going to have some sort of criticism. They've never

170 | They're Playing My Song

criticized a song in their life, and you say, 'Hey, I wrote this'; they'll say, 'Well, that one part there needs changing.' So, I tried to write songs that nobody could possibly criticize. But after doing that, and after recording and everything, I still have people come to me and tell me they loved a song for the wrong reasons. They really didn't understand it at all. I thought the songs were basically self-explanatory, but they weren't. So, I just went ahead and let people like them for the wrong reasons. But I figured, I don't really have to knock myself out to explain things. I can be a little more abstract.

"A song is not finished until I consider that I'd do it for anybody. But when I finish it, right there and then it's certified. I've heard other writers give suggestions years later about changing a line or something, but once I finish a song—this is even before I record it—I figure it's like a book on a shelf. It's already done and I can't do anything about it. When you hear somebody else do the song, that's when you get a chance to criticize lines that you wrote. Whenever I hear my own records, I know it's my voice. I'll end up listening to the arrangement. But when I hear it done by somebody else, sometimes it brings up lines I thought before were just a link between two other lines, and all of a sudden that line stands out, depending on how someone interprets the song.

"Another thing, and this is a result of being a recording artist. Around the time a record is finished I refuse to write for at least a couple of months, even if I feel like it. Mainly because a lot of people haven't heard the new stuff, and I'll be going around doing it, and it's impossible for me to have a song finished and not go out and perform it. It's impossible for me to keep it locked up for six months or more."

∽

Roots rock legend John Prine recorded eighteen studio albums before his death in 2020.

Bruce Springsteen (1973, 1984)

On the night of January 31, 1973, we were present for a little bit of rock and roll history. The "we" I refer to are a few dozen of the New York City pop culture cognoscenti who were urged, cajoled, tipped, hipped, or otherwise hyped into joining the paying customers who saw Columbia artist Bruce Springsteen open up a five-day stint at Max's Kansas City—one of the last remaining oases of good music in a city of deserted singles bars, beat-up coffeehouses, and broken down concert halls.

Already something of a word-of-mouth, underground, and trade press instant legend, Springsteen seems about to leap into the daylight of mass acceptance, household status, and bandstand furor via the resounding clatter of praise issuing forth from some of your favorite magazines. The crowd at Max's was prepared then—somewhat—for his set, armed and waiting to fling the hype back into his face like a custard pie.

"It's strange, very strange," Springsteen said, later, at the sumptuous Columbia Records café. "Let me tell you, Max's was the first gig where people came to see the band. Before that, it was like we were playing at football games, you know? People just didn't relate. And I figure this would be that kind of scene. But then people started to get interested. I've met a lot of nice people who honestly like the music and are really excited about the band. But then you get people who come with an attitude toward us. I just get up and play every night—if somebody runs around saying it's good or it's bad; I don't have a lot of control."

Clad in dungarees, baseball cap, and T-shirt, Springsteen, twenty-three, ascended to the spotlight at Max's with acoustic guitar in hand, accompanied only by an accordion player. He dedicated his set to John Hammond Sr.—Columbia's musical tastemaker supreme—who hadn't been this high on a discovery since he flipped his superlatives at Folk City some eleven years or so ago on Bob Dylan. Dylan advanced from Folk City to the Gaslight, where Sam Hood put him to work. Eventually, Bobby departed for the western skies of New Jersey. Bruce is from Asbury Park. Sam Hood now takes care of business at Max's. And John Hammond Sr. came down early in the evening just to shake Springsteen's hand.

"*The New York Times* compared me to *El Topo*," Springsteen remarked with a laugh. "They said, if you like *El Topo*, you'll like Bruce Springsteen. I think they compared me to Allen Ginsberg, Rod Stewart, and *El Topo* in the same article. There's a cat with an original point of view. My songs have been compared to Ginsberg's 'Howl.' But I just write what comes out of me. The stuff I write might not be the kind of stuff I'd read. I'm not really a literary type of cat. I've hardly read any poets. I was never a serious reader. I went through a year and a half of college, which I don't remember a darn thing from. All I remember is being hassled to no end."

After his opening number, a dirge called "Mary, Queen of Arkansas," which is one of the nine songs on his debut album, *Greetings from Asbury Park*, the pace picked up with a rocker about Indians and flapjacks made 'em fat, and bishops, and James Garner's one-eyed bride. Following this was a piece about the big top, complete with flute and tuba, chilling the air just enough to set the stage for some electricity.

With the band joining him now full blast, Springsteen put down the guitar for piano and began to show this crowd what he was really all about. Before he was through with "Spirit in the Night," the halfway laid-back, still somewhat unconvinced and cynical New York audience came to life. He did a song about a bus ride (now playing electric guitar) before slamming into an epic opus that might have been called "Her Brains They Rattle and Her Bones They Shake," and while this stomping, romping rocker was going on, the realization came upon you that the kid and his band were only warming up, getting loose. This was but the first set of three tonight, of five days here, of other days and weeks, present glory, future fame.

"I was into messing around with words when I was eighteen," he told me. "But I quit and got into R&B. It wasn't until now that I figured out a way to fuse the two. It didn't come together easy for me then. I've been playing for ten years. I was out there by myself for five. That's how I made my living. By playing hard and sometimes getting groups. I played down South a whole lot, went out to California with a band when I was about twenty. We played the old Matrix, second billing to Boz Scaggs. But it got to a point where things got so tough we had no way to get

Bruce Springsteen (1973, 1984) | 173

Figure 24. Bruce Springsteen, 2012. Photo: Bill Ebbesen, Wikimedia Commons, CC BY-SA 3.0.

the equipment around. We had no PA system and no manager, and no nothing. So I said, maybe I'll try it by myself for a while. The only club I really played by myself was Max's. Sam would give me some jobs. In a way, it seems kind of funny now.

Part of the magic is the relationship between Springsteen and his group. More than organ, drums, bass, guitar, and sax, more than just a bunch of good musicians, they are a grease ball, dancehall jazz band five, who relate to each other as if they've been playing for years, like they grew up together in the Jersey flats, shared the same vision forever, and are just now getting around to laying it on an unsuspecting public. They seem to be having a ball, too.

"There used to be a little club around town in Asbury," said Springsteen, "a joint called the Upstage, three floors of solid black light. I would go down there quite a bit, three or four years ago. That's where I met the drummer, Vini Lopez, and that's where I also met the organ player, Danny Federici. Me and Vini's been playing together four years. Me and Danny played together about three years, then we used another cat for a while, and now Danny's come back to the band. And Clarence, the sax player, wandered into this club where I was playing about a year ago, the Student Prince, and said, 'Hey man, can I sit in?' He sat in and we got something going. And that's the band. They're all great guys and they push. They work as hard as I do. It's the kind of scene where we're all in the same boat. If it happens, it happens for everybody."

Bruce Springsteen's intensity and humor onstage is contagious. You can bet he won't be playing second billings for long. After leaving Max's he starts on a winding uphill route of roadside dives, college gyms, and noisy after-dinner clubs. After a return to Asbury Park and a tour of the East Coast, the Springsteen Five will be like a basketball team playing fourteen games in twelve days, covering Denver, LA, San Francisco, Seattle, and Portland.

"Lately you know what I do when I'm not playing—I sleep, period. I go home and go to sleep, get up and play again. Run to Baltimore to play, run back. Believe it or not, I used to be a real Solitaire freak, but I haven't been lately. This week I've got three days off, which is a really big vacation."

If Springsteen's crew of managers, press agents, publicist, grooms, and groupies can keep his head and his band together, can disregard the frantic hype that's bound to trail him, can manage to avoid falling prey to the nitpicker vultures who like to snipe at any moving target, they might bring him home again to the metropolitan area a winner. But it will be no easy task.

"All I want to do is write some good songs," he said. "It's my trade. It's how I get my satisfaction. The main problem is not to lose sight of what is actually going on. All the ads and the hype . . . anyone with any sense just ignores it. It's just one of the unpleasant things you have to do to make a record. I've never been a door knocker. I don't try to push myself on anybody. I just don't believe in it. I mean, if people want what you've got, that's good. All this other stuff is very new to me."

Part Two

This interview was for a five-part series in *USA Today* in 1984, representing a high-water mark in the Boss's career. This was the year of his biggest commercial breakthrough, with *Born in the USA* scoring seven hit singles. Befitting his towering stature, there were hoops to jump through in securing the interview, where few had existed before—even for a five-part feature in *USA Today*. The main hoop I encountered was at the Madison Square bowling alley, where the man and his security staff had commandeered lane 12 while every other interested onlooker hit the pins on lanes 1 through 6. When I was finally granted access to lane 12, Springsteen hailed me like a long-lost war buddy. Assured of the interview, I had only one more hoop remaining, which was rolled in front of me just as the interview was about to commence after his first show.

"Bruce is really exhausted," said his PR rep, "and he's got to save his voice for tomorrow night. So you're going to have to ask him all your important questions in the first five minutes."

"But this is for a five-part article," I cried.

Luckily, in the Springsteen tradition of giving at least two hundred percent onstage or backstage, five minutes stretched to an hour and a quarter.

"Nobody is going to demand that I play harder at night than I myself would want to play," he said. "A lot of times I'm out there for me. I'm out there doing something at night that I have to do for myself. I get a feeling from playing that I can never get from anything else."

Especially therapeutic are the long stream of consciousness anecdotes he unspools between songs, mainly about his troubled relationship with his father, the staunchly working-class Douglas, encountered sitting at the kitchen table in a preface to his interpretation of the Animals' "It's My Life."

"I get along real good with my parents and have for some time," he said now. "When you're a teenager, you tend to dehumanize your parents and it's kind of a shame. Finally, you realize your dad is just a guy and your mom is just a girl."

So, it comes as no surprise during his five nights in Jersey when he invited his mom, Adele, up to the stage to dance! "She got a tremendous round of applause, one of the biggest of the night," Springsteen said. "She felt so good. I felt good, too."

As Springsteen's followers have celebrated his return to family values, they've also embraced some of the darker epics. Where his early imagery was devoted to saints and angels and spirits in the night, he segued into tales of the working class, kids corrupted by real life, the death of the American dream, kids leaving home, marrying too young, turning to crime, dreaming of escape, hungry hearts, burning with desire, dancing in the dark, the dark side of success. "The whole thing basically in rock 'n' roll is dancing on your problems," he said. "So a song could be about something that is not necessarily uplifting and still be uplifting. I think it's the recognition of the emotions that people find uplifting. It's just the feeling of sharing the same emotions. For the *Born to Run* record I established a certain set of values: hope, faith, friendship, a certain type of optimism. After that I felt I had to test those things to see what they were worth, what they would mean in real life, which I began to do after *Born to Run* through *Nebraska*. Those records were kind of my reaction, not necessarily to my success but to what I was feeling. What I felt the role of a musician should be, what an artist should be. I was trying to find something to hold on to, something that wouldn't disappear out from under you. *Nebraska* was about the basic things that keep people functioning in their communities, or in their families, or in their jobs. The idea that they all break down. They fail. The record was a crisis album, a spiritual crisis. Families fail, your job fails, and you're gone, you're lost. Everything goes out the window. I was interested in finding out what happens, what do my characters do, what do I do?

"I always felt free when I was young because I was playing in a band and I liked my job. I'd get up when I wanted to get up and go out to play at night. I was writing songs and just going out and playing to the people. As we became more successful, the idea was to maintain that particular freedom because you can lose it easily. It can confine you or, hopefully, give you more room. It's all in knowing the things that are really valuable as opposed to the things that appear to be valuable. It's knowing that thing on the inside that keeps you alive, keeps you vital, gives you strength, knowing what that is and not getting lost in the distractions. The main ideal is to just do it better. Just keep going at it. I'm interested in getting as good as I can be. I think that's where I'm most useful."

∽

Springsteen's twenty-first studio album, Only the Strong Survive, *released in 2022, was his sixteenth to hit the album chart top ten. His marathon concerts continue to draw a loyal fanbase.*

Allen Toussaint (2014)

"Southern Nights"

Even though Glen Campbell took "Southern Nights" to number one in 1977, the song didn't have any discernible impact on the already established career of its writer, New Orleans legend Allen Toussaint. "It was just one of the songs that was out during that time," he said. "I was busy doing many things and having a good time. We were kicking with the Meters and things like that. Lee Dorsey was still around, and I was writing for him a lot. Shortly thereafter came Patti LaBelle doing 'Lady Marmalade,' which I produced. I had a partner, Marshall Sehorn, who was drumming up business and answering the questions on whether we would produce an artist for a company, and I was just back there making music and writing songs and producing and arranging."

According to Toussaint, there wasn't even much of an uptick on his regular BMI checks at the time. "I didn't notice anything special from that song, because the checks come with payments from the tiniest song to the most major. I didn't notice it, because I never was paying attention to the amount of the check. Never."

But Toussaint does have a theory as to why the song wasn't as life changing as one might assume. "It took people quite a while to realize I'd written it," he said. "I wasn't out there performing, so I guess some people thought probably Glen Campbell had written it. Which I don't mind. It was just like all the rest of the songs I've written in my life. People didn't know I wrote 'Mother-in-Law' or 'Java' or 'Working in the Coal Mine' either." As opposed to "Southern Nights," Toussaint regarded "Mother-in-Law," the number one tune he penned for the great New Orleans showman Ernie K-Doe, as more of a commercial effort. "I understood that it was the kind of a song with a tempo and a message that anyone would understand and either like or dislike. But again, even at that time I never paid attention to its success or failure, because I was always on to the next thing, like I still am these days."

The story goes that "Mother-in-Law" was rescued from the trash by one of Ernie K-Doe's backup singers. Allen doesn't dispute the legend. "What happened is I wrote four songs for him to do, because we always recorded four songs at a time, and 'Mother-in-Law' was one of them. When I tried it out on him the first time, he began to shout and preach at it, and I really didn't like his approach to it. I thought it was a waste of time to try to get him to do it, so I balled it up and put it in the trash can, like I did with other songs. One of the backup singers, Willie Harper, thought it was just a wonderful song, so he took it out of the trash can and said, 'K-Doe, why don't you calm down and listen closer to the way Allen is doing it and try to do it like that? This is a good song.' So he

Figure 25. Allen Toussaint, 2009. Photo: dsb nola / Derek Bridges, Wikimedia Commons, CC BY 2.0.

calmed down and didn't preach at it but did it like it finally came out. Ernie was a cocky individual, but I thought he was a dear man and he loved the business so much. I think he thought that James Brown had his slot, and he was going after it. He liked James Brown's energy and he really wanted to let the world know there's an Ernie K-Doe."

These days Toussaint remains one of the finest emissaries of the New Orleans tradition he has helped to create. "I'm glad to say it's a wonderful day for us," he said. "We're still turning out good people, like Trombone Shorty, John Boutté, and people like that. And those youngsters are still blowing their horns in front of St. Louis Cathedral and down on Jackson Square right now. It's a wonderful music scene, I'm so glad to say. They're holding on to some tradition, as well as growing into the future. They're taking a tradition with them."

"In 1974 I was busy producing. I wasn't thinking of myself, but that song was written for me to sing. That was unusual, because writing for myself wasn't my normal forte. I enjoyed writing for and producing others. But I was asked to do another album for Warner Brothers, and I did it. That was the last song for the album, the very last song. I had written and recorded all of the other songs, and for some reason I couldn't come to terms that I was finished with the album. I had trouble being satisfied. I always take forever to do an album, because when I do an album, I don't plan to do another. The only reason I ever did another album after any album was because I got a request by some company. Left to my own devices, I wouldn't record me.

"While I was finishing the album, Van Dyke Parks visited me in the studio. He was a wonderful guy, a genius of a guy. He said, 'Well, consider that you were going to die in two weeks. If you knew that, what would you think you would like to have done?' And after he said that, I wrote "Southern Nights" as soon as he left. I stood right there and wrote it. It all came at once, because I lived that story. It was one of those things that writers would like to happen all the time. We would like to write from total sheer spiritual inspiration, but many times we just write from our tools and our bible. That song was a total inspiration. It felt like a soft, clear white flower settled above my head and caressed me. I really felt highly, highly inspired and very spiritual doing that song. It's the only one I felt that much about. Some others have been inspired highly, but not as high as that one.

"It probably took about two hours to write. Then I went down and recorded it in the studio with just a Fender Rhodes and another guy beating on an ashtray, that little tinkling sound. It was just me on the instrument and singing, and Tony Owens playing on an ashtray. No one remarked on it, because it didn't sound much like a commercial song, and it wasn't. I didn't write it to be a song like all the others on there. I just wanted to share that story with this album. It wasn't supposed to be a commercial song, and I didn't think it would sound like one to anyone else. But I did feel quite complete after I wrote 'Southern Nights.' I felt totally finished with the album. But that didn't mean I was ready to die!

"The album had a very good reception. In fact, Warner Brothers sponsored a marvelous tour, and I was able to take a full complement of musicians and singers on the road. I went out on the road with Lowell George and Little Feat. That was quite a charge, because he was just so hip and I admired him and his work so very much. He also liked what I was doing a lot. He was a wonderful guy and very savvy and wide awake. I performed the song on the road because it was part of the record. I didn't talk about it like I started doing much later on. Now when I do 'Southern Nights,' many times I tell the story of it. I didn't tell the story in those early days. I did a shorter version, because I didn't think people would have the patience to sit through a story, because it was just so personal to me. But I knew it wasn't a mainstream tempo beat, so I didn't impose that on people. Sometimes I didn't play it at all, or I may have played just a little bit of the ending of it or something like that. I just knew it wasn't a mainstream song and I always assumed that people would rather hear something that moves.

"I found out Glen Campbell was going to do it after it was done. I love the story of how it came about. Someone told me that Jim Webb introduced Glen Campbell to it. He said, 'Man, you ought to give that Toussaint song a listen and pick the tempo up, and I think you'll have something.' And he was so right. I'm so glad he did that. I love Glen's version. I had never thought of it as an up-tempo and mainstream song before. I first heard it on the radio and I was delighted. It was so good to hear it like that, because I just hadn't imagined that someone would listen closely enough to it to want to cover such a thing. I already liked Glen Campbell, because of all those marvelous songs he'd done, so to include this as one of the most important ones in his life was just a joy.

"I never watched it on the charts. I was so busy doing other things and by the time I heard it, it was a hit. I met Glen Campbell afterwards many times. We would meet and chat like friends. I guess after that song he began to pay attention to me more as a writer, knowing that I had written it. He knew other songs of mine, and he liked them.

Allen Toussaint (2014) | 181

"I was just so surprised that 'Southern Nights' would become a mainstream hit. It's most interesting. These days, when I introduce it, I put it in another light, forty years later. In those days, when someone would hear my version, they'd hear some words and maybe not hear some others, and they'd be waiting for the next thing to happen. But now, after I tell the story, I think everyone hears it in a better light and understands the significance of it."

Prolific songwriter and producer Allen Toussaint released eleven solo albums before he died in 2016.

Chris Frantz / Tom Tom Club (2014)

"Genius of Love"

Tom Tom Club was a side project drummer Chris Frantz and his wife, bassist Tina Weymouth, came up with during an indefinite Talking Heads hiatus, when lead singer David Byrne got a gig scoring the Twyla Tharp dance project *The Catherine Wheel*. At first Chris and Tina weren't interested in having a side project, even when the fourth member of the group, guitarist and keyboard player Jerry Harrison, announced he was doing a solo album. It was actually their accountant who convinced them. He said, "Yes, you're doing well, but you just did this big tour of the world with an eight-piece band, and you've only got about $2,000 in the bank. So you'd better do something."

"Tina and I looked at each other. Neither of us were singers, at least at that time, and we thought, 'What kind of solo album could we do?'"

Taking advantage of the early eighties hip-hop/dance era, they concocted the Tom Tom Club, whose first album, *The Tom Tom Club*, produced the massive club hits "Wordy Rappinghood" and "Genius of Love," propelling it to instant success. How much success? "Well, let me tell you this story," says Frantz. "When the first Tom Tom Club album was raging, we were riding in a cab from Fifty-Seventh Street downtown to Irving Plaza. In the car was Tina, myself, our manager, and David Byrne. I wish our manager had waited until David wasn't in the cab with us. But he said, 'Hey, guess what? *The Tom Tom Club* album went gold today.' Tina and I were like, 'Oh, that's great.' But David was just sitting there, not making any comment. Talking Heads had not had any gold albums in the United States to that point. I think we had one in New Zealand, of all places. So 'Genius of Love' is right up there, in terms of sales, with the best of the Talking Heads.

"Our manager was good friends with Chris Blackwell of Island Records. We already knew Chris because he'd passed on Talking Heads. In fairness to him, he said, 'I'm putting all of my power into breaking Bob Marley in America.' Anyway, our manager said to Chris, how about if Chris and Tina come down to Compass Point and make a record down there. Being keen on reggae, he understood the power of a good rhythm section. So he said, 'Sure, send them down and they can record a single. And if I like the single, then they can do a whole album.' The first song we recorded was called 'Wordy Rappinghood.' We recorded it and mixed it in three days. Chris Blackwell came into the studio and said, 'I love it. Get started on a whole record. And in the meantime, I'm going to release this as a single in Europe and Latin America.' It did really well. In quite a few countries it went to number one. So we got to work on an album.

"We worked with one of the house engineers at Compass Point, Steven Stanley. At that time, he wasn't getting a lot of work, but Tina and I liked him, and we thought, 'We can work with this kid.' We had worked with him a little bit on *Remain in Light* when the first engineer, Rhett Davis, a very famous British engineer who came down with our producer, Brian Eno, got mad at Eno and left after three days. So we had Steven come in as sort of an interim engineer while this other guy got himself together to come down. Stevie had recorded all the tracks for 'Once in a Lifetime,' so we knew he was a good engineer. And he became coproducer with us. We mentioned to him that we liked Lee Perry. Stevie was totally into that sound, except he was much more precise and had a more international outlook. Like, Stevie wasn't just thinking about what would be hot in Jamaica, he was thinking about the whole world.

" 'Genius of Love' was the second song we started. We didn't finish it until a couple of weeks later. I had the idea for the title and Tina wrote the rest of the lyrics and the melody, except for the last line. We wrote all the songs for the album in the studio. We had learned to write that way on *Remain in Light*. It's a good way of coming up with surprise things. If you just sit down with a piano and a vocal and you make a demo, chances are it's going to sound like something that came before. Same with a singer-songwriter with a guitar: chances are it's not going to be a real surprise to your ear. But if you go in with no preconceived ideas, or maybe a slightly preconceived idea, but not a fully formulated idea, then it can just go anywhere.

184 | They're Playing My Song

Figure 26. Chris Frantz and Tina Weymouth, 2023. Photo: Cory Doctorow, Wikimedia Commons, CC BY 2.0.

"In the studio I'd play the drum part. It's played by hand, but it's a loop part. It doesn't have any fills or anything, but it does have some tom-toms, so I would record a groove with bass drums, snare, and hi-hat. Then Tina would put down her bass. Then I would add a little tom-tom here and there. And then we added the keyboard part, which was actually two keyboard parts combined. Then Tina worked out the vocals with her two sisters, Laura and Lani, and a little bit of screaming by myself. Then we added Adrian Belew on guitar. We also had a Bahamian guitarist named Monty Brown playing a simple rhythm part. He had recently left T-Connection, a Bahamian funk band that had had a few hits.

"Lyrically, things would get changed as it went along, but Tina had a good idea of what she wanted it to be about. We also wanted to pay tribute to all these great soul artists that we really enjoyed and appreciated, like Smokey Robinson, James Brown, and Sly and Robbie. 'There's no beginning and there is no end / time isn't present in the dimension.' I didn't hear that line coming. Tina came up with that. That stuff in the middle, that's Tina's sister, Lani, who invented this language when she was a little kid. It's gibberish, but it sounds like it might be Hindu or something. People at the time were asking, 'What kind of language is that?' Well, it's this language that Tina's sister Lani invented as a child.

"I would say it probably took two sixteen-hour days to complete, but once we had the bass and drums, we already knew we had a hit. Usually, you wouldn't say, 'This is a hit,' because you don't want to jinx it, but I think everybody in the room knew it.

"It was the next single in Europe but it didn't really happen there. It was a hit in the dance clubs but it was not a commercial radio hit. But before the album came out, Island pressed one hundred thousand twelve-inch singles and exported them to the US. We were signed to Island only for the UK, Europe, and parts of Latin America. Actually, we didn't make the deal in the US until one day after Island had sold one hundred thousand import singles in the United States. Seymour Stein at Sire, bless his heart, woke up that morning and said, 'Whoa! I'd better get on this.' And he then offered us a deal. But originally he wasn't interested.

"First time we played 'Genius of Love' live was on the tour that became the movie *Stop Making Sense*. We had never intended for Tom Tom Club to be a live thing. To us it was just an interim thing while Taking Heads waited for David Byrne to be finished with *The Catherine Wheel*. But in fact, on that tour some people would say, 'I didn't come here tonight to hear Talking Heads, I came here tonight to hear Tom Tom Club.' That was mostly in the big cities, with people who liked urban music. In New York it would be the Mudd Club and Danceteria and Hurrah. All of those places would play music to dance to, but it could be any kind of genre—it wouldn't necessarily be disco. It might be new wave from England. It might be something from France or Africa. It wasn't necessarily your cookie-cutter disco bands. But down at CBGB's, where Talking Heads started, there was a whole 'disco sucks' thing. Those people just disdained anything having to do with dancing. To them it was all disco and it was all bad. They didn't like rap either, but Debbie Harry and Blondie did. They had a big hit with 'Rapture,' and then just weeks later we came out with 'Wordy Rappinghood,' which was also a white girl rapping. Neither of us knew that the other was doing it, because we were recording in the Bahamas, and they were recording in New York.

"The song came out in '81. So the checks started rolling in as early as '82, continuing through '83. And then there might have been a little dry spell. But the song still sounds fresh even today. It still gets used in movies and on certain TV commercials. Recently, it was in *Anchorman 2* and *The Wolf of Wall Street* at the same time. But it was a pity that we didn't have time, after the initial thing, to really take Tom Tom Club seriously until after Talking Heads was over. Because with Talking Heads we were touring a lot, and when we weren't doing that, we were working on new records. We did do several Tom Tom Club records after that, but they were all kind of squeezed into a certain period of time.

"The only comment David ever made was when we went to see the premiere of *The Catherine Wheel*. Tina and I sat with him in the VIP section with Baryshnikov and all these dance people, and afterwards there was a party at Studio 54. So we went to Studio 54 and what should be playing when we walked in but 'Genius of Love'? It sounded so good, and you could tell everybody in Studio 54 was really getting off on it. David leaned over and he said, 'How did you get that hand clap sound?'

"That was the only thing he ever said about the record."

"Genius of Love" is one of the most sampled songs in pop history. It was used on the single "Fantasy" from Mariah Carey's best-selling album Daydream. "Fantasy" remained at number one on the Billboard charts for eight weeks.

Marc Campbell / the Nails (2012)

"88 Lines About 44 Women"

A tone poem unmatched in the annals of rock literature, "88 Lines About 44 Women" emerged in the studio. "It was so simple it was uncanny," Campbell told me. "I was in the studio dicking around; we had a studio in our loft in Manhattan, the Nails, and it was back in the day when you could rent the entire floor of some old factory for $1,000. And we had put in a little recording studio / rehearsal space in there. And I and my keyboard player, David, were playing around and shifting our positions in the band around by me playing drums and him playing bass. And we were just laying down some riffs. And we jammed; well, actually, he had the thought to use the new Casio, the little GC Casio keyboard that had some preprogrammed rhythm tracks. And the track that you hear, the little rhythm track that you hear on '88 Lines,' is taken directly from the Casio. So he had turned on that little rhythm track, and we were playing along with it. You know, I was on the drums and playing this kind of big primitive, *boom boom, boomboom, boomboom*. And he was on the bass doing a riff. And I liked what I heard. So I took the cassette tape that we made of that riff and went home—which was this third-story, third-floor walkup—and put the cassette in, and realized that there was about four or five minutes' worth of riff in there, and that that would accommodate eighty-eight lines, or forty-four couplets. That was what determined the length of that song. And curiously, eighty-eight is a pretty cosmic number, it turns out. There's eighty-eight keys on the keyboard, I think. But eighty-eight pops up a lot. Rockin' eighty-eight, just the number pops up a lot in life, I've noticed. It could simply be because I wrote that song, so I'm really attuned to it. But nonetheless, I realized that, Hey, what can you write eighty-eight lines about; what can you write forty-four couplets about? Well, I mean, really what is there other than women? Maybe cars for some guys. Don't have any drugs. Oh, there are. But what are the big things that, you know, that were in my life at that time? Sex, drugs, rock and roll. So it came down to women. And I didn't have to really think twice about it. I'm actually making it sound as if made a choice. I didn't. It just was obvious.

"The way songwriting works for me is always kind of like a trance-type state. I really believe that most good writing kind of takes the writer by surprise. Why write what you already know? So I write what I don't know in order to find out. And that's what happened. It just came flowing through me. It was very easy. One line leading to another. And some of the women are real, some are made up. I had a goal to achieve. At that point I don't know if I'd ever had forty-four really important women in my life. And the song was basically, many people thought, 'Oh, he's boasting about his sex life.' If you listen to the song, that's not true. I created women that I thought were kind of, again, it wasn't like I was sitting there faking through this. But as I was flowing along and writing it, I instinctually felt gaps needed to be filled in terms of my characterization of women as a whole. And I wanted to achieve some kind of epic uberwoman. You know, one that kind of encapsulated all of these women, woman as a source of energy and inspiration, et cetera, for me. And that's kind of how it panned out. It was written about in two hours. It came flowing out. I sat at my beat-up typewriter, and when it was done, I stuck it on the nightstand, went to sleep, and the next day took it into the guys, the band, said, 'Let's get together and record this.' What you hear on the original 4-track, which was the one we released originally as a single, was the rhythm track that David and I laid down in one take. In fact, if you listen to the original single, you will hear me drop the drumstick and then pick it up and lean into the mike and say, 'Are you receiving me?' So, what I did was, I got the band together and they did overdubs on top of that basic riff. At that point that riff basically combined, gelled David's bass, my drums, and the Casio riff kind of gelled into one rhythm track. It almost sounds sampled. Because of the rinky-dinkyness of it. But that was it. They came in, and not much was done. Some horns were thrown down and some guitar. And then I sang over it. And it was done.

"A lot of people are, of course, reminded of "People Who Died" by Jim Carroll. It was just a listing of names. And there was a poem by a New York underground poet named Joe Brainard in which he did a listing

Figure 27. Marc Campbell, 1984. Photo: Louie Lucchesi, provided courtesy of Marc Campbell.

of, I think it was just stuff he liked. But it was a book-length thing. 'I like this,' or whatever it was. What I liked about it was that it's a great 'I Remember.' Okay. That was the name of the poem. 'I Remember.' Which is great, because to begin every line with 'I remember' and then go into your brain and pull this stuff out. And that was part of it. 'I Remember.' Okay. So I really need to give Joe Brainard props for giving me the idea of just a simple list and how compelling that is and how it has this kind of power as you're reading Joe's poem. Which, again, I say this is a book-length. It really has this mantric theme going on where you kind of become hypnotized by it. And the same is true of '88 Lines.' I kind of got into this hypnotic reverie, and it did bring up all kinds of great memories, and it's something I could address over and over again. That song could be, every ten years, it could have a sequel. In fact, I'm writing a book called '44 Women,' which is my memoir. And I'm just using the women as the chapter headings. Because you look back on your life, and really it is, and this is such a cliché, for me it really is sex, drugs, and rock and roll. I don't remember that most influential English teacher I had. I don't remember some of my closest friends' names. But I do remember the first time I took LSD; I do remember the first time I ever got laid; I do remember the first rock and roll song that I went and bought was 'Return to Sender.' So it's a cliché, but it's fucking true. I decided to hang this memoir around the women. And so the very first chick I tried to impress when I was in a garage band in 1964, all the way up to the divorce, my divorce of forty years ago. And these were all important beacons.

"Sometimes what I sang is so true it can get spooky, because you don't know which lies are the truth anymore. You don't know if I dreamed that, or did that really happen? I can't think how many times I've said that. Leonard Cohen certainly has to figure into any discussion of '88 Lines,' no question. And Patti Smith. And Jonathan Richman with 'Roadrunner.' These people all opened up the doors through which I realized that a rock and roll song, or any kind of song, any mantra that doesn't necessarily have to have a melody, though there was a hook in '88 Lines.'

"I'm living with one of the girls in the song right now. Tanya Turkish liked to fuck while wearing leather biker boots. Well, I got divorced after eighteen years of marriage three years ago, and it was devastating. I really thought my life was over, at my age to try to start all over. I owned a home, I had business in Taos, New Mexico. It all came to a grinding halt. And I left it. And I really thought it was over. And somebody said, 'Marc, have you checked out this thing called Facebook?' And I checked out this thing called Facebook, and I hooked up with some old friends in Manhattan, and we decided I was going to drive to Manhattan from Texas and visit my old friends and have dinner with them. So good old friends of mine in the music scene and fashion scene, we all got together. And one of the women that attended was Tanya, who's actually part of the song. Well, she's living with me now.

"I'd always thought about doing it in video. We never did a video for '88 Lines.' Which is weird. RCA gave us like $35,000 to do a video for 'Let It All Hang Out,' our cover of the Hombres. Because we're scared of '88 Lines.' Which is ridiculous. Because at that point '88 Lines' was being played on the radio, John Peel was all over it, the United Kingdom. But RCA, it was so fucking out of touch. And I had this scenario, basically, it was me in a lounge, like a Ramada Inn in Atlantic City. And I'm now in my fifties or sixties, I'm overweight, and I'm singing to our one hit. Which

I've been milking for thirty some odd fucking years. And I'm singing, and I'm looking like fat Elvis style. And the camera pans across the audience, and it's all these old women. They're the women in the song. They're all swooning. Can you imagine how much fun that would have been? It would have really been the kind of thing that I think people really would have adored on MTV and all that stuff. But for '88 Lines' the big hit that really never was. It became a bigger and bigger phenomenon after I'd say a year after it released.

"I never thought I would be a part of the music industry. I wasn't one of those guys who sat on the end of his bed with a guitar writing songs and having visions of being a rock star. I was doing it because I loved rock and roll, and I thought rock and roll needed some new energy. And I loved what was going on in London with the punk scene and in New York at CBGB's. I wanted to be a part of it. It had very little to do with anything commercial or financial. I wasn't expecting to be paid. So we wrote that song for an EP, remember those? A twelve-inch vinyl EP, which was going to have four songs on it. We hooked up with a little indie record label and both that label and ourselves pooled our money and we bought some time in a nice state-of-the-art recording studio in Manhattan. And we went in and recorded some pretty layered multitrack, somewhat bombastic rock songs. And '88 Lines' was not part of that project. But it was sitting there. We had recorded it in our studio. And it was sitting there gnawing at me. And I said, 'I really want to include "88 Lines" on this EP.' And the guy who had partnered up with us said, 'No, Marc. It's just too low-fi. Up against all these other songs it's going to sound rinky-dink.' And I said, 'That's why I want to include it.'

"I pretty much decided that what we had recorded in this big studio was not really all that honest. And '88 Lines' seemed to me to be a lot purer. And so after much arguing we included it on the EP. Somehow that EP got into the hands of John Peel at BBC. And he started playing '88 Lines' on his radio show. And was inundated with phone calls from all over the United Kingdom. Suddenly he contacted us to get our address. I don't know how that took place. I think at that point we maybe even had some help in management or something. He broadcast it on his show, and we were inundated with fan mail. It was really heartfelt stuff. It was people saying, 'I knew a girl like such and such, she broke my heart, and blah blah blah.' Or 'This is the best song I've ever heard.'

"And it was all handwritten by kids from all over, Great Britain and elsewhere. And any kid within earshot of John Peel's radio show, and he was so hugely influential and so cool. And suddenly the record label started coming at us, and I mean, coming at us. I think somebody said, 'Well, do you think you want to clean it up for radio play?' And we said, 'No, no. If Warner Brothers releases it, we want the dirty bits.' So we had the big showcase gig for all these record labels, the reps in Manhattan and all the labels show up. And the Nails got onstage. And I refused to do '88 Lines.' I was so drunk; I tore my clothes off and fell into the drum kit and blew it. The only ones that stuck around were RCA. Dude, it was punk fucking rock. And it pissed off my band. But at the same time, it was like what they expected of me. You just never knew. I mean, it was a fuck-you to all these guys that were up in the balcony to be able to pass judgment on us and offer us a fucking deal. They'd all come because of '88 Fucking Lines,' but I had written twelve, fifteen new songs since that. And those were the ones we played.

"I guess, RCA contacted our manager and said, 'We'd like to see them once again. Let us know when they're playing again.'" And this time we played some gig at a place called Trax. And I remember being in the dressing room drinking vodka and trying to pace myself so I wouldn't be too fucked up onstage. And I looked out the dressing room door, there was nobody there but the guys from RCA. So we just laughed. And a few minutes later I stuck my head out the door and it was packed, and it was packed with all of our fans. And the crowd went apeshit when we played it. And the next day we get an offer from RCA. At that point I'd made my point. There were other battles to fight at that point.

"I think the only time we played it live was maybe that time, and of course we had to play it because radio stations were playing it and we were touring. And we'd go to Boston. And everybody at the Paradise or whatever would expect to hear it. And I always begrudgingly played it and made a big deal about not wanting to play it. But there's a video of the Nails doing '88 Lines' at the Bottom Line in New York City. And I'd make it quite clear that I'd had a cheat sheet of the lyrics that's ten feet long, and I'm making a very, very big production of the fact that I'm reading the lyrics, and the band is struggling with trying to reduce their sound down to the '88 Lines' song. There were six great musicians onstage to back up a really bad four-track recording. Eventually, the band would leave the stage. The way that I finally dealt with it was the band left the stage, and I did the song, I was sitting on a stool to a taped backing track.

Marc Campbell / the Nails (2012) | 193

And kind of made it clear that this was unofficial. And I wasn't hiding the fact. Instead of trying to get the band to sonically dumb down and try to replicate that song live, I just said, 'Fuck it.' It's a song that revolves around a really low-tech Casio rhythm thing. So let's not pretend it's anything more than that. And it really is about the lyrics. And no question it has a hook. But again, it was so hard to pull off live that I almost changed it to a performance piece, you know, performance art piece or almost reduce it down to a poetry reading.

"It was just too almost embarrassing to do live. Because again, the band was big and '88 Lines' was an atypical song of ours. The other songs were big and fat and Doorsy and Gothy. And here was this thing that really kind of stuck out in our set. And so by setting up a stool and doing it on a backing track, it was effective. It was dramatic.

"That's the amazing story about '88 Lines.' If there's a story about '88 Lines,' it's that the song that can only be found on compilations when compilations popped up. It was the song that everybody heard, but nobody could buy. This was before downloads; this was where you had to go to a record store and buy a record. This was before CDs. The Nails catalog wasn't released by RCA on CD until 2007, believe it or not. So this, '88 Lines,' is a song that everybody heard, but nobody could buy. RCA, after the first hundred thousand records were sold of our first album on which '88 Lines' appeared, RCA did not do a second pressing. Why, I don't know. They gave us money to do a second album. But they never did '88 Lines' as a single. They didn't even do a dance mix. I think the first time '88 Lines' became available on CD was a kind of one-hit wonder new wave compilation. Do you really want to be on a compilation called *Living in Oblivion*? And it was put together by Bruce Harris, the guy who signed us to RCA. So up until then you could never buy it. So '88 Lines' is the one that we will never know what it might have sold had people been able to go in and buy the single. It would have done well.

"Recently it was in a Mazda commercial. We got the call from an ad agency in Detroit saying they were working on an ad campaign for Mazda, and they wanted to use '88 Lines About 44 Women.' And our lawyer contacted us to discuss it. He said, 'This is the deal. They want to offer you,' I think it was, '$75,000.' Which was good money at the time. And he negotiated the deal that was really a smart deal. And that was if they used it for a second commercial, they'd have to pay us double that, and if they used it for a third, they'd have to double it again. And they did use it in three commercials. But my immediate response is we're not

194 | They're Playing My Song

going to do it. Totally against this idea of rock songs being used to promote big corporations or whatever. It ain't going to happen. Of course, my band, who are married with families, 'You're going to say what?' So I finally caved and said, 'We'll do it.' But they wanted me to sing it, for the band to play it, and me just sing it with the new lyrics. And that's where I drew the line. I said, 'No way, our fans will never forgive us.' The bottom line is, I agreed to sing it; that would really be a lot of money. What really changed my whole decision from a no to yes, was that the guy who was at the ad agency did something very cool, but uncool for his agency. He was the one that had suggested '88 Lines' because he had grown up in Southern California and it was a staple on KROQ, and he loved the song. And he contacted me privately. Probably could have lost his job for this. He said, 'Marc, if you don't sell us the rights to this song, we're going to duplicate it. We'll change it slightly. But we're going to go ahead and do it anyway. You're going to get fucked.' That's what made me go, Okay. And that's what they would have done.

"It's been done time and time again. '88 Lines' has appeared in many, many forms to promote many, many things. Not long ago it was used in the *Dexter* ad campaigns for the TV shows. It was twenty-six lines about thirteen psychos. We sued them and won. It's been used in fucking soda commercials, the State of Massachusetts used it in an anti-drinking campaign, and you know what, we sued them, even though we were behind what they were doing. And they came back, they got some hotshot guy whose job is to dissect songs, some professor of music, who came back with this thirty-page rebuttal to us stating how I had actually ripped the song off from some fourteenth-century madrigal or something. He had me completely convinced I had stolen this song from a fourteenth-century madrigal.

"I just think we got lucky. That's all I can tell you. We got a deal with very little effort because of a song called '88 Lines About 44 Women.' I never had to struggle. We played gigs in Boulder, we did the CBGB's and Max's scene. It was all fun. And if you look at YouTube, if you just put in '88 Lines About 44 Women' in a search on YouTube, you'll be shocked to see how many people have made their own videos for the song. I mean, there're dozens of them. One guy made one about fishing, eighty-eight lines about forty-four fish. With their own lyrics. When the guy did the one about the fish, I actually through YouTube sent him a message. I said, 'I got to hand it to you, man. This song has covered a lot of territory. But this is the first one about fish.' A lot of the people who made these songs

Marc Campbell / the Nails (2012) | 195

are high school students and stuff. So, eighty-eight lines about forty-four anime characters, you know, Japanese animation. They're clearly really young people. Most of them are terrible, but I'm thrilled that the song has this life of its own."

Says Campbell, who passed away in 2004: "The only money the Nails have ever made off of '88 Lines' is from commercials and suing people."

Neil Peart / Rush (1986)

Downstairs, in the labyrinthine chambers of the Meadowlands in New Jersey, at two minutes to midnight, is neither the place nor the time one would expect to discuss the course of American Literature. "When you look at Herman Melville and Henry James, Nathaniel Hawthorne—the turn-of-the-century American school of writers—and how writing developed through Sinclair Lewis, Theodore Dreiser, and then up to Scott Fitzgerald and Ernest Hemingway, there was a tremendous progression, but at the same time an elimination. That progression of writing was a process of stripping things away and eliminating the inessential, making, in effect, the right word do the job of five approximations."

And neither would you expect the drummer of a world-renowned arena-resounding rock band to be conversant with the subtleties of black humor. "I love writers like Thomas Pynchon and John Barth and Tom Robbins. To me Robbins is the quintessential modern writer because he's funny, he's profound, he's sexy, he's irreverent, he's dirty, he's hip. He's everything I would like modern writing to be."

If you're talking rock lyrics, you'd have to consider Neil Peart, Rush's resident drummer/lyricist, as one of today's quintessential songwriter. Unashamedly intellectual in a world of lip-readers, Peart is the thinking man's word slinger equivalent of Yngwie Malmsteen. What the flashy Swede does with notes, sheer manual dexterity, the loping Canadian accomplishes with words, a verbal drumbeat that is as much part of Rush's sound as Alex Lifeson's guitar or Geddy Lee's bass. Speaking, in fact, in the same shifting time signatures that characterize Rush's music, Peart is in total command of his mental resources, analyzing, conceptualizing, pontificating about the lyrics that are near and dear to his heart, and near and dear to the hearts of Rush fans the world over.

"I can take someone like T. S. Eliot, who has influenced me greatly over the last few years, and realize that what he was doing was just throwing so many images at you all the time that you were left dizzy. But at the same time, you were left with something. You were stepping into another dimension. So, I use that idea. On a song like 'Red Lenses' from the *Grace Under Pressure* album, I tried to construct a series of ongoing images that just came at you. The color red was the theme of it, but I twisted it in so many ways. It was the hardest thing I ever wrote, because I was trying not to say anything, and each line was saying something but at the same time it was trying to be so obscure and so oblique about the way I went around saying it—on purpose. It seems confounding, but in the end, you're left with something. T. S. Eliot's poetry is the same way to me. At the end of it I don't really know what I've read, but it comes back to me. When I think of 'The Love Song of J. Alfred Prufrock' or 'The Waste Land,' I can't quote lines from them, and I can't say I understand everything that was said, but they move me."

With a catalog of standards that includes "Big Money," "Tom Sawyer," "Closer to the Heart," "Vital Signs," "Distant Early Warning," and "Limelight," you'd think Neil Peart would be content to relax atop the shelf of lyrics he's given his many fans to ponder. But, like the relentless perfectionist he is, Peart is driven to grander vistas of achievement. "For me, prose is where it's at," he says, a rare lapse into the vernacular. "I'd love to throw away the limitations of verse and be able to express myself in a much broader medium. To be able to write in sentences and paragraphs and whole chapters and subchapters appeals to me greatly. Someday I would love to turn out just one good short story."

[Author's note: Ten years later, in 1996, Peart turned out his first nonfiction travel book. In the next ten years, he published six more.]

While we've got him on our turf, working in the medium of the song lyric, we sat Neil down and grilled him extensively about his approach to his craft.

Were you a student of songs before you started writing them?

"No, but I was a student of words and a student of rhythm. I think as a listener of music; lyrics were strictly tertiary for me. First there was the song and then there was the musicianship, and then, after I already liked the song, there were the lyrics. There's no way I'll ever like the lyrics to a song that I don't like. It's an essential relationship. So, I never really paid a lot of attention to lyrics until after I started writing them, and then it became a craft, like drumming. If I weren't a drummer, I don't think

I'd spend a lot of time thinking about drumming or drummers. It's something I became aware of as my involvement with words became more and more active and intense. At that point I started to become more aware of the techniques. I learned about rhymes and learned what's a good rhyme and what's a false rhyme, what's a rhyme for the sake of convenience and what's a carefully constructed one. I have a very rigid set of values in those terms. I'll never rhyme just for the sake of it. I hate semi-rhymes."

With some of the words you use in your songs, it seems the lyrics must have been written before the music.

"It essentially goes both ways, but I think being a drummer has been very helpful to me. I have a good sense of the music of words and the poetry of words and what makes a nice-sounding and even a nice-looking word. For instance, 'Territories' as a title appeals to me as much to look at as it does to listen to. I find that the more layers a word or series of words offers to me, the more satisfied I am. If I can get a series of words that are rhythmically interesting and maybe have some kind of internal rhyming and rhythmic relationship, plus at least two ideas in there too, the more pleased I am. I love to sneak little bits of alliteration in—even if it would never be recognized. It is recognized. It's like, the more you put in, it's always there and even sometimes the more you take out, it's still in. I do like to get away with unusual words, but there are limits. There are some words that are not good to sing. They can sound and look good and feel right in the context of a piece of verse, but when I go over them with Geddy, he'll complain that either I've gone overboard with the alliteration or there are certain vowel-consonant combinations that, from a singer's point of view, are very difficult to deliver because you have to think so much about the elocution of those syllables that you can't possibly deliver them with the necessary emotions. There are things that Geddy suggests to me from a singer's point of view that help me a lot."

Are you thinking with the drum track in mind when you write lyrics?

"Oh, definitely. Being a drummer helps me a lot, because words are a subdivision of time. Sometimes I give my verse to Geddy and he's perplexed by how he's supposed to deliver it, and I have to express it with my toneless delivery. Things have to be phrased in less obvious ways sometimes, across a bar line, with one syllable stretched and another compacted. In a song like 'The Manhattan Project,' where it is essentially a documentary, I wanted the delivery to be like punctuation, and the chorus had to be more passionate and more rhythmically active. It was hard to express exactly how I wanted it. The first time we worked on the

Neil Peart / Rush (1986) | 199

music, they had phrased the lyrics in a very slow manner and I had to protest. The phrasing of the line was two short lines and then a long line and two short lines and then a long line. There were internal rhymes and internal relationships among the words and within the delivery that had to remain intact for it to make sense at all. It was so carefully crafted that it couldn't be delivered any old way."

When you come up with lyrics, do you have your own melody?

"Yes, but it's purely arbitrary. Sometimes it can be the most childish melody or the most unrealistic one, or sometimes the melody to another song entirely. But it's just a framework; it's a written structure in my mind that allows me to go forward and to have something on which to hang all the rhythms, and it allows me to be adventurous and not be satisfied with the rhythmic basics. Being fairly adventurous rhythmically as a drummer, I'm driven that way lyrically. I like to stretch lines and play with phrasing. The more I became appreciative of singers, I understood what phrasing could do for lyrics, how it can make them come alive. The first time I hear words sung is really when they come alive for me. When they're written on a piece of paper, it can be satisfying technically, but whether they work or not really happens when I hear Geddy sing them for the first time."

You obviously don't turn these songs out in one sitting.

"Definitely not. Sometimes the gist will come at one sitting, but the process of refinement will be very laborious. A lot of times I'll have a basic idea and a layout; usually I like to have a verse/chorus organization before I go to the other guys with it. Geddy, being the singer, has the greatest amount of input lyrically and he might suggest some little key twists that will help."

Do you have certain parts of the year when you do your writing?

"Yes, but the important thing is to keep those divisions external. They're limitations as opposed to compromises. What I find important are two other things—inspiration and craftsmanship. Those are things you cannot compromise. When an inspiration comes to you, it doesn't matter how inconvenient it is, you must take advantage of it at the time. I keep a notebook all the time and always force myself to write down any cogent thought, however sketchy it might seem, whether it's a title I like or a phrase I like or even just an image that I would like to develop or a theme I would someday want to address. By the time we reach the writing period, I'm prepared. That's the ironic part of it—you set aside a month or two months and say, okay, we're going to write songs now. But creativity doesn't work that way. But if you already have that part done,

200 | They're Playing My Song

if you've already yielded to the spontaneity and the inspiration at the proper time, then you can literally sit down at a writing desk on the first Monday morning of the writing period and start sifting through pages and pages. I keep things forever, and then, as I use them, I cross them out. As a page gets too full of things crossed out, I recopy the things that haven't been used yet. Some things sit in my notebook for ages and ages, and then sometimes a catalytic idea comes, because it's never just one idea. For me no song is ever written on just one idea. It takes probably four or five things and then I have to find the common parallel that will either unite all of those things, or at least give them some kind of linear flow. I think in anyone's experience, your thoughts will tend to follow a pattern and evolve around a nucleus of things that you're sensitive to at a particular time. All those things will collect together automatically. If you write a short story, you have the luxury of developing all those things in a very relaxed form. Lyrics are a tremendously demanding form of discipline; it requires precision."

Do you have a special room where you work?

"Yes, but it's been a different one every album. Basically, I just need a table and a chair and my rhyming dictionary. On the last four or five albums, we've worked each time in a different place, but in each there's been a room where I can go to have quiet and to be able to think. You need solitude for the amount of concentration that it takes. I try to get to writing as early as possible, before anything else becomes distracting. I'll generally spend the whole day writing. Geddy and Alex work on the music during the daytime while I work on the lyrics, and we'll all get together after dinner to work on arranging and rehearsing the songs. So, in essence, days are devoted to individual work and the evenings are devoted to collective work."

Did you all ever work together in a kind of spontaneous atmosphere?

"Not very comfortably, because for me the craftsmanship is important. I'm not happy with spontaneity musically either. I think you take such a chance. It's the same with those ideas you wake up with in the middle of the night. Sometimes you write them down and you wake up in the morning and go, 'What?' And you rip it up and throw it away. Other times you save it. We do, musically speaking, have improvisational periods during our sound check or just when we're playing together, and we record them and look for anything that happened that was magic. And there are ideas that we can mine out of there, taking advantage of the spontaneity of one day's mood. But to go onstage and expect people

Neil Peart / Rush (1986) | 201

to indulge you; that doesn't work. I prefer organization. I don't like lyrics that are just thrown together, that were obviously written as you went along, or the song was already written and the guy made up the lyrics in five minutes. I can tell—craftsmanship speaks. It's the same with reading books. I admire writers who have obviously worked and worked over what they've done, to make sure it's clearly presented and as beautifully presented as it can be. And there's nothing like time and careful work to make that happen."

Have you adjusted to your own rhythms of writing?

"For me, the important thing is to do the inspirational part of it when it happens, so I never have to go there with an empty book. At worst, if I'm stumped, I can just put the work in progress aside and I have pages and pages of other things to look at. I'll just sit there and leaf through those and hope something will connect, and generally it will. But the important thing is to be enough ahead that it's not scary, because if you get frightened, that's when writer's block will occur. I never want to be in that position. There have been things that I've tried to write that haven't worked out, but I've been able to find out early. You don't have to write two hundred pages and then discover you're working at nothing. By the time you've gone through a verse and a chorus and you've shown it to the other guys, you can see if it's working. It might be a satisfying technical exercise. I can be satisfied that I achieved what I set out to achieve even if the song wasn't used."

You do a verse and a chorus and show it to the others?

"More often than not it's complete. I'll have a series of themes or a series of verses. Sometimes they become reversed. I'm very much in love with the middle eights. It's something I really love as a musical and lyrical departure. So, a lot of times I'll have a song that'll have a verse, chorus, verse, middle eight—the classic thing. But when the other guys get ahold of it, it'll be turned around and the middle eight will become the chorus or the verse will become the chorus."

Someone will come back and say, we need four more lines?

"Or the opposite, where there'll be two lines too many. Or a song just wants to be structured a different way musically. Those things are never negative. They're always a challenge. Sometimes it can't be done, and if you have truly done a good job and distilled the lyrics down to their most essential form, there's not much you can do with it. But if the music's demands are stronger, and if the lyrics can be messed around with, that's very exciting to do."

Do you ever work to a finished melody?

"Very often the guys will have worked on something musically and made a tape of it for which they have nothing particular in mind. 'Grand Designs,' on the last album, was done that way. They had the musical ideas laid out and just made a little tape for me with guitar, keyboards, and drum machine, and I had that. So, again, if I'm stumped on something that I've been working on, I pull out that tape and try to close my mind off for a minute and listen to the tape. 'Chemistry' was a true collaboration between the three of us. The other guys had a couple of key phrases they wanted to express, so they gave me the music. That was easy because all the groundwork was done. Playing with words comes so much easier than having to dream up the whole thing."

Does the concept of each album start with you?

"Usually there isn't a concept. This album was the first time that I decided from the beginning that I wanted to address as many vignettes of power as I could. In the past there have been themes in each of the albums, but they have been more after the fact. For instance, on *Grace Under Pressure*, the theme of that title seems very obvious in each of the songs, but in fact it came after, and the songs were each being written about different reactions. The theme of that album, to me, is pathos, and it came through sometimes thirdhand experiences, but most often secondhand, observing my friends. That was a period of time when a lot of people were out of work and having difficulties in terms of self-esteem. They had reached a point in their lives where they felt they should be established and they weren't. People were having life crises not only in employment, but also in terms of their romances. All of those things came to a head in my perception and I was writing with a great deal of empathy. It wasn't always understood by either listeners or critics, but that was the stem of it all. So, after the fact I realized that the theme of the album illustrated the 'grace under pressure' concept. That album was made under a great deal of difficult circumstances for us personally, too."

Doesn't it seem to you that sometimes a group is categorized for its music, but its message isn't considered as important as that of an individual singer-songwriter?

"That's okay; as a member of the audience it was that way to me, too. If people don't take all the trouble interpreting lyrics that I took in creating them, that doesn't bother me, because I'm a musician first and not just a lyricist. I only spend two months out of every two years doing that and the rest of the time I'm a drummer."

Neil Peart / Rush (1986) | 203

Do you feel that Rush is the best vehicle for your self-expression—or do you have a goal to express yourself elsewhere too?

"That's complicated, because being a drummer first, the kind of liberty I have in Rush is important to me. Stylistically I never feel limited as a drummer and that will carry over lyrically, too. There's no way I'll ever write anything good that won't be suitable for Rush. On the other hand, I have written things with which I was happy but which didn't fit into the scheme of things at a given time. But I have no trouble putting those away. Those things always lead me on to something else. We have musical ideas all the time that never get fully developed, but at the same time they lead us to another area. Or even things that do get developed and recorded, from an artistic point of view, a lot of times we're not satisfied. At this point we've gone through several periods of different stylistic approaches, different areas of influence, and at this moment they might seem indulgent to us or naïve, but without that experimentation we couldn't have arrived now at the ability to write a five- or six-minute song and put everything into it that we do. We can write a song that will have complicated time signatures but it won't be five minutes of that. It'll be two minutes of that. But the point is that we can change types of signatures three or four times in a song very comfortably.

"I went through periods the same way lyrically of being over-ornamental and spending a lot of time developing an atmosphere lyrically. I don't do that anymore. I want five words to do what I used to use five lines to do. I'm fairly satisfied with my body of lyric writing over the last four or five years, but prior to that it was strictly kindergarten, strictly groundwork and experimentation. Musically too, I don't have much use for our stuff prior to 1980. That's not negative. That's the way it should be, because we were honestly experimental. We pushed ourselves over our heads lots of times and we were grappling for some kind of grip on the technique that we were aiming for."

Do you feel you have to distill your material to get it played on commercial radio?

"No, I don't. The hardest thing is to have something that's both personal and universal. To me, that's the aim. I try to find something that moves me—a lot of times it's anger, but sometimes it can be pathos or it can be joy. I can be thrilled by the world at large or by nature or some small experience. Adolescence is a common theme for me. The crossover between innocence and disillusionment is something I have addressed a lot, because it's something I can personally relate to and illustrate, but at the same time it's universal. I don't want to just be confessional, like a Joni Mitchell. That's an area I've tried to avoid; at the same time, that's what gives you personal involvement, and without that impetus, sometimes it's hard to get going. Fortunately, I'm very prone to anger, very prone to outrage in the way people act and the way they treat each other and the world we live in. So, all these things act as an impetus to me, but I couldn't write only about my own areas of outrage. I like to find those and translate them into something that is universal."

Do you feel that your best lyrics have become your best songs?

"No, not always. It's weird how it goes. There's so much chemistry involved and there's so many intangible things that happen. There are ones where the music has been better than the lyrics or the lyrics better than the music. 'Middletown Dreams' is a good marriage of lyrics and music. 'Mystic Rhythms' is another one."

You said there's a magic moment when you hear a song for the first time. Is there another magic moment when you conceive of a song for the first time—or finish it for the first time?

"That's a good point. I think the joy of creation is very overrated. The irony is that the moment goes by so fast. When I'm working on a piece of lyrics and I have the theme of it going and I'm working away, there is that moment when I realize, yes, this is going to work. But then I'm gone. I'm gone into making it work. And then the knots in the brain start to become untied. I'm figuring out, okay, this line goes to that line, this verse to that verse. You can't sit back and go, oh, I'm great. The moment is great, but you can't just sit back and feel fulfilled by it. To me the most satisfying time of making an album is the writing period. We listen to a demo, and yes, this is exciting, and it's what we wanted it to be and it gets you off. That is the ultimate return that you will get from the song. And then you'll spend another six months recording the basic tracks, doing the overdubs, doing the vocals, doing the mixing. At the end of it all there's no joy of creation; there's no sitting back and going, 'This is finished and wow, I'm so happy,' because you're so tired and drained from all of the mental demands. You don't have anything left to throw a party. In the demo period the rewards are instantaneous."

Is there another level where you see a song you've worked on and believed in going over with the audience?

"You picked out a very important thing, because at the end of an album it's impossible for us to judge which songs will truly be popular and which won't. We're inevitably surprised. And then there are songs like

Neil Peart / Rush (1986) | 205

'Vital Signs,' from our *Moving Pictures* album. At the time, it was mixed it was a very transitional song. Everybody had mixed feelings about it, but at the same time it expressed something essential that I wanted to say. That's a song that has a marriage of vocals and lyrics that I'm very happy with. But it took our audience a long time to get it, because it was rhythmically very different for us and it demanded the audience to respond in a different rhythmic way. There was no heavy downbeat; it was all counterpoint between upbeat and downbeat, and there was some reflection of reggae influence and a reflection of the more refined areas of new wave music that we had sort of taken under our umbrella and made happen. That song took about three tours to catch on. It was kind of a baby for us. We kept playing it and wouldn't give up. We put it in our encore last tour—putting it in the most exciting part of the set possible—and just demanded that people accept it because we believed in it. I still think that song represents a culmination, the best combination of music, lyrics, rhythm. It opens up so many musical approaches, from being very simplistic and minimal to becoming very overplayed. Everything we wanted in the song is there. That song was very special to us. But we had to wait. We had to be patient and wait for the audience to understand us."

෴

Starting in 1980 through 2013, Rush charted eleven top ten studio albums, one live album, and six video albums. Neil Peart passed away in 2020.

Mike Watt / Minutemen (2012)

"History Lesson, Pt. 2"

I always refer to 1984's "History Lesson, Pt. 2" from Minutemen's classic double album *Double Nickels on the Dime* as the song with the saddest riff in the world. One day after playing back a mixtape I made I noticed how perfectly it segued into the Byrds' version of Bob Dylan's "My Back Pages." The song's writer, bass player Mike Watt, even name checks Dylan, saying, "This is Bob Dylan to me. My story could be his songs." He also name checks punk icons, Richard Hell, John Doe, and Joe Strummer, while paying homage to his pal, guitarist D. Boon. The opening line "Our band could be your life" was later used by writer Michael Azerrad for his 2001 book on the Indie rock scene of 1980–1990. He called Watt to ask for permission to use it. "I thought it was good that Michael was writing a book about that period, so I said, sure," Watt said. "I mean, up to that time they went from Sex Pistols to Nirvana and they didn't talk about anything in between and here's Black Flag, who built that whole circuit we still tour on."

The song was part of the soundtrack for the 2004 movie *Levelland*, one of the closing songs in the documentary *We Jam Econo: The Story of the Minutemen*, a lynchpin moment in the 2011 documentary *A History Lesson Part I: Punk Rock in Los Angeles in 1984*. Lately the Hold Steady performed it live in LA, changing the lyrics slightly to reflect their own band, their own life, their own story.

One of a handful of tunes to top the two-minute mark in an album that is universally regarded as one of Indie rock's crowning achievements, Watt said most people still misunderstand the song.

"The meaning is like, I'm going to tell the story of this band and show you guys that we're not elitist over you, but I never really heard the meaning of the song described to me like I wrote it. It means something different to other people. What I always get from fans is that it's a true friendship song. That's what people tell me. And it did come out of my friendship with D. Boon. And I was even using that for an example. But in a way, it was also like an ode to the scene. Nowadays, when people talk about the old days, I don't say scene. I say movement. Because I really believed it was. I don't believe the Minutemen would have even existed without that movement.

"On *Punch Line* (the band's 1981 debut album) there's a song called 'History Lesson.' It's a nightmare song. It's about human slaughtering over power and money. I was thinking, well, maybe there's another kind of history, too, about this crazy scene. You've got to understand, punk in the US in those days was this tiny scene. But we were so involved in it, it seemed important. So this was a history lesson. I guess when you write a song, you don't want it to be too generic. You want to put feeling and something human in it. As a lyric, it just came right out. Usually I start with the title and when I got the title, I got the focus. The music track was a little different for me, because I wrote it on the guitar not on bass. Even in those days I didn't do it that much. We had just played in Europe with Black Flag for our first tour over there and we were listening to a lot of Velvet Underground. There was a song of theirs called 'Here She Comes Now' that influenced the music part. The words don't have anything to do with the Velvet Underground, though. The words came out of reading the fanzine *Flipside* in the early eighties, where people would write in letters. From reading some of those letters I got kind of a feeling that Minutemen were in a strange place.

"We learned punk in Hollywood during the seventies. Minutemen started in January of '80. So when we started really playing gigs as Minutemen by that time a lot of those seventies punk people were into glitter and glam and artist types. And a lot of them stopped going to gigs. You didn't really have a lot of teenagers in seventies punk. And then it moved to the suburbs and that's where hardcore came from. So the Minutemen are strange because we have a foot in each world. So anyway, this stirred up the people writing letters to *Flipside* saying we were 'posers,' right? You know, these guys are posers; us and a band called TSOL. They were from the hardcore scene. You can understand the perceptions of young people. When you're young, there's a lot of peer pressure in who I'm

Figure 29. Mike Watt, 2016. Photo: Phil King, Wikimedia Commons, CC BY 2.0.

supposed to like. Anytime someone gets a little too popular, they're always considered posers.

"So, in 'History Lesson, Pt. 2' I was commenting on this thing where even though Minutemen was kind of from a different world from these young hardcore people, we weren't old men yet. I think I was twenty-five years old when I wrote that song, but you know when you're younger, five or eight years is a big jump. A high school guy and a guy in his midtwenties, big difference. When you get down the road, there's no difference at all hardly. But in those days and in that time period, it was big. So I was trying to say, the way I looked at the aesthetics of this punk scene, there's not a lot of difference between us, except some stylistic things, which is natural, because we've all got different kinds of expression. But that's okay. I was trying to use the example of how I got into music, which was to be with my friend. I wasn't even a musician. I just wanted to be with my friend. One way was by playing music. I had D. Boon sing the words, so he changed them around to 'me and Mike Watt,' cause otherwise it would have sounded stupid.

"Seventies punk was a reaction against people who went to arena rock shows. They'd never even been to clubs, except maybe some of this glitter and glam stuff. The Ramones started it all off. And that became the paradigm for hardcore. But I would say for us it was a little more hard rock. The Ramones didn't play so much with the Eddie Van Halen kind of guitar. Some of those guys played like that in the hardcore bands, or were moving towards that. Actually, the Ramones provoked a whole bunch of crazy shit, too, like Devo and No Mercy, a San Francisco band that was just a singer and a drummer. And Zev. He was one guy who just beefed-up pieces of metal hanging on ropes. Anything you could get away with, right? The Ramones had a huge influence on us. They got us to play faster and faster. They did these slam dancing shows. They liked that. Fast, fast. You listen to the other seventies punk, it ain't really that fast like the younger people got it to go. And arena rock bass was like the bottom of the totem pole. It's like right field, where you put your worst player in Little League, where nobody hits the ball. So I had an insecurity thing about that. And then I found out about Richard Hell and the Voidoids, and this guy not only was a trippy bass player, but he wrote the songs for his band. And so I put a picture of him on my bass in 1977 when I got that record, and it was like I didn't want to copy him exactly, but he was an inspiration to me. And so, I was saying in the song that's the way many moments are in the healthiest manifestation. You're inspired, you bounce off, you don't just become clones or an army or a mindless herd or something. You're all connected in a way, but it's to inspire each other.

"What really blew our mind about the punk scene was these people, who you could tell were just learning and stuff, but they sang words, like if you talked to them, you could tell it was very personalized. Even the bands we didn't see, when we heard their English records with their accents and their slang, it wasn't just trying to use the cool rock and roll words. They were using music for personal expression. We were very influenced by that. There was one English band called the Pop Group, that put Captain Beefheart with Parliament. And we were thinking, you know what, bands like the Stooges and Beefheart were already playing punk and nobody had given it a name yet. Beefheart was definitely an influence. We got to see them play live. The *Doc at the Radar Station* tour. He was a tripper. His music has still got a big blues influence. It's rooted in something. With slide guitar and a kind of Howlin' Wolf voice. It's a trippy mixture. There was another English band called Wire that had an album called *Pink Flag*, which had little songs. That gave us the idea of little songs. I mean, really little. And in the form, too, where you didn't have to have chorus/verse/chorus. They were really instrumental

210 | They're Playing My Song

in opening or knocking that door down for us. I'd never really written about the scene that much. Usually, our thing was more like thinking out loud. That's what we called our technique. What's ever on your mind, you're going to just start talking about. But in 'History Lesson, Pt. 2' I was actually talking to those younger guys, the younger punk guys in a way, saying we don't look down on you.

"The album *Double Nickels* was inspired by the Hüskers, you know. We had an album done and ready to go. They didn't have a title for it yet, but the Hüskers came to town and recorded *Zen Arcade*. And we go, 'Wow, they made a double album, we should do that, too.' So we wrote a whole bunch of songs and recorded another album and put them together. We couldn't really have a concept as much, except this idea that Sammy Hagar couldn't drive fifty-five miles an hour. You know, that stupid thing. 'We'll drive the speed limit and we'll try to play crazy music.' The album still sells. The documentary, *We Jam Econo*, came out in 2005 and that revived a whole bunch of interest in us. The guys who made it were too young to even see us. So this documentary's kind of the story of them finding out about us by talking to people who were there. I agreed to it because they were genuine in their feelings. But also, I thought it was a way of paying back the scene, because I wasn't trying to say Minutemen was the best band of those days, but I thought if younger people saw bozos like us making a band, then anybody could try to make one. Because that's what the scene did for us, it empowered us. You could see that these guys did it and are trying it. Why don't we try it? To me that's the story of the Minutemen and of a lot of the bands from that scene. Buddies getting together, no matter what the style. You understand, we didn't really believe punk was a style of music. That was more up to the band. But the scene was more like a kind of state of mind, a style of living, a set of ethics. I don't know. It was about people who couldn't fit in with the other people.

"Ultimately, I guess, the song is a eulogy for D. Boon. He got killed in that car wreck a year later. I couldn't even listen to Minutemen for a long time after that. I didn't listen to Minutemen until I was asked to help make that documentary, because it would make me sad whenever I'd hear it. But during the filming, they wanted me to drive them around town and do history stuff and go through the album. I was like, whoa I kind of like these little things. Man, I want to try this again. So I kind of used Minutemen format for my 2010 rock opera *Hyphenated Man*. The last part is called 'Wheel Bound Man' and it's in the 'History Lesson, Pt. 2' vein. Maybe not a lot, but in some ways. I've done three rock operas now. Stuff I never, ever thought I would be doing, but it just seemed like I couldn't say what I wanted to say about those things in two minutes or less. Actually, the first one, *Contemplating the Engine Room*, is about the Minutemen.

"But *Double Nickels* is probably the best record I've ever played on. I didn't realize it while we were making it. Maybe it took until a year later when we tried to make *Three Way Tie*. Then it was like, whoa. The way we were thinking was hills and valleys. People that are around for a while, the journey's full of valleys. But we realized when we were making *Three Way Tie* what an intense record *Double Nickels* was. That was definitely a hill, we thought. That was a peak of ours. And now looking back even more so. But what can you do about that? You get put on the path. The worst thing to do is stop trying. So I just keep trying. I'm about to leave on a tour next week; I think it's my sixty-sixth tour. I've been doing this for thirty-two years, so I keep trying. Even though it ain't the same. It can't be the same because D. Boon ain't there."

Rivaling his contemporary, Dave Grohl, bassist Watt has appeared in over two dozen different bands and contributed to many more album projects. A gentleman and a scholar, a photographer and a diarist, he claims as one of his influences, James Joyce. He participated in an international project setting Joyce's Finnegans Wake *to music (Waywords and Meansigns, 2017).*

Billy Steinberg (2012)

"Like a Virgin"

The songwriting team of Billy Steinberg and Tom Kelly had to endure a long period of waiting before "Like a Virgin" got the green light as a single in 1984. In the meantime, the career of the fairly unknown Madonna started blossoming with hits like "Borderline," "Lucky Star," and "Holiday." The career of Steinberg and Kelly took off as well. Steinberg had been to the top ten once before, in 1980, when Linda Ronstadt released his "How Do I Make You." But the Madonna experience was very different.

"That was very intense," he said of the hit with Ronstadt. "It was a huge thrill and a huge redemption for me. It showed me that I wasn't deluding myself. When you've never had a song cut before and you submit things and you get no response, you start to worry, well, maybe I think I'm a good songwriter but maybe I'm not. So it showed me that I wasn't just a songwriter in my own head. That I had the capacity to be a world-class songwriter. But 'Like a Virgin' was a hundred times more intense. For one thing, 'Like a Virgin' exploded all over the world. It was number one for six weeks. Someone could live off the income that song generated, not in high style, and maybe not in LA. But if you lived very modestly and watched your expenses, you could live. There's no question a lot of performers can tour for forty years off of one giant hit like that. For me it was this enormous culmination of relief and excitement and it really lit a fire under Tom and me to do more and better work. We went on to have five number one songs in five years.

"I met Tom in August of '81 at a party given by producer Keith Olsen, who had recorded two of my songs with Pat Benatar. I had never done much cowriting, but I suggested to Tom that we try cowriting together.

Tom did a little checking on me, and when he found out I'd written 'How Do I Make You,' he decided that it would be worth his while, because he'd liked that song.

"Right away we realized we had a certain ability to write together. But we didn't write any hits for a couple of years. One thing that was a bit of a distraction was that we got signed as artists to Epic Records. We called ourselves I-Ten. But that record didn't meet with any success.

"We continued to write maybe two weekends a month. Tom was making a living doing background vocal sessions, while I was working in my father's vineyards. As often as possible I would come up to LA or he would come down to the Coachella Valley, where I lived. When we wrote we just tried to write songs we liked. We weren't thinking of what was currently in vogue. We weren't thinking about who was in the studio. We were just writing songs for the love of it. And because we took that approach, I think that's why the best songs we wrote are enduring. Because we wrote as if we were writing them for ourselves as artists.

"In 1983 after I-Ten was gone, we wrote a new batch of pop songs and one of them was 'Like a Virgin.' I probably wrote the lyrics to it sitting in a pickup truck on the vineyard in the Coachella Valley. I got together with Tom and I showed him the lyrics. Tom and I had become very close friends, and he knew in my personal life I had been trying to extricate myself from a very difficult relationship. I succeeded in doing so and met somebody new and I wrote the lyrics: 'I made it through the wilderness / somehow I made it through / didn't know how lost I was / till I found you / I was beat /incomplete / I'd been had / I was sad and blue / but you made me feel shiny and new / like a virgin.'

When I put that lyric in front of Tom, who was sitting at his keyboard, he tried to write a ballad to it. But when he got to the chorus it just sounded ridiculous singing 'like a virgin' in a sensitive ballad sort of way. So we put that lyric aside and started to write something else, but eventually I kept pushing that lyric because I felt it was something special. One day, out of frustration, Tom started playing the bass line for 'Like a Virgin' using his left hand and singing in a Motown-style falsetto. He was known for having this Foreigner type of high rock voice, and the first things we'd written together had all utilized that instrument. So when he started singing falsetto a la Smokey Robinson, I went 'That's it. That's it.' He was just clowning around, but I said, that's perfect. So we finished the song together and then made a really good demo. Tom sang it falsetto and it really put the song across. I started submitting it to a&r people and our

Figure 28. Billy Steinberg, 2006. Photo by Art Streiber, provided courtesy of Billy Steinberg.

first responses to it were, 'Are you kidding me? No one's going to sing a song called "Like a Virgin."' Somebody said, the song is catchy, but why don't you change the title? But we stayed with what we had.

"Eventually Tom and I had a meeting with Michael Ostin, Mo Ostin's son, who was an a&r man at Warner Brothers Records. Our main reason for meeting with Michael was because Tom and I were still clinging to the idea of making another record. We played him a couple of songs that demonstrated what we would like to do as artists. Then he asked if we had anything that might work for Madonna. They were looking for songs for her follow-up record. She'd already made the record that included 'Holiday' and 'Borderline.' So Tom and I said yeah, 'Like a Virgin,' and as soon as we said it a lightbulb went off in both of our minds. Madonna. 'Like a Virgin.' It was as if the song were handwritten for her, like you couldn't come up with something more perfect for her than that. Even on that very first meeting, before she ever heard the song, I threw out the idea to Michael that you could have her wearing a wedding dress in the video and be on top of a wedding cake. It seemed so perfect.

"He got back to us a couple of days later. She loved the song and she was going to cut it. Needless to say, we were thrilled about it, even though she wasn't by any means a superstar yet. She cut it with Nile Rodgers producing in New York. Nile Rodgers has said in interviews when he first heard the song, he didn't like it. I think it was Michael Ostin and Madonna who insisted she was going to cut the song. Tom and I weren't involved in any way with the recording process. We didn't hear it until it was done. But I can tell you one thing, she was faithful to the demo. The recording Madonna made of 'Like a Virgin' copies every little nuance of our demo. Even as our demo fades out and Tom is singing these little ad-libs, right to the fade where you can't hear anything, she copied every little ad-lib.

"She recorded the song and it was set to be the first single off her next album, but her first album kept yielding these hits: 'Borderline,' 'Holiday,' 'Lucky Star'—so they kept pushing back the release of 'Like a Virgin.' But then, when she was asked to sing at the MTV video awards, she chose to sing 'Like a Virgin' even though the song hadn't been released yet. She went on TV and sang this song with this provocative title that no one had ever heard before and she rolled around the stage. Tom and I were watching it on television and we thought, oh, we're doomed now. This is an embarrassment. This is never going to succeed.

"But they released the single and one day a short time later I was driving in my car, and I turned on KISS radio and they played it, and then when it ended they played it again. It was the most requested song for weeks on the station. They would often play it twice in a row. I've never heard that happen before.

"After 'Like a Virgin' Tom and I felt that Madonna would be receptive to wanting another one of our songs. Or want to cowrite a song with us. We wrote what we felt was a great follow-up and showed it to Michael Ostin, but she didn't elect to do it. We would call Michael frequently to ask if she'd want to cowrite but she never did. I've always thought she was perhaps a bit resentful that her signature song was written by somebody else and she had no part of it. If I'm not mistaken, her people tried to get her on the song as a cowriter or to get a piece of the publishing, and we just said it's out of the question. We boldly stood our ground and we didn't give it, because we felt there's no way they're going to drop it from the album, it's too good of a song.

"People always think because I'm in the music business I can get free tickets to any concert, but there's no truth to that. Even when 'Like a Virgin' was number one and Madonna was on the Like a Virgin tour, when Tom and I tried to get tickets to her show when she came to LA, it was very difficult. We would call her manager's office and they'd say we'll get back to you, we'll get back to you. We figured it was modest enough request to see the Like a Virgin tour. Finally, the day before the concert they called and said we have two tickets for you. Not four, not eight, two. No backstage passes, either. They weren't even good tickets; they were in the nosebleed section. During the concert, Madonna sings 'Like a Virgin' and the roof blows off the amphitheater. Everyone in the audience is singing our song and, ironically, we're sitting back there where we could hardly see. Then the concert ends and we see all these paparazzi groupie-type people flocking backstage with their backstage passes and we don't even have any.

"I met Madonna once, very briefly. It was probably five years later. Madonna's manager was turning fifty and Tom and I were invited to his birthday party. He and his wife lived in a mansion in Bel Air. So Tom and I were standing on a terrace outside the house chatting with a guy named Steve Bray. Steve had dated Madonna and had also written a couple of songs with her, including 'Into the Groove.' So when she started walking toward us I thought, this is perfect because Steve Bray will make the introduction and we'll finally get acquainted with her. She was dating Warren Beatty at that time. So she's walking across this terrace with Warren Beatty and they walk up to us, and Steve Bray says, Madonna, I want you to meet Billy Steinberg and Tom Kelly. They wrote 'Like a Virgin.' And the first thing I remember is that Warren Beatty started to chuckle because I guess he thought that it was a pretend introduction, because she must know the guys who wrote that song.

"Anyway, I sort of gushingly said, 'Oh Madonna, I've wanted to meet you for so long.' And she said, 'Well, now you did.' And she grabbed Warren Beatty and walked away. And that was the end of it. Tom Kelly started laughing, 'cause he saw that I was kind of crestfallen and I'd set myself up for it. Part of the dynamic of our relationship was him laughing at some of my personality traits, but always in good fun.

"So that was our great meeting with Madonna and I've never seen her since."

Billy Steinberg and Tom Kelly were inducted into the Songwriters Hall of Fame in 2011. Although Kelly retired in the 1990s, Steinberg continues to collaborate with other composers and artists, among them Susanna Hoffs, formerly of the Bangles (see "Eternal Flame" below).

Narada Michael Walden (2012)

"Freeway of Love"

"The song was written for my own album about two years before that. I kind of got started on it but never recorded it. It wasn't until I started working on Aretha's record that my friend Preston Glass said, 'What about that song "Freeway of Love" for Aretha? So I dug it out of the vaults, looked at it, changed the lyrics around so it would be a little bit more for her, and I cut it at the same time I cut 'How Will I Know' for Whitney Houston at Tarpan Studios in San Francisco.

"The first thing Aretha and I did for the album was 'Who's Zooming Who,' 'cause that came from a conversation I had with her. I tape recorded her phone call and I'm so glad I did because she talks so eloquent, beautiful, street, hip, and wise that I couldn't remember it all at the same time. So I asked her, what do you do at night to have fun? She said, 'Oh, I go out to nightclubs. Maybe I see someone in the corner who looks kind of cool. He looks at me, I look at him, and it's like who's zooming who. But as soon as he thinks he's got me, the fish jumps off the hook.' Then she started laughing.

"After I hung up the phone, I said that's kind of a cool concept for a song. So we started writing that. But after it was done, she didn't really like the song. Clive Davis had to convince her to do it. I did that song first and then 'Until You Say You Love Me.' Her father had just passed away after being in a coma for a long time, so she was really delicate after not being in the studio for two years. I had to be gentle with her and massage her shoulders and be really, really soft. So she did the first two songs, which were stellar, then I came back with 'Freeway of Love.' By that time we were working well together and it was all good and she sang the hell out of it. In fact, she had the whole thing memorized, even down to all the ad-libs on the ending. Everything about the song was memorized. So I went, 'Damn, now I know why they call you the Queen of Soul.' When she comes in she's really well prepared.

"The song peaked at number three (number one R&B), but anything up in that range of the charts where they hear your song every hour on the hour is the same thing. It's great to say you're number one, but there's no difference between number five and number one, when you're hearing it every hour on the hour. After that, people who I'd never thought about would call. Great singers I'd always wanted to work with started reaching out. It's funny how things work when you hit the top ten—managers start reaching out. That's what happened. The phone started ringing with all kinds of people from all around the world.

"What I learned from that experience is to never turn anybody down before I meet them. I may think I can't work so well with a certain artist, but then I meet the artist and I love them. I almost turned down working with Whitney Houston because I was busy cutting 'Freeway of Love.' I got a call from Arista and I said, first of all, I'm right in the middle of making this album for Aretha. I can't take my attention off that. But they said, you've got to make time for this girl because she's going to be incredible. So they sent me the demo on 'How Will I Know.' I said, the song's only half done, will it be okay if I mess with it? Eventually, the writers said it would be okay. So I rewrote it and cut it on the same session as 'Freeway of Love.' It didn't come out until December, but it was a monster hit. And it was all because when I met her, she was just mind-blowing. All that range and power and beauty and sex appeal coming at you with a kind of confidence you've never known before. I said, oh my Lord, you are really too much. She said, yeah, I know.

"After that a bunch of things came down the pike. I had so much in the next couple of years it was crazy. God blessed me. I always wanted to have my hits on the jukebox and the radio. Even when I was playing drums in the Mahavishnu Orchestra, we'd always eat at this little café in Queens and I'd throw my nickels and dimes and quarters into the little jukebox there, and I'd imagine my songs coming out of that thing. I really prayed for it. There's nothing better than having your songs on the radio nonstop. Everywhere you go you're hearing that vibration. Music is a vibration of love, if you put love into it, it comes right back at you.

"So I did 'You're a Friend of Mine,' with Clarence Clemons (who played saxophone on 'Freeway of Love'). Then 'We Don't Have to Take

Our Clothes Off' with Jermaine Stewart was a top five hit. After that was the Starship, with 'Nothing's Gonna Stop Us Now,' which was the first number one hit for Diane Warren. I always dug that sixties thing with Grace Slick. She's a very outspoken woman. We're all from the Bay Area, so it's like family. I actually played the drums when I laid the track out. I got Grace to come in, flipped it around so instead of the low part, she wound up singing the highest part. I gave her the highest part and she just killed it. That's when I realized it could be a smash. And when I got happy in the studio, she got happy.

"Having a hit never surprises me. I don't mean to sound overconfident, but I feel like everything I work on is a number one. I put that kind of energy into it. I get chills and I get the feeling and I get the vibe, and then it's just a matter of whether the timing is right. From my side I'm always shooting for number one. If it doesn't happen, then it's just not the right divine timing.

"Each artist I work with is different, but they all need so much love in the studio. They give so much; you have to give them a lot of love in return. The more love you give them, the more love they pour into that microphone, like honey, like syrup on a pancake, like hot buttered soul. You rub their feet. You rub their neck. You give them teddy bears or flowers; you ask them how's your love life? You have to make a connection. Then when you're on the other side of the glass, you say, honey, maybe we have to bring the pitch up more, put more soul into it, put more heart into it. And they do. All of a sudden these diamonds start coming out, chunks of gold come flying out. Guys need that love too, but it's not the same.

"When I got with Mariah Carey, bless her heart, she was so shy and so timid it took her a while to really adjust to hearing her voice. She was brilliant. She would sing the most staggering, knockout, stellar runs you'd ever imagine. But she'd say, to her it sounds rancid. I'd say, honey, it's absolutely magical. No, no, no, it's rancid. You had to find a way to let her calm down and live with it, so she'd come to her senses. Oh yeah, this is good. Maybe she'd want the tape flown to New York so she could do one punch in on one thing that really bugged her. Now you really wouldn't hear a difference, but it would make her feel better, that she gave it her best shot, which I understand.

"On the other hand, Aretha and Whitney love almost everything they do. When they put their heart into it they love it. You have to convince them, maybe it could be a little bit better. They go, why? Aretha would say, I know, you want what's called a straight reading. I'll sing it a little

Narada Michael Walden (2012) | 221

more to the melody, which would need another take. Because you want another take just to make sure. Then she'll give you a straight reading and it's a little bit more like the melody, not too much, but at least you have another take to draw from when you're putting it together, so you appreciate it. But she was really satisfied with the first take, and frankly, when you get it back to listen to it, you go, damn, this is good. Same with Whitney. She did 'How Will I Know' in one take. Maybe I'd fix one thing here and one thing there, but the majority of it is one take.

"Sometimes you've got to be like Angelo Dundee, the great trainer for Muhammed Ali. If you want Muhammed to jab more you could say, hey champ, jab more. He'd go, who are you talking to? You've got to be like, hey champ, your jab was great today. Then he goes, it does look good, don't it? So then he's jabbing more, which is want you wanted. You've got to be roundabout sometimes, but that's okay. The ego and the spirit and the soul, all those things have to come together, so you have to make it where you can relax that person enough to be vulnerable. Because you want to make a record that'll last a hundred years.

"Things finally started slowing down for me when you could download music for free. Companies weren't spending money on budgets anymore. Everybody was losing their jobs. Hip-hop came on strong, but not when it first came out. Early on it was that Teddy Riley–type of new jack swing. When rap took over, my phone stopped ringing as much, because ballads went out of style. So I slowed down my train. I went out with Jeff Beck a couple of years ago, playing drums, reconnecting with my beginnings playing live. I realized all over the world people want live music. They may not be buying CDs as much but they're sure showing up in clubs. And when you're clobbering with that funk and that sweat and passion, you're blowing people's minds. So that's what inspired me to go back in the studio and make more music.

"Anyone who calls me now I'm open. Anyone who wants something beautiful I'm open for. I wrote my first symphony two years ago and performed it with Carlos Santana. I'm doing a big charity album with a lot of superstars, a We Are the World type of project to raise money for people in Africa, who always need it. Another project will be for America, because we need it in America too. I have my own new band now and two new albums called *Thunder* and *Rising Sun*, which is a remix of my early fusion music. We're doing live shows with that music. I've gone full circle. Go back to where you start from and reinspire yourself. I feel as inspired now as I did when I was thirty years younger.

Since 1985, Narada Michael Walden has produced tracks for numerous pop artists and groups, including Patti LaBelle, Al Jarreau, Elton John and Kiki Dee, Diana Ross, the Temptations, Ray Charles, Santana, and Journey. Songs of his have appeared in the films 9½ Weeks, Innerspace, Mannequin, Bright Lights, Big City, License to Kill, The Bodyguard, Free Willy, Crooklyn, *and* Jason's Lyric.

Julie Gold (2013)

"From a Distance"

God was definitely watching Julie Gold that Saturday morning in the winter of 1985 when she sat down at her childhood piano and wrote "From a Distance." Delivered the day before from her parents' home in Philadelphia, to her pad in Greenwich Village, the piano had to thaw out overnight before she could play it. But as soon as it did, Julie was there to receive its welcoming message of hope and love and peace.

"I had come to New York with an electric piano," she said. "That was a hideous relationship, but it was all I had. And then for my thirtieth birthday, my parents thought it would be a beautiful thing for me to be reunited with the piano of my childhood. So they sent it to me in December 1985 as my birthday present. I wasn't allowed to play it for a day because it was frozen like a block of ice. I slept in this loft bed that was over it and all night I looked over the edge and there it was. And then I came down that steep ladder in the morning and the first thing I wrote was 'From a Distance.'"

Julie likes to say the song took her three hours and thirty years to write, summing up in a song almost every relationship to music and the culture she ever had, especially to John Lennon's repetition of the line "Nothing's gonna change my world" in "Across the Universe." But she'd already come up with "God is watching us," repeated three times, along with the title, while doodling at her day job as a secretary at HBO. "I had some preliminary lyrics," she said. "My songwriting ritual is always scales and arpeggios and chords, but that specific day I remember just feeling so connected to my instrument. And when these majestic chords came out of me, I knew they were going to be something I could use. Usually, if I get one good keystone, then I can build the house."

When she finished the song, she performed another ritual on the piano; she kissed the keys. "Why? Because I know what it feels like to write a song and I wonder if I'll ever be given that opportunity again. So I'm grateful every time. I certainly didn't think, 'Oh, my God, this is the song that's going to change my life.' I just knew it was a beautiful experience, a cathartic experience. Then, like I did with all my songs, I immediately went into the studio and made a demo and started pitching it. And it was rejected by everyone I knew.

"The first person I sent 'From a Distance' to was a guy who in my notes it says, 'Music man I met by accident in a shoe store.' That was early in 1986. It's the fifth song on a tape that I sent to somebody at BMI. Let's see, I sent it to Kate Wolf and I got back that she had died. How do you like that? I sent it to a guy who worked with Ronnie Milsap who rejected it for Milsap Music. Then there was this guy who used to work with Tom Rush. Most of these things had no response at all. The first person who

Figure 30. Julie Gold, 2015. Photo: Bruce Johnson, Wikimedia Commons, CC BY-SA 4.0.

loved it was Christine Lavin. Christine and I had met when I still lived in Philly and was coming up to New York to do songwriting workshops. She'd give me her songs; I'd give her my songs. We had management, we lost management; we knew each other's careers very well. She was playing at this little club on MacDougal Street called the Speakeasy, and she told me, 'Bring me ten cassettes and let me see what I can do with it.' Within three weeks after that, Vince Scelsa played it on K-Rock. I sat down on the floor in my apartment and listened. Introducing it, he said, 'So I play this for everyone out there who still cares.' And then he played my demo of 'From a Distance.'

"On May 5th, 1986, Nanci Griffith called to ask to record 'From a Distance,' because Christine had sent her a copy. This was the first song of mine anyone had recorded. Nanci has since recorded about seven or eight songs of mine and she has also recorded 'From a Distance' live and multilingual, with Donna Summer, may she rest in peace, and with Raul Malo. And it's because of her recording that other artists heard it, like the Byrds and Kathy Mattea, and Judy Collins, and, five years later, Bette Midler.

"I was still working at HBO. I'd be at my desk and Nanci would call me from Belfast, and she would tell me, 'Julie, you don't know what I witnessed last night. Catholics and Protestants were crying in the aisles, embracing.' And I was like, 'Wow!' And then I'd go right back to work. I finally quit my job in July of 1989, only because I had already played Carnegie Hall with Nanci Griffith, and I had heard my song sung by all these other artists. But I was still stone broke. I can't even begin to tell you the difference between an album cut and a hit. It's like when you look at a map of the galaxies and you see Pluto next to Jupiter. Album cuts don't get airplay; even if it's on college radio, it doesn't compare to the top forty. So your royalties are all based on sales.

"Yes, I got significant royalties from all the covers; it bolstered my income as a secretary, but I was still in one room. I couldn't go anywhere; I couldn't buy anything.

"Here I have to thank the love and support of my parents. One night I was crying on the phone to them. My father would be on one extension; my mother would be on the other. And they would tell me how great I was and that I shouldn't get discouraged and these things take time and blah blah blah. And my mother said, 'Julie, what can I do? What would help you?' And I said, 'Truthfully, pay my rent. Please, please, please, please, please, please pay my rent.' And my mother said, 'Do you want it one month at a time or you want the whole six months?' I said, 'One month at a time so I feel like I'm working and getting a paycheck.' That was $500 a month, and during that time I did God's work with my music. I sent out songs to Dear Ms. Streisand, Dear Mr. Manilow, Dear James Ingram, Dear Natalie Cole. Everyone was looking for songs then. I knew my UPS man; I knew my FedEx man. I knew my copy center man. I knew my mailman. I knew everyone. For six months, I did the greatest work of my life. But I didn't catch one single fish. And at the very end of those six months came a check from BMI for Nanci Griffith's accumulated royalties overseas. And that let me have another six months, which brought me to 1990.

"Meanwhile, another interesting thing that happened with Nanci Griffith's version was that it was seen by the editor/publisher of *American Way*, which is the magazine for American Airlines, and they did this sixteen-page magazine spread with an accompanying video on all their international and national flights. It was Nanci Griffith singing 'From a Distance' and it was called 'From a Distance: The '80s.' There was the guy in the tank. There was the guy who was married to Tammy Faye Bakker. It was every world event that happened in the eighties set to 'From a Distance.' Steve Popovich [from Polygram Records] was already a champion of the song. He called me and said, 'Jules, who do you want to get it to?' So I said, 'Clive Davis; that's my number one goal.' Popovich says, 'Okay, he's waiting for you. Bring him the "American Way" video.' So I brought it and I wrote him a note. One day later the note was back in my hands and it said, '"From a Distance" is a beautiful song worthy of a Joni Mitchell authorship. Unfortunately, I am only looking for hit songs, as the writers have their own album cuts so I have to pass. But thank you and congratulations.'

"That didn't stop me. When I teach songwriting, the first thing I say to my students is: 'Let me teach you my mantra.' And I say, 'Are you ready?' And they go, 'Yeah.' Then I say, 'They're wrong. Repeat that. They're wrong. Repeat it. Louder. Louder. THEY'RE WRONG. THEY'RE WRONG. THEY'RE WRONG.' And then I tell the Clive Davis story and I say, 'So what did I say to myself when he rejected it? I said he was wrong! And guess what? He was.'

"Because I came home one night to my answering machine flashing. And the guy said, 'Hello, my name is Mark Shaiman and I work with Bette Midler. Steven Holden at *The New York Times* told us you have a song called "From a Distance," and we would love to hear it.' I sent it out to him, but I always tell myself it's not going to happen. That's the only way you can protect yourself. But I heard back almost instantly. And that's when my life changed.

"I started getting courted by publishers and one of them was Lance Freed at Almo/Irving. I remember they flew me out to LA while Bette was recording it. I was thirty-five years old and it was the first time I ever went to the West Coast. At the airport, they had my name, 'Gold,' on a placard. And a limousine drove me to my fancy hotel that had a switch where the fireplace went on in the summer. It was crazy. Mark Shaiman picked me up at the hotel in this little white 1967 Mustang convertible and he took me first to a Chinese restaurant called Genghis Cohen. Do you believe it? He excused himself to make a phone call, and he came back to the table and he said, 'Guess what. We're going over to the studio and you're going to see Bette Midler and Arif Mardin.' I was tingling. I had never met Arif Mardin, but he'd just won a Grammy for Bette's last hit, 'The Wind Beneath My Wings,' so I knew what he looked like. He came running up to me with childlike jubilation. He's wearing a plaid madras shirt and he's holding a Walkman in his hand. The Walkman had an external speaker on it, and he pushed 'play' and I heard Bette Midler singing 'From a Distance.' Then in his heavy accent he says, 'But don't tell her I played it for you. It's a scratch vocal and she'd be very upset with that.'

Bette Midler arrived, hours late. During that time Diane Warren showed up. So when Bette finally came, she was much more attentive to Diane Warren. Not only that, we sat in a room with Diane and Diane said, 'Will you call my mother?' And so, Bette Midler called Diane Warren's mother and said, 'Hello, Mrs. Warren, this is Bette Midler.' I wanted so badly to say, 'Can you call my mother, too?' but I didn't dare. So Diane Warren watered down my first meeting with Bette Midler. But it was still thrilling.

"However, nothing gave me a clue the song would be a single. But then the first ground war for the Persian Gulf War broke out. I don't know if they debated what would be the first single, and what wouldn't. But when the song was released, it was unstoppable. It became completely and entirely intertwined with the Persian Gulf War. It was the most requested song on Radio Saudi and I found myself being invited to these military events where I was presented with honorable awards thanking me for what 'From a Distance' had done to boost the morale of our troops. The whole period while it was on the charts was surreal. On the other hand, I had wanted it, envisioned it, and I believed in it for so long that it almost

228 | They're Playing My Song

seemed natural. I had rehearsed it in my mind for so many years without a moment of doubt that it would happen.

"Nevertheless, I still lived in my one-room apartment. The expression is 'the money's not in the pipeline yet.' So I was still stone broke. My song was playing on the radio and I had nothing to show for it yet except that it was beloved. I remember one night when I was sick; I didn't have a thermometer; I didn't have an aspirin. I had nothing. I went to the drug store in the snow; my hair was greasy and I was feverish and wouldn't you know it, 'From a Distance' is playing on the radio. So I run over to the pharmacist and I say, 'Did you hear that song?' And he's like, 'Yeah.' And I said, 'I wrote it.' He looked at me as if he had just seen Elvis. And I realized how absolutely outlandish the whole thing was.

"The next year at the Grammy Awards, let me tell you, my competition for Song of the Year wasn't too shabby. One of the nominees was Phil Collins for 'Another Day in Paradise,' and the interesting thing about that was that he was an Atlantic Records recording artist, and so was Bette. So if, in fact, record companies were encouraged to vote for their own, then they had a divided voting bloc. I was also up against Mariah Carey's first hit, 'Vision of Love.' Then there was the Prince song sung by Sinéad O'Connor, 'Nothing Compares 2 U.' I don't know for sure, but it might have been around the time Sinead O'Connor came out against the pope, so that might have hurt her chances. And there was also the big Wilson Phillips hit called 'Hold On.'

"I'd come there in a white stretch limo with an attendant, which Almo/Irving paid for it. Ultimately I had to recoup that, but, nonetheless, they paid for it. My parents came up from Philly, and my brother Danny was also with them somewhere in the balcony. I brought Christine Lavin with me and we sat next to each other. Earlier that day I got a call from the Recording Academy telling me, 'Your seat has been moved up ten rows forward.' So I said to my brother, 'What do you think that means?' And he said, 'Well, what do you think it means?' I said, 'Well, I don't think they would be so blatant.' He said, 'Well, just enjoy it.'

"I'm much more sophisticated now than I was then, but that whole world was unknown to me. So I had someone shop with me for something and I bought it at Bergdorf Goodman, this colorful jacket that was later trashed by *The Globe*—not *The Boston Globe*. It was in Radio City that year, so I hired a makeup artist who I had met from working at HBO, which was right at Forty-Second and Sixth, and I used an old friend's office. I looked like a ghoul with a Halloween mask, if you ask me. The makeup ended right at my chin, so my neck is three shades lighter than my face. But nonetheless, I thought, I am nominated for a Grammy, I need to wear a jacket from Bergdorf Goodman and I need to have makeup.

"I always thought the Song of the Year was one of the last awards, but this time it was on very early in the show. They had told me my presenters were going to be James Ingram and Natalie Cole. So I'm sitting there and all of a sudden I see James Ingram and Natalie Cole walk onstage. And I'm like, 'Oh my God, this is it already!' I could have been in the ladies' room. I could have heard it from a stall in the ladies' room. But instead, they came onstage and they said, 'The Song of the Year is a writer's award.' And they read the nominations. Carnie Wilson was across the room, but we were in the same row. When they read my name, she leaned forward and she gave me a good luck sign. And I always thought that was really gracious of her, because she was up against me. It was really a loving, gracious sign. Recently I friended her on Facebook and I wrote her that, but I never heard back from her.

"I have to say, that period did affect my writing process a little bit, because I wondered what do they expect now? I kept hearing the word 'anthem.' 'We need an anthem about popcorn,' 'We need an anthem about ear drops.' 'Anthem, anthem, anthem.' It was like, come on, man. But it was never really a burden. Since then I think I have written many songs that have measured up to 'From a Distance,' but what can I say? If someone came into your garden and picked a beautiful rose, and then every time they see you they say, 'We never got another rose like that,' well, come back to my garden and you'll see that not only is there another rose like that, but there's an iris and a lily . . . but it's a strange business. Thankfully, I've always been grounded and I never saw myself in any way other than what I've always been. I still sit at the piano and I write with a pen, and I hope for an inspiration, and then I demo my song and I pitch it. I was signed to two different publishing deals along the way. For about ten years I was a paid songwriter, which is a beautiful gift.

"I can't say one negative thing about what that song has done for my life, for my family's life. It just continues to bless my life. Because of the Internet, at least once a month, but sometimes once a week, a stranger will write to me and tell me what the song meant to them. I've traveled and I've met and performed for people simply because of that song. I heard from a lot of people who came out of the woodwork. But it was all about love. Nothing was opportunistic. I have a lovely life and my friends have always been my friends. So all this did was reverberate deeper from the love of my friends. No one came out of the woodwork that I was unhappy to see.

Eventually the checks started coming and they were amazing for years and years. I've never been a reckless person. I had a publishing deal for ten years, so I was able to bank all my 'From a Distance' money. I didn't buy a car. I didn't travel. I didn't do anything, except buy this condominium where I live. Because I am a struggling songwriter still. And thank God I have this gorgeous cushion to save me from being a secretary again, I hope. But I can't say for sure."

"From a Distance" has been covered by many artists, including the Byrds, Judy Collins, Jewel, Kathy Mattea, Donna Summer, and the African Children's Choir.

Andy Partridge / XTC (1988)

"We call it Billy Bolts or Billy Bolts Upright. I just sort of sit up and become this person Billy Bolt. You just get into the process of thinking and sending your brain out to search, getting those tendrils going everywhere. You find a piece of string and you think, this is a really good piece of string and you're pulling and pulling—God, there's something on the end of this—and I can't turn my head off from doing this at night, and there I am, I'm awake and I'm yelling like I'm being murdered, and I'm facing the wardrobe and it's four a.m. and I don't know what I'm doing."

The archetype English preppy down to his rubber soles, Andy Partridge is as unique a musical and lyrical voice as XTC is a band, on the cutting edge of the forces that drive the universes within, both psychic and psychedelic. Over the course of a decade and nearly a dozen albums, the changes upon changes that define his career, the ineffable Partridge touch, one part grouse the other part dove, has gradually brought XTC into a hallowed geologic region occupied only by two other such hermetically sealed stalactites of the rock iconosphere.

"We usually get either the Beatles thing, or if not it's the Steely Dan thing." Andy acknowledged, "which I think is much too high praise, 'cause basically they sound much more melodically and rhythmically together than we'll ever be. Comparisons are always flattering, but in a way, it makes it scarier, 'cause you know the next thing you write has got live up to it, so it's best not to think about it, it's not going to resolve itself."

With a mind as hyperactive as his, Partridge covets no extraneous stimuli. "I always have a terrible dilemma that the last song I wrote is going to be the last song ever and it gets worse every time," he stated. "It always resolves itself, but I feel like I must worry about it. If I don't worry about it, it's not going to resolve itself."

And yet, if his experiences making *Skylarking* can serve as an example, Partridge is a veritable songmaking exemplar of prolificness. "What happened was that we actually wrote about three albums," he said. "We did a load of stuff and it was more orchestral feeling with more sort of countryside textures. We literally took an album's worth of demos to the record company in England and they said, 'Well, this isn't the album we want from you. We want something that's going to sell big.' What do we do now? So we started writing again. But that sort of telling off obviously must have affected us, because I thought, I'll perk it up and try something different, and a load of songs came that were harder sounding; they were beefier, more stripped down, R&B sort of stuff. We figured this is what they want. So we took it to them and, 'Oh, I don't know. These songs aren't quite as good as the early songs; do you want to try again?' So we go away and write another load of songs, not with anything in mind, just more songs. So we ended up with a choice of thirty-five songs, and we used some early stuff, very little from the middle, and some stuff from later on. We gave it all to our producer, Todd Rundgren, and he rounded up elements that sort of connected with other elements and the way that they felt right together is the way that they came out. And it means that a lot of your personal favorite tunes get left out, and it means that you don't necessarily agree with where those songs should be on the album. But I generally agree that the songs do flow very nicely into each other and he did his homework."

Part of that homework, of course, is the by now legendary subtraction and then addition of "Dear God," from the American edition of the album. When this catchy ditty found a cult audience as the B-side of an English single, the powers that be in the US realized they had their ticket to the big bucks after all—*and they'd thrown it away*. They hastened to amend this stunning faux pas, and XTC suffered their biggest hit to date. But for Partridge success has not changed his creative process all that much.

"To write you have to kind of tune the head in to receive this stuff from somewhere, because you can't be receiving it if you're managing the band, if you're doing interviews, if you're doing the artwork or whatever. You have to kind of tune in the head and empty it of all the other stuff. We've only recently finished another Dukes of Stratosphere record, so by the time I finish talking in England about 'Dear God,' there'll be some more Dukes talking. Then I shall have an empty period where I can tune this receiver in and start getting things out of the atmosphere. But it's not like I can plan it. At times, I can write a song a day, but sometimes I can

Andy Partridge / XTC (1988) | 233

go for months without anything, absolutely nothing comes up. I have to just click into a writing mode. Songs come, but if I don't run home and sing them into my answering machine quick, they go. There's tunes that come just as you're falling asleep. A few times it's happened where I'm dozing off and I get into that incredibly relaxed state, and a whole song will just pop out—melody, great lyric line—and I think, 'Oh, I'll write it down in a little while,' but I never do. They're the best thing you've ever heard and then you go to sleep. And you've just dreamt 'Hey Jude' or something.

"We try not to give ourselves really specific deadlines, but you begin to see one on the horizon, like some big distant city, and that increases the anxiety. A sure sign of desperation is when you just turn on a drum machine and play anything. Sometimes, just by the brute banality of it, you might kick down a door that you thought was never going to open, and suddenly you'll see something in there. You hit a chord and you think, I'm just going to keep squeezing and squeezing this chord, and you just play it for hours and hours and the drum machine is bashing away, and then suddenly you'll slip with your fingers and make a mistake, or you'll think, this is so banal, it's a battleship. Battleship! It sounds like a battleship! Some stupid thought will blow the thing wide open. But usually the case is, you get tuned in and this stuff explodes, takes you over. You play too late into the night and your dinner's going cold downstairs. Then it gets like the air changes or something, and you're breathing a sort of different atmosphere somehow. It's like you really have tuned in and the first program's come in, and suddenly you feel wonderfully receptive to a load of stuff—things that wouldn't have meant anything a couple of weeks before suddenly all come crowding in real quick."

It's at times like these, all channels open and the air electric, that Partridge's wife will bring him down to reality. "She tells me off for drumming," he said. "Like we'll have friends over in the evening and I'll sit there drumming. I've got this sound in my head and I don't realize I'm playing; it's leaking through my mask. So she'll say, Oh, stop drumming! Five minutes later I'm back to drumming again."

In the daylight hours, she's one of his severest critics. "I used to do a lot of lyrics at night when everyone had gone to bed. But most of *Skylarking* was done in the afternoon. You get up and crouch over your poor studio and sing the songs really quietly so as not to upset the neighbors. Sometimes I'd come up with something really exciting and I'd start tingling, so I'd run downstairs and force it on my wife. She's very cool and my worst critic, my stabilizer. Her opinion is usually, it's not commercial enough, or I don't like the bit about the porpoises."

Always a student of nuance and shading, Partridge is perhaps most concerned about certain of life's more tenuous balances: between man and nature, art and commerce, music and lyrics. "You have a lyric," he said, "the lyric says, What must I set this stage with, what scenery does this lyric want? And so you find the scenery from the instrument. Or you have the scenery and you think, What sort of actors should I have; what lines must they say? Things suggest other things. A chord can mean a phenomenal amount; just one chord brings you a lot of pictures. You hit a chord and think, that chord is so foggy; if somebody could get fog and turn it into a chord, it's that chord. And it'll be like the tip of the iceberg for a song, and you'll work on this foggy chord and you'll think, fog, fog . . . and all these lyrics cascade out under fog, like some sort of school essay. You know, give me five hundred words on fog. You try some other chords; no, that's not foggy, that's too rainy, that's too sunny. Oh, that's really foggy. How does it sound with the other one? Oh, not too bad. Maybe I'll use that as a middle. Then you kind of round up all the foggy chords and you build this set for yourself. What I used to do was find chords and then hit a note that seemed comfortable with it in no relation to the chord. But now I actually hear myself singing notes in some way uniform with the chords, like the notes will ascend. The chord structure may go all over, but I'll find one line in the chord that will appear to be like an ascending line, or a line that appears to descend. You actually follow notes in the chord that have this kind of worm that floats through them. In some cases, I'd like to be more melody dominated, but I find I'm highly rhythm dominated. I'm finding it very difficult to get out of being locked into a rhythm and to make the transcendent leap from rhythm to melody. I build lyrics still for their rhythm feel, or I'll get the lyrics I'm really happy with about a given subject and I'll insert a load of ifs and buts and stuff to give it rhythm.

"Sometimes I'll phone Greg up with a chord change and say, can you try these notes and tell me what they sound like on piano? And he has to lay the phone down and run away, and I have to listen to it on piano and see if it's going to work or not. Songs I've written on keyboards are much less predictable than the guitar things. I can play nearly anything on guitar. The only thing I've found interesting with the guitar in the last five years is working with different tunings, 'cause that's thrown me off course. It's been like a different instrument, and I can come up with

Andy Partridge / XTC (1988) | 235

exciting accidents. You play the easiest, most banal shapes and with different tunings you get the most wonderful stuff. It gives you things you wouldn't think of playing or trying out. On piano, I've got no restrictions, because I haven't got any technical ability, so the songs are all accidents."

A father himself now, Partridge's early songs were the stillborn accidents of his wild seedless youth. "The first album, *White Music*, was just snotty, naked baby photos," he recalled. "I don't know if I'd want to see them now. Don't get them out, Mother. I'm not like that anymore. I get embarrassed by *White Music* now because I was really trying too hard to find a style in which to say these things. But the paradox was, at that point in time I had nothing to say. I was just writing lyrics and they never gave me any pictures other than the total thing of that sort of modern, loud, noisy guitar, bass, drums, organ mess. The chords were picked because they upset more than they were musically well crafted. After *White Music*, I started to feel like I really wanted to get out cohesive ideas."

And after *English Settlement*, in the early eighties, Andy's well-documented bout with the sweats caused him to abandon the performing arena. "The venue I perform in now is usually Dave's front room and it's usually on an acoustic guitar," he said. "And just as a panic it'll be Greggsy grab a strap or sit at the piano and do this for me and let's see what it sounds like. To me a song doesn't grow in front of an audience; if anything, it gets stifled. You can't do it justice when you're thinking about your pants falling down, or is your guitar strap lock on well enough, or are the monitors feeding back. It's not a relaxed, creative environment. It's at best a getting by environment. You're doing a performance and all these aspects crop up. You know, when someone is slinging a mud-filled bra at you, it's not really conducive to ornamenting the song."

Instead, Partridge finds the get-off in the thing itself. "The release is getting the sleeve in your hand and taking out the disk. That's a great sensation. Usually while we're doing an album, I take it home and I play it until I'm really sick of it and then I forget about it. Then the album comes out and I get excited again." As the years go by, and the albums multiply, his chances for accidental pleasures increase dramatically. "I like to play our records when I'm really drunk and my vanity completely disappears," he admitted. "The family goes to bed, and I get really drunk and get over the guilt of listening to my own stuff. I ram the headphones on and lay there on the floor with the empty cans rolling on the carpet, and I go, Yeah, great; I'd forgotten about that. Like playing something from *Drums and* Wires or *English Settlement* and I'd forgotten the chord changes; I'd forgotten the lyrics, and right in the middle I go, Of course, Yeah."

And yet, as honest as he is, Partridge would not admit to entertaining the one maudlin thought that usually accompanies such sentimental binges of the artist in a world of commerce, the one that goes: If I'm so good, how come I ain't more famous? "Feedback is nice," is all he'll allow, "but it doesn't affect what I want to write about one iota. In fact, if they say something one way, I'll want to go the other way to spite them."

So ornery is this Partridge that he's even prepared to spit in the face of the biggest success of his career. "I think 'Dear God' is a piece of dull music," he said. "It's dull; it's average. And I think it's going to become our '(I Can't Get No) Satisfaction.' But any way someone can get into the band it doesn't matter. It's like, what's a key? A key is a scraggy lump of metal, but it gets you through the door," he says, as aphoristic as Leonard Cohen, and not entirely tongue in cheek, ". . . to the riches beyond."

The erratic, sporadic, and quintessentially chaotic career of Andy Partridge, in and out of XTC, with various spinoff groups and album reconfigurations, continued into the twenty-first century and as yet shows no signs of relenting.

Kool Moe Dee (2001)

"What changed my life from being a fan to becoming an artist was one night in November 1978 when I was up at the Audubon Ballroom in Manhattan. Basically I went to see Lovebug Starsky. That particular night Grandmaster Flash turned the music down on Lovebug Starsky, who got off very reluctantly, because he was in a good space and everybody was dancin'. Now there's dead silence. We didn't know that Flash was doing that intentionally. He didn't really care if you danced. I mean he wanted you to dance, but he mainly wanted you to pay attention to him. So, he brought the music to a dead stop and the spotlight came on. It wasn't really a spotlight; a light came on and one of his DJs, Kid Creole, basically gave the crowd in echo form a big, long, elaborate introduction: 'Ladies and Gentlemen, welcome to the greatest show on earth. Never before have you seen anything like this . . .'

"And I'm like, an introduction for a DJ? I've never seen anything like this before. He's using the echo chamber and it's like he's saying who he is and it's like, 'Kid Creoooooole. Solid . . . solid . . . solid. Gold . . . gold . . . gold.' This is something new. I'm not as skeptical as before. Shortly after that he said, 'Are you ready??' And simultaneously he cued Flash and he came on and got another MC who was called Cowboy, who I'd never seen before either.

"Soon as Kid Creole and Flash hit the music, Cowboy started rhyming. I'm blown away by this point. I'd heard an echo chamber, I'd seen a DJ cut on cue with another MC coming in at the same time. Cowboy's rhyming and saying, 'What's my name?' and the crowd is responding back, and he's saying the most colorful things I have ever heard. A guy who's spelling his name out seems very simplistic now, but back then I was like, What the hell was that? Say what's my name? Champagne! Say what's my name?

"He had all of these sayings that everybody knew and we suddenly felt like we were behind in something. These Bronx people knew what was happening. We were like, who are these kids from the Bronx coming down here with these crowds who already know what to say? We had to learn what to say real quick if we wanted to participate. You didn't want to be left out of hip-hop at that time.

"After he finished, he passed the mic. Which we'd never heard of either and you heard: '1, 2, 3, 4, Melly Mel what ya waiting for?' Melly Mel gets on and he proceeds to do metaphors. This is the changing point for me from being a fan, to this is what I want to do for the rest of my life. He goes, 'I make Alaska hot, I make Africa cold.' That was ingenious to me. He went on this long rhyme and he said, 'from Melly Mel from the top of the World Trade to the depths of hell.' And I was like, 'That's it. That's the formula. How many incredible things can you do? How many can be put into rhyme form to wow the crowd?'

"Shortly after that, Grandmaster Flash started scratching, which we also now take very much for granted. He's doing this record called 'Apache' and everybody went berserk. And while he's playing the record, he's scratching it back and forth and it's like warp speed, and we can't comprehend what's happening. I'm watching it with my mouth wide open like a little kid. I just couldn't believe it. Shortly after that, Kid Creole stops the music again and says the 'never before have you seen this greatest show on Earth' thing again. Grandmaster Flash is now doing what's commonly known as back spinning. That was it. I was literally not thinking about dancing anymore. All I'm thinking about is how I was going to be onstage doing what I just saw. I was blown away and that was the moment that changed my life.

"I'd wanted to do it before, but now I had a passion for it. I was just starting high school and I began writing rhymes secretly. My legacy is that I was going around to all of these parties, following Grandmaster Flash. But, anywhere anybody had parties I would go to them. Sometimes three or four a night. And I was always like Mr. T, standing at the front of the ropes with my arms folded, and I would look at the MC that was rhyming and shake my head and give him the thumbs down. Very slowly, very wrestling-like. So I was already known before I even said a rhyme. Who the hell is the little pipsqeak always standing in the front of the

Kool Moe Dee (2001) | 239

crowd shaking his head as we rhyme? So I just went around from party to party, standing in front, usually in something all white or all red, from Kangol to sneaker.

"Finally I decided to test my stuff. I got on the mike as we sat at the café on lunch break in school. We were one of the first schools to play music, and I remember everybody danced to records like 'Good Times.' I did the same thing that Flash did, in reverse, from an MC's standpoint. Don't play anything that they can dance to 'cause I wanna rhyme. I wanted them to hear my rhyme. My DJ at the time was a guy named Dano B., and he basically cut the record to a very slowed down beat and I started rhyming, but I rhymed double time. I wanted a slow beat and to rhyme fast. I knew that would blow the crowd away. I became kinda popular overnight. I started raising the bar early on.

"When I was young I planned on being a boxer. I was always an Ali, Bruce Lee, and Sugar Ray Leonard fan. The one thing that they all had in common was flash. I was like, okay, I have to be flashy, but with substance. I couldn't just come in dressed like Liberace and rhyme. I was planning rhymes before I knew what hip-hop was. I would have rhymes for each of my opponents. It worked out differently, but at least I didn't have to get punched. Basically that's when I started to figure out that I needed an angle to separate me. I had to stand out.

"One thing I never respected was off the top of the head rhymes. I get it now, but I never respected off the top of the head before, even though there's an art to that. For me it's absolutely about putting thought into rhymes. After putting thought into it, then you go to the styles and how you're going to say it. You have to be passionate about it. I think nothing on the planet can be done without passion. A lot of people take it for granted. Some of it is a God-given talent. But a lot more of it is hours of practice.

"In 1980 we made our first record, *New Rap Language*, which was all of the fast rhymes. Being our first record, we knew nothing about production or sound. The technology wasn't what it is today. We were in a situation where we thought we had to get it right in one take. We didn't know we could do it over. The bass player, the guitar player, and the keyboard guy were all in the same room. The stuff was bleeding over. As a matter fact, we might have even recorded it in mono.

"This was the early days of rap, when people were skeptical, and we were ahead of the curve. We were on tour with the Barkays. The crowd was going berserk for us, and the Barkays would have to go on after us. That's where some of the backlash in hip-hop started coming from. To those guys, we were not musicans. They would say, 'They don't play instruments. They cover other peoples' songs and basically we just rhyme over records. Where's the band? The DJ's scratchin' and he's rhyming and the kids like this? It's not real.' Shortly after that, we started getting our own tours.

Eventually, I wound up going solo, which was a learning process in itself, in terms of signing with a record label. I used to talk every day to a guy who was working as a box boy in that company. I kinda felt sorry for him because he had all this knowledge and ambition and he was just a box boy and nobody paid him any attention. So he was like, I know a guy named Teddy Riley who plays music. You're one of the best guys over here. You should hook up with him. So he hooked me up. He introduced me to Teddy Riley and we made a record together, "Go See the Doctor." The rest is history.

～

A pioneering artist in the new jack swing era of hip-hop, Kool Moe Dee released five solo albums from 1986 to 1994.

Dave Alvin / the Blasters (2013)

"4th of July"

Dave Alvin is a man of many layers, one part fierce guitar slinger out of the roots rock tradition, one part hard-bitten author out of the Raymond Chandler school of pithy prose—and no part naturally gifted warbler, whether in the Blasters, X, or on his own. With the writing of the future anthem "4th of July," Alvin joined the disparate parts of his persona into a mythic tone poem of romantic alienation, never a hit but played to this day at ballparks across California to celebrate Americana's national holiday.

"What I've always tried to do is be a combination of my musical and my literary heroes," he said. "When I started writing songs for the Blasters, I felt the music I really love and listen to was slowly disappearing as far as being a cultural force. I felt there were a lot of bar bands or even some national acts that were playing, we'll call it traditional electric roots music, whether it was blues or rockabilly or R&B. But the one thing I always felt was lacking in a lot of them was the Dylan influence. And one of the things Dylan was great at, and still is, is basically taking Elmore James and making 'Leopard Skin Pillbox Hat' out of it. So my feeling was to take, say, Little Junior Parker or Howlin' Wolf or Jimmy Reed or Carl Perkins or Chuck Berry and write my own lyrics. So there's certainly a little bit of Raymond Chandler in there.

"In college, one of my poetry teachers was a guy by the name of Gerald Lockland, who really enlightened me as to the beauty of the mundane. You drive through a neighborhood of tract homes and all the houses look the same, and you can just see there's nothing going on there. But inside all of those friggin' houses is a poem, maybe a short story, maybe a novel, maybe a song. A lot of my songs in those days came out of free verse prose poems, which I would shape into songs if I found a good image. '4th of July' started as a three-page prose poem. It was written about a year or two before the song. There's only one or two lines from the prose poem that are actually in the song. 'Mexican kids are shooting fireworks below,' and 'She turns out the lights and lays in the dark.' It also had Fourth of July in it, but it wasn't a chorus.

"I think the poem was called 'Fourth of July in the Dark.' It was about a previous girlfriend and I living in a neighborhood in our hometown in South Downey. We were living in a little duplex apartment and both working day jobs, and I considered myself old and done at the age of twenty-one. There's a line in the song, 'On the lost side of town.' And when I sing it, what I'm thinking about is where I come from. It's a part of town where great things don't come out of it. It's the kind of place where your job in life is just to work, eat something, sleep, and pay your bills. I think any relationship in that kind of situation has its difficulties,

Figure 31. Dave Alvin, 2024. Photo: Joe Mabel, Wikimedia Commons, CC BY-SA 4.0.

where you're sort of transitioning from your youthful dreams into possible adult disappointments. That can put a lot of stress onto a relationship.

"I don't know if '4th of July' is my most Chandleresque song, but it was definitely trying to say a lot with a little. Sometimes I try to say a lot with a lot. But that song was trying to say a lot with a little. When I was writing it, I had a third verse, which I threw away, because the weight of the song with the third verse felt too heavy. On the other hand, with just the two verses and the little part that goes 'whatever happened / I apologize,' it felt like, 'Is that enough? Is that possibly enough? I get it. But will anyone else?' Here's what I've learned over time, and my only advice to a young traditional roots rock songwriter is that a song you think is entirely personal and no one else will get it is sometimes the most universal. I don't know too many songwriters who were 'trained' or schooled as songwriters. So it's a feel thing. When X wanted to record the song and we recorded a couple of demos for Elektra, one of the producers, who is a notable musician who shall remain nameless, said, 'I'm not getting enough. It needs more.' So, I thought, well, maybe I should pull that third verse back into it? But then I thought, no, it's getting the point across. They're either breaking up or they're staying together.' "

Thus, with the music and the lyrics out of the way, the stage was set for something totally unexpected. "What happened next," said Dave Alvin, "changed my life.

"Technically, I'd already left the Blasters and was a member of X when I wrote the song. In the Blasters, besides being the loud, noisy guitar player, I was the songwriter. And when I left the band, they were kind of up the creek without a paddle, because there was nobody else in the band who could write songs. In the Blasters' contract, there was a leaving member clause, which meant if either my brother or I left, Warner Brothers had the right to drop the band. But Warner Brothers decided, if we get another guitar player, everything will be fine, and they agreed to let the guys do another album. And then because I grew up with these guys, I felt like, okay, I'll write songs and I'll even play on the record. But when the recording and the writing is done, you guys get another guitarist. I'm not part of this band. Is all that clear?

"Then Warners sweetened the pot, so to speak, by suggesting that Nick Lowe produce the band. We knew Nick. We had toured Europe with him earlier in our career. So we thought that was a great idea. Early in 1986, we were scheduled to go in and cut two or three songs and I had to come up with them. So, one night I was with my girlfriend and some

244 | They're Playing My Song

other friends at a bowling alley. Normally I write sober. But we're sitting there having a beer watching our friends be bad bowlers, and at some point, the little inspiration muse walked into the bowling alley and sat down next to me and said, "You know that poem about 4th of July, that's a song." So I grabbed my girlfriend, drove her home, drove to my house, grabbed the guitar, and about two hours later I called her up and said, 'What do you think of this?'

"Now, I was never a singer. When I was a little kid, I got kicked out of choir. My older brother Phil was one of the star choir singers of the Catholic church and I was asked not to be part of it. So when I wrote songs for the Blasters, I'd go to rehearsal and sing them for like an hour and my brother would sit and listen and say, "Sing it again, sing it again." Then when he would step up to the microphone, he'd say, "Okay, I got it," and I'd never sing the song again. I mean, I had this brother with this big, loud, magnificent blues voice.

"So Nick Lowe flies over from England and we get together. I'd written '4th of July' and I'd written another song. I sat down with Nick, played him the one, and then played him '4th of July.' And then he said something that changed my life, which was, 'Your brother can't sing this.' I said, 'What are you talking about?' Although I knew kind of what he was talking about, because structurally it was different from anything the Blasters had ever done. He said, 'It doesn't fit his voice. Melodically, it's not what your brother does.' Then Nick said, 'You should sing it.' I said, 'Well, I can't sing.' Then he gave me my motto for the rest of my career, when he said, 'I can't sing either, but I've somehow made a living doing it.' And that registered. Because in those days there was still enough of a sort of do-it-yourself punk rock underground that I was attached to. So I go, 'Yeah, that's right. That guy can't sing and that guy can't sing, and she can't sing, and that other guy can't sing either.'

"We go into the studio and we start tracking the song with me singing in the same way I would at a Blasters rehearsal two years before. And Phil and Nick had, we'll call it a disagreement. Because Nick was like, 'You know, your brother's going to sing this.' Which put my brother into a real uncomfortable situation, because, as he was trying to explain to Nick Lowe, 'Well, that may or may not be true, but he's only here to help us make a record so that we can continue touring. He's not going to be in the band to sing the song.' And I'm in this weird situation, too. Once I heard my brother singing it, I knew that, yeah, it's not in his comfort zone. And yet I'm not in the band. So we cut a demo for Warner

Brothers with me singing. Nick went back to England and my brother went in with the engineer after Nick left and cut his own vocal on it, and both versions were delivered to Warners, and then Warners had the same reaction. 'This is great, but he's not in the band!' So, long story short, that album never happened.

"Once I played X the demo, I was really high on the idea of me singing. I just thought the song was frigging *great*. It was one of those things that as soon as I heard it coming back through the speakers of the studio, I was like, 'That could be a *hit*.' I played it for Exene and John Doe, and John was instantly, 'I want to sing that song.' And I was like, 'Oh, fine.' Because I knew that he could. So that's how it eventually wound up on an X record called *See How We Are*. But even while that was going on, at the same time Demon Records over in London approached me. 'Well, hey, we'll give you x amount of dollars if you want to make a solo record.' Elektra released X's version as a single and I still think it should have been a hit song. I'll put a couple of other songs of mine in that category. Back in Blasters days I could never figure out why this song I wrote called 'Marie, Marie,' which was a huge international hit for a guy named Shakin' Stevens out of England, wasn't a hit in the United States either for Shakin' Stevens or for the Blasters. Warner/Slash never released it as a single. 'Fourth of July' should have been a hit, too. But in 1987 there was still enough of a pushback from radio against anything that even remotely resembled punk rock, which kind of doomed that record. This was before Nirvana, before Pearl Jam, before all the bands that got on the radio because a shift in who decided what got on the radio happened in the early nineties. Bands that were influenced by X or Hüsker Dü or the Replacements were getting on the radio then, whereas the bands of ten years before were strictly on college radio. I had left X by the time the record was released, but I know Elektra tried their best to break that song. On the other hand, out here, and several other places, they play it leading up to 4th of July at baseball stadiums. It gets played at Angels Stadium; it gets played at Dodgers Stadium. So in some ways it was like having a hit.

"I think I've written three songs, maybe four, that'll be around when I'm gone and that's one of them. When I'm writing songs, I don't think that way, but over time you start going, 'Wow, people really like that song.' You get messages through Facebook or whatever from fans, 'My dad used to play that song and dance me around the room when I was a little girl.' As in any song that gains some sort of cultural popularity, they start taking on the qualities of folk music in that they touch people

246 | They're Playing My Song

and they remind people of certain things that are timeless. The songs take on that kind of timeless patina. So I can't complain. I mean, I was a fry cook in Long Beach, which was the era I wrote about in the song. I'm a really lucky guy in that when I did go solo, I couldn't sing a note and somehow I stuck with it and learned.

"When I look back on my time in this racket, the one thing I know is that you never know what people are going to like. I didn't think anyone would like '4th of July' when I was writing it. All I knew is that I liked it. But as a songwriter, you have to persevere through that board of critics that's in your head going, 'You might as well just throw this away. Nobody's going to like this one.' You just have to get to a place of acceptance."

Alvin has continued to tour, record, produce, collaborate, and write poetry. A collection of his writings appeared in 2022, New Highway: Selected Lyrics, Poems, Prose, Essays, Eulogies and Blues.

Susanna Hoffs / the Bangles (2012)

"Eternal Flame"

"Whenever I write with Billy Steinberg and Tom Kelly, we would always start first with me getting together with Billy and working on lyrics. This was actually a new way to write songs for me, because I'd always written songs the other way around, where I'd just sit down with my guitar and write music. So I told Billy the story about this official private tour of Graceland the Bangles had been given. The day we were there we were taken out to the Garden of Memories, and there was this little box which was supposed to have a lit flame in it, an eternal flame. Actually, that day it was raining so the flame was not on. That led to Billy saying, 'Oh, eternal flame is a good title for a song.' So we crafted the lyrics at Billy's house and then we took it over to Tom's studio. I was really thrilled when I had a demo of this somewhat simple, pure, melodic, almost like a lullaby that I came up with.

"So I had this cassette in my purse and I was always taking it out and playing it for people. Finally, I brought it into the band as we were sifting through songs. Everybody had gone off and written with outside people for this album, so there was a lot of little mini a&r sessions within the band. We were working with a new producer, Davitt Sigerson, and I played him the song. There were four of us in the band who were writing and singing, so I knew there were only going to be a few songs for each of us ending up on the record. I really had a lot of faith in 'Eternal Flame,' but I don't know where it landed on the list. After I played it for Davitt, he said, 'You know, I have an idea for that song. I know you love Patsy Cline.' I was into a very heavy Patsy Cline phase where I was listening to those records and singing along and loving them. So he said, 'I'm envisioning a very kind of crafted little arrangement, kind of like a music box.' I said, 'Wow, that sounds great.' After that conversation with Davitt, we started making the record. We were tracking everything like we normally did with drum kit, bass, everyone playing in a room, laying down a scratch vocal. And then everyone went in and kind of did their main vocal after we had tracked the record. But because 'Eternal Flame' didn't really have drum kit on it, we were halfway through the making of the record and we hadn't worked on it. So I said, 'Hey, are we going to do "Eternal Flame"'? I was sort of afraid to mention it. And Davitt said, 'Oh, yeah, yeah. We're going to do it. I found a keyboard player and you and me will get together with him and we'll just work on the arrangement.' So I'm glad I brought it up. I'm not sure what would have happened if I hadn't.

"We ended up working on this little music box arrangement with the keyboard player [John Philip Shenale], so the song was kind of keyboard driven. We created a little track, brought it to the studio, and then we laid down these incredible harmonies. It was so much fun putting the track together because it was different from everything else on the record. It was all kind of pieced together in the studio. Vicki played a really beautiful guitar solo on it. I remember our manager at the time, Miles Copeland, came in and said, 'Nice song, but this'll never get played on the radio. It doesn't have drums on it.' Everything with the history of that song, I had to keep sort of protecting it and fighting for it. It just seemed like at any moment it would disappear, like something would strike it down. So it was a very sweet success when the song finally came out in the form that it was when Miles heard it.

"There is a famous story about the making of that record which is pretty funny—but it's true. Like I said, we tracked most of the songs during a period of a few weeks. And then Davitt had this great idea that whichever one of us was singing lead vocals would come in in the evening. His theory was you can feel more relaxed and more in the mood to sing in the evening. He went out of his way to do something special for everyone and he kind of pulled a prank on me. He told me that Olivia Newton-John, who he'd just worked with, sang in the nude on all her songs, and she'd never sung better. Well, it wasn't true, but I fell for it. I said, 'Really? You're kidding!' I kind of thought, well, that's like skinny dipping. So I developed this whole routine on the record where, of course, they put in like a folding screen between me and the control room, so no one could see in. And it became this funny thing where I sang most of the songs on that record in various stages of undress, including 'Eternal Flame.' It was just for that record; it's not something I ever did again.

Figure 32. Susanna Hoffs, 2015. Photo: Justin Higuchi, Wikimedia Commons, CC BY 2.0.

"I'm so amazed by that song, how it connected with people around the world, and continues to be played and remembered. That never gets old. When you realize that something you wrote is actually being played on the radio, it's one of those things that just never gets old. But I think by the time that song came out and the eighties were winding up, just the strain of being on the road for so long and never having a normal life away from living by committee, and decisions being made by committee, that's a really difficult thing. I mean, that's true of anybody who has partners in business. Sometimes you find yourself doing more than you think you can handle, and that was true for all of us. I think of bands as families. I don't know of any families that don't have some sort of dysfunction built into their personalities. It's just the nature of it. It's incredible to be part of a team, but at the same time, it definitely takes communication skills and being able to know how to keep it going, how to figure out what kind of rules you're operating under. And we were young and sort of burned out by the end of the eighties. It had nothing to do with that song specifically. We were all approaching our thirties and had other things we wanted to do. Personally, it was hard for me to maintain a romantic relationship with anyone when you're never home. My biological clock was ticking really loudly at that point, and I craved having not necessarily a white picket fence but having a home base where I could just wake up in the morning and be there a few days in a row. Everybody said, 'Really? Why now?' It was hard, at that point, but I think we were all feeling it."

Married with two children, Susanna Hoffs expanded her domain into acting and writing fiction, starring in several movies directed by her mother and producing the novel This Bird Has Flown *published in 2023.*

Sophie B. Hawkins (2019)

"Damn, I Wish I Was Your Lover"

Sophie B. Hawkins's first single received some of the most remarkable reviews of the year. It was called "pop perfection," "searching and seductive," "about as complex as music can get." She was compared to Madonna. Her music was tabbed "swoon pop" and her personality celebrated as "a true eccentric." You'd have thought Sophie would have been walking on a cloud during this period in the spring and summer of 1992, when she was twenty-seven. And you'd be right.

But it was a dark cloud.

"I was totally frightened by fame," she says. "I always feel, no one's going to want to take a picture with me. No one's going to know who I am. I admire people like Katy Perry, people who can feel their power and feel their fame. It's part of their persona and part of their being. I never felt like that. It's so horrible in a way because maybe I could have had more fun with it. I'm always more concerned about the thing that's happening next."

When she was pitching the demo with "Damn" on it, it seemed like everyone in the industry knew who she was. Seymour Stein wanted to sign her to Sire, Clive Davis wanted to sign her to Arista, Donnie Ienner wanted to sign her to Columbia. The reason she went with Columbia was because of . . . Laura Nyro.

"Laura Nyro is a huge influence on me," says Hawkins. "She's someone I dearly and desperately loved and wish I could have met. Rick Chertoff, who coproduced *Tongues and Tails*, and some of the musicians on the record, like Rob Hyman, loved Laura Nyro, too, and that was a huge bond in signing with Sony [Columbia is a division of Sony]. Another reason was because I didn't think they would change the song. I really had a sense that Clive Davis was going to change it. Maybe it would have been a multiplatinum hit if he did, but I wasn't willing to do it at that point. I would never have been willing to do it."

Next after "Damn, I Wish I Was Your Lover" was the second single Columbia released, her cover of Bob Dylan's "I Want You," the only track on the album over which there was some critical differences of opinion. The top forty listening public didn't care for it. But one particular artist did. Bob Dylan himself.

"I was on a plane going to Los Angeles, sitting in coach, and Dylan's manager came back into coach to talk to me. He said Bob heard my version of 'I Want You' and really liked it." They invited her to Dylan's Thirtieth Anniversary tribute concert coming up that October at Madison Square Garden in New York City. Still miffed by the song's poor chart showing, Sony didn't include Hawkins's performance on the album or the video of the concert. Which hurts her to this day. "People still stop me on the street, and they say that I was the highlight of that concert. Every time it appears on YouTube it disappears just as fast. One person said to me the other day that it changed his life. So, I don't know why they didn't include me."

The song that changed Sophie's life was written at the end of the eighties. She'd just been fired by Bryan Ferry after two weeks as his marimba player (an instrument she'd studied at the Manhattan School of Music). "So then I went home and I don't think I was disappointed. I think I was proud of myself for having lasted that long. I just said to myself, 'Well, good, now I get to write songs.'"

As far as who originally inspired the song, Sophie wouldn't commit to an answer. "I'm going to be very honest with you. There may have been a person that triggered the feeling, but I feel strongly that the most meaningful teachings come from our child self somewhere back in time when we couldn't express these incredible feelings. When we finally start developing as artists, we find a way to express them. So, 'Damn, I Wish I Was Your Lover' truly is my anthem, and I'm learning things about it all the time. Only as I grow do I grow into knowing why I wrote it. And so, while I want to say maybe somebody triggered the song, that person is irrelevant and long forgotten."

Musically, the song was the result, as so many of rock's greatest moments are, of an accident. "The demo version was probably done around '89, but it could have been '88. I remember it was the end of the summer and it felt to me that for the whole summer, I was looking for some music to really move me. I had written a lot of songs, but I remember, for instance, going to my aunt's house in Massachusetts, or going places and always playing on someone's piano, looking for that something. When the chords finally did come out, it was because my hand slipped. Maybe I was tired, but that was the mistake I was looking for, because the change sounded so big and it also sounded so serious. Those emotions were what I was looking for, something unlike what I had done before. I almost shivered because I thought, 'Now, this is the big song you've been waiting for.' There was this strange sense. It was like something big was coming. You've never been able to do it before and now you have to do it. It was like a baby coming out. Now that I've had a child, I can sense it was like the feeling that you may not be able to do it or that it may go badly—just an indescribable fear—but also knowing that you can't do anything about it.

The first lyrics came right out, "That old dog has chained you up alright." I'm pretty sure the first verse came out at the same time. Using the word 'damn' wasn't the part that worried me. The part that worried me was the sixteen-bar bridge and the three verses. I thought, *It's not going to fly*. But I also thought it's integral to the story that I felt so emotionally attached to.

"I never show anything until I fully record it. So, I recorded it. I had a reel-to-reel recorder that I had borrowed from a cab driver. It probably took two days of really enjoying recording it, because once the song started to come out and I had the rhythm of the verse and the rhythm of the chorus, the phonetic feeling of the lyrics, then it was really fun to record and write the rest of it. And that's the original demo that sounds like an unwieldy beast, but I loved it. Probably the first person I played it for was my roommate a few months later and she didn't get it. She didn't think it was good. And I played it for another person who didn't get it. He didn't think it was good. But I was attached to it. I thought it was good.

"I made copies of my demo tape, adding as many songs as you can fit on a cassette. I would write my name on it and my phone number, and I always had that demo tape on me. I had no illusions of being a singer. I was a songwriter and that's what I wanted to be.

"So I was working as a coat-check girl in Manhattan on Forty-Sixth Street. A lot of people would talk to me because I was this coat-check girl reading *Anna Karenina*. Steve Martin gave me a big tip. David Bowie asked me how his lipstick looked. Mark Cohn came in one day and he said, 'You have such a beautiful speaking voice. I bet you're an amazing singer.' I said, 'I'm a terrible singer, but I am a songwriter.' So, I handed him my demo tape.

"Maybe two weeks later this guy Ralph Schuckett called me and he said, 'I picked up this demo tape on the desk of JSM Music and I listened to it on my Walkman on the way back to Brooklyn and I think you should be making records.' He said, 'Come meet me at my studio in Brooklyn.'

"So, I put a kitchen knife in my pocket and I went to meet him because I thought he could be a rapist, you never know. He said, 'We just have to clean these demos up a little bit and I think I can get you a deal.'

"That, of course, started a fight. I'm not changing anything. But he did convince me to at least work with him and clean up the demo. We never changed the writing at all, but he made it better, with a simpler percussion line. He tried to make my vocals better because he probably thought I was an awful singer. And that was the demo we sent around. But it ended up being the original demo that people heard and that we worked off when we were doing the album.

"I didn't play the song live until the record was done. The first time was probably a performance for Sony. Then they went to radio and it became a huge radio hit. I'm not sure how long that took. In those days, you really had to hand it to the program directors. Then listeners had to call in. So, I remember doing radio from six in the morning 'til twelve at night. I went to truck stops. I went to McDonald's. I went anywhere that they wanted me to show up. I was asked to open for Neil Young and I wanted to open for Neil Young, but it didn't happen. So, then I went out on tour with my band. The first gig I had was at the Montreux Jazz Festival. I guess they wanted me to get my feet wet in Europe. Then I played First Avenue in Minneapolis and Toad's Place in New Haven, Symphony Space in New York.

"The song was going up the charts, because I remember getting faxes from Donnie Ienner, head of Sony Music. At shows, my encore was usually 'I Want You,' and 'Damn' was the song just before the encore, because I wanted people to stick around for it. I didn't want people to leave right after hearing it. It's such a hard song to sing, but I've always loved singing it."

Hawkins made three albums for Columbia. The second, *Whaler*, contained the hit "As I Lay Me Down," which, like *Tongues and Tails*, sold over five hundred thousand copies in America. Her last Columbia album was *Timbre* in 1999; since then she's released her own material on her Trumpet Swan label.

"These days, I started writing my own show, and I also recorded the songs and kept writing songs for a new album. I started looking for a producer, then I finally just recorded them in Brooklyn and I love what I have. I have a play that I'm three years into working on, and I have an album that I haven't released, because I didn't want another album to go nowhere like *The Crossing* [2012]. So, slowly but surely, I now have a team. What's also really been great is doing solo shows. That was frightening but so good for me, because even though I practiced all those years to be a drummer, I'm not really in my mind a good musician or a good singer. And so, to get up there alone was scary, but I've been doing that and I really got a lot out of it. All these things have led to a really good point now where it seems like I'm going to get a beautiful release for the album in Europe and maybe a deal so it can come out here.

"It's funny, I always thought of myself as wanting to write great songs. I still dream of making a connection based on writing a great song. And 'Damn, I Wish I Was Your Lover' is my anthem. It's my reason for being. So is 'As I Lay Me Down.' Those songs became the Sophie B. Hawkins classics. There are other songs that I really love that I wish would go somewhere, but you can't hope for that kind of support. Well, you can hope for it. I tried so long to make things happen. And then when I finally just observed what was going on, I said, 'I could do it myself.'

❧

Hawkins's first album in over ten years, Free Myself, *was released in 2023 by Lightyear Entertainment.*

Todd Thomas / Arrested Development (2001)

"Tennessee"

Todd Thomas (aka Speech) founded Arrested Development in Atlanta after first experimenting with gangsta rap. "But that turned out not to really be our style," he said. He and cofounder Headliner did most of the work on the album in their respective bedrooms, using a sampler and a drum machine. "And then we would do some shows in clubs—open mics and battle-of-the-bands types of thing, where we didn't have live instrumentation but we would come in with our sampler and a sound man."

According to Speech, the group, which eventually expanded to six members, evolved organically. "I was looking more for image and vibes than musicianship. It totally happened by accident. We were at a show once where I met Dionne Farris and her fiancé at the time. We got booed that night, and they happened to be backstage encouraging us, and I looked at his dreads and I looked at her vibe and I was like, man, why don't you join us? And they said they would."

Farris was the lead voice of "Tennessee," their first single. " 'Tennessee' was the last song I wrote before we got signed. We had shopped for a label deal for over three years with no success. Then Chrysalis wanted to do a single deal with 'Mr. Wendell' on the A side and a song called 'Natural' on side B. Right about that time my brother and my grandmother died within a week of each other. The last place I saw both of them was in the state of Tennessee. So, I wrote the song 'Tennessee,' dedicated to my brother and grandmother. The label was ready to release 'Mr. Wendell,' but I said this is something I just wrote and I really feel emotionally attached to the song and want to put it out first. Luckily, EMI liked it.

Figure 33. Arrested Development, 2018. Photo: Madison Colt Studios, Wikimedia Commons, CC BY-SA 4.0.

"We did a tour of Black colleges and no one came to see us. We would be in these huge auditoriums. The curtain would open and there would be five people in the audience, so we would invite them onstage with us. Those early shows definitely helped to refine me as a musician and why I like to do it. If you don't get booed a lot in the beginning you might do it for the wrong reasons. I do it because I love music.

"At first, we were a little nervous because many of the fans were older Black people. Even when our first single was released, most of the first buyers of it were older people. So, we were worried because we just felt like the hip-hop community wasn't going to embrace this. But we were wrong. They definitely wound up embracing us. I didn't realize this until one night in Charlotte. We'd been touring the South in a twelve-seat van with a U-Haul in the back. When we pulled up to the club, I saw there was a line around the block. I asked my road manager, who was also the driver, 'Who else is performing tonight?' She said, it's just us. I said, 'Wow.' That's when it hit me, when I realized the line was for us.

"'Tennessee' hit the number one on the R&B chart and crossed over into the pop top ten. Being successful definitely put on a whole lot of pressure because the band was so communally oriented. People joined the band just because of the vibe of the music. What happened once the money and fame got involved was that everyone wanted their own manager. Everyone felt that they weren't being represented and partially that was true. We were all naïve as to how the business should go, so there were a lot of contracts done by mistake and a lot of agreements that weren't the best for myself and everyone else included. So everyone got management, everyone got lawyers, and everything got very complicated."

Thomas has continued to tour and record, both with Arrested Development and as a solo artist. The song "Tennessee" was among the best reviewed of the year, hitting the top ten in the US and charting around the world.

Travon Potts (2001)

"Angel of Mine"

Good old R&B got a fresh face in the rap revolution, as collaborators upon collaborations and sample upon sample reduced the songwriting pie to a veritable sliver. Still, great groups and great voices managed to break through the clutter with songs that scaled the pop and R&B charts. Travon Potts (Monica) was a beneficiary of this new world.

"I'd studied classical music since the age of three," Potts said. "By age twelve I started playing for my church's youth choir. In high school, I was introduced to one of the creative directors at a publishing company. She took an interest in me from hearing me play and I recorded some demos. I wound up getting my first publishing deal right after graduating from high school, for a whopping $17,000 a year. I knew at this point I was on my way to becoming like my music idols.

"In about two years I was dropped from my publishing deal and picked up by Motown music publishing. I had not written any hit songs at that point, but I felt that being with Motown meant that every song I wrote would be viewed as a hit and Whitney Houston would be knocking on my door. I also felt that if I wrote about five or six songs a year, that would be five or six hits. My publishing representative urged me to be a tad more prolific, but I felt that was unnecessary.

"In a year, I was on probation with Motown because of my low song output and lack of song placements on commercially released CDs. I was able to get a few remix gigs here and there to pay off some of the debt I was mounting. At this point Polygram bought Motown. My publishing rep survived the merger and somehow had enough belief in my raw talent not to drop me. To motivate me she figured out a way to advance me money to purchase some studio equipment to add to the equipment I already owned.

"One day I got a call from an old friend, who told me that the popular producer Rhett Lawrence had an opening for a staff writer/producer. I had a meeting with Rhett and in a week, I moved my small studio into one of his studio rooms and his engineers integrated my small setup into a computer program called Pro Tools. In his studio, I cranked out about two to three tracks a day, and with each one he became more and more impressed.

"One particular track I liked I took to Rhett. He listened to it in passing and didn't say much more about it. But I didn't give up on the track. I played it for him again in a different setting and ironically he loved it this time. He went into my studio room and asked me to set the track up to be played over and over as he wrote lyrical ideas. He was stumped on lyrics for the second verse and bridge so I wrote those parts. When we finished 'Angel of Mine,' we sent it to Tamia. I don't think it even got to Tamia. Whoever intercepted it didn't like it and thought it wasn't a hit. So, we sent it to Clive Davis as a long shot for Monica, and the next day he called us and put the song on hold. Six months after Clive's hold a popular act from England named Eternal came to town with their manager. They

Figure 34. Travon Potts. Photo: Brandon Williams, provided courtesy of Travon Potts.

heard the song and loved it. Two days later we recorded and produced it, and the following week it entered the European charts at number five.

"Clive still wanted the song but he wanted Rodney Jerkins to produce it here in the States. Knowing Rodney is not cheap told us just how interested Clive was in the song being a single. We made calls and found out it was going to be the second single on the album, but I was not sure until I saw ads for it in the trades.

"I don't remember how long it took to go to number one, but I remember it entered at number eighty-five. I thought that was too low for it to go to number one. It's a ballad, so I thought it would move slowly, but it seemed like it took forever. But more and more the video kept being shown, and more and more my family would call and tell me they saw it. And pretty soon I started hearing it over and over on the radio, which was cool, because when I would look over at other people in their cars, they were bopping to it. It wound up being number one for four weeks on the Billboard charts! But it only started to sink in that it was a hit when I met Jam and Lewis and LA and Babyface for the first time.

"Before this, my only other big hit was a song called 'It's About Time,' which was a top five R&B single for a Chicago-based group named Public Announcement. Needless to say, 'It's About Time' was one of the biggest songs of the year in Chicago. I met the program director at WGCI at the group's record release party, and after having such a big hit he asked me to come speak on a panel at WGCI's conference. I thought the panels would be led by a bunch of midlevel writers like myself. Little did I know that Jam and Lewis and LA and Babyface would be there. This program director did not know I wrote 'Angel of Mine' until he saw my discography. Then he made it a point to make sure everybody at the conference knew I wrote that song. What was weird was that Jam and Lewis and LA and Babyface, the two songwriting teams that are the reason why I even wanted to write and produce, congratulated me on the success of the song. I mean, they even came up and shook my hand. That's when I started thinking to myself, 'Wow, this must be a hit!'"

A fantastically popular single, "Angel of Mine" was first recorded by the British group Eternal, where it hit the top ten in the UK, Scotland, Sweden, and Norway. In 1998, Monica's cover went to number one in the US for four weeks, was certified Gold in Australia, and hit the top five in Canada.

Shelly Peiken (2018)

"What a Girl Wants"

Overcoming the glumness of the pop star males of punk and grunge, Madonna's minions came to dominate if not define the female pop landscape of the nineties, with show-stopping stage antics and manufactured songs set to manufactured beats. Many, if not most of these songs and beats come from the stable of Karl Martin Sandberg (aka Max Martin), the Swedish pop tycoon who started scripting top ten hits in the US as far back as the Backstreet Boys, with his then-partner Denniz PoP: a combination of Abbaesque pop, eighties rock, and nineties R&B.

Following Disney grads NSYNC to the spotlight, seventeen-year old ex-Mouseketeer Britney Spears was the lucky recipient of Martin's "Baby One More Time," which launched her career, after the group TLC turned it down. (Karma returned the favor when Spears passed on Rihanna's career-making "Umbrella.") With her bad girl persona and lavish concerts straight out of the Madonna playbook, Spears reigned for the next ten years in mortal opposition to fellow Mouseketeer Christina Aguilera, who modeled her vocal approach more along the lines of Mariah Carey, with one of her biggest hits scripted by the veteran songwriter Shelly Peiken.

For most songwriters, achieving the vaunted pinnacle of a number one single on the Billboard Hot 100 chart would represent a breakout moment, a professional coming of age, leading to a long-awaited hot streak of unprecedented visibility. For Shelly Peiken, who'd been placing songs with major artists like Celine Dion, Brandy, Cher, and Britney Spears for twenty years, the feeling she got when "What a Girl Wants," the song she wrote with Guy Roche for Christina Aguilera, peaked at number one in January 2000, was more like "the universe saved that little cherry on top for me.

"I've got to tell you," she added, "in the nineties and the two thousands lots of records went platinum. I'm sitting here in my office and I've got platinum records all over my wall. Lots of records went platinum and many of them went double and triple platinum, because there wasn't any other way to hear the music than to buy it."

This situation has changed dramatically in the new century, and, for songwriters, not for the better. "What really changed things is when Napster came about," says Peiken, who is at the forefront these days of the fight to get songwriters their proper rewards. "Then iTunes thought, well, we're going to put a Band-Aid on it. We're going to sell tracks for ninety-nine cents. The album format disappeared because everybody was listening à la carte. In the early days, whatever you bought, whether it was a single or an album, had to be a physical copy. Right now, there's no physical copy. I used to make a really nice living from songs that were album cuts that nobody ever heard on the radio. It didn't have to have a big hit. Publishers were signing writers because they could recoup from album sales, but there aren't any more album sales. The only thing you can make money from is airplay. Fortunately, there are so many more

Figure 35. Shelly Peiken, 2005. Photo: Shelly Peiken, Wikimedia Commons, CC BY-SA 3.0.

stations than there were twenty years ago. So, when you have a hit, it's played more repetitively because people are more connected to the familiar. On the other hand, it might not be a copyright that you're going to remember in two years, because everything is coming and going so much faster right now."

Peiken's two biggest hits are a case in point. The Aguilera title (as well as her part in the team that wrote her next number one song, "Come on Over Baby") doesn't get licensed as often as her other major hit, "Bitch," by Meredith Brooks, which peaked at number two in the summer of 1997—kept out of the number one slot by Puff Daddy's "I'll Be Missing You."

The inception of "What a Girl Wants" came about on an otherwise ordinary day. "My friend Todd Chapman had called me to come over to his house in North Hollywood. He said Ron Fair, an a&r guy at BMG, wanted to make a record with this girl. She was an ex-Mouseketeer. He was collecting material for her first album. He said, why don't I send her over and you can see how compatible you are? So, Todd called me to come over and meet her. She wasn't glamorous. She was very shy and quiet. We worked with her for a couple of weeks and she tried her voice out on some songs. Then I went to work with my friend Guy (Roche) and we wrote the song called 'What a Girl Needs,' and we sent it to Ron. It was sort of like cheating on Todd, but I mean, you can't worry about that.

"Ron asked me to switch the title to 'What a Girl Wants.' The demo we sent over was way different from the single. First of all, it wasn't Christina singing it. We hired somebody. It was slow and plodding and, honestly, I can't believe that Ron heard through it. They sped it up when she cut it. He wanted it immediately but we probably thought about it for a week before letting him have it, because she wasn't really anybody. Right now, it's almost impossible to get a song cut unless you write it with the artist. Back then we had choices, so we probably waited. They took it right away. They didn't say, well, we've got to hold on to it for six months before we decide. But honestly, everything's on hold until the album comes out.

"I didn't go to the studio on that one and it's always sort of been a little thorn in my side. I think I would have liked to be there. Very often I am at the studio when somebody's cutting my song. That's half of the thrill. Some producers might think it can be a distraction. They tell you not to come or just don't tell you to come. I could have said, you know what, I wrote the song. I'm coming. I do remember being a little sore about not being there.

Shelly Peiken (2018) | 265

"I think 'Genie in a Bottle' was already out when they told us the next single is going to be 'What a Girl Wants.' Sometimes you just don't even listen when people say that because half the time it's not like they're lying. But there's just no way they can tell right then because so many things can happen.

"Christina and I didn't party together. We didn't go out to dinner. But we wrote a couple of times together and I took her home a couple of times. Or if she would perform at a concert, I'd see her backstage very often and give her hugs. She was always very sweet. But she didn't cut any more of my songs after the first album. Sometimes I think artists want to distance themselves from the cluster of the first stuff that they recorded. She probably felt like she was really young and she wanted to get into more sophisticated stuff. Often artists like to try out new people and move on to new producers.

"When you're on an album that's on its way to selling eight million copies, you never realize it right away. You know it's showing signs of doing well, but you try not to jinx it. It's always exciting when you have a hit going up the charts. 'What a Girl Wants' was exciting because it went number one. I was reading my daughter *Winnie the Pooh* when I got the call that we went number one. As much as I wanted to jump up and down and scream, as a mother, knowing what's most important in life, I couldn't interrupt story time. I finished reading, tucked her under the covers, and sat in the rocker in the dark like I did every night until I was sure she was sleeping. And then I left the room, closed the door gently, and jumped up and down in the hallway. I still couldn't scream because that would wake her up. That was the extent of my celebration. And that was enough."

∽

Shelly Peiken has had songs recorded by Celine Dion, NSYNC, Cher, Bonnie Tyler, the Backstreet Boys, Joe Cocker, Taylor Dayne, Idina Menzel, Meredith Brooks, Lisa Loeb, Selena Gomez, Natalie Cole, Lulu, the Pretenders, and many others. Her book, Confessions of a Serial Songwriter, *came out in 2016 and an album of her own songs,* 2.0 etc. . . , *in 2020.*

Tom Higgenson / Plain White T's (2020)

"Hey There Delilah"

Although a number of music fans probably regarded the Billboard Hot 100 after the year 2000 with the equivalent of an asterisk, the appearance of "Hey There Delilah" by the Illinois power punk outfit Plain White T's in the number one slot is a significant post–rock era milestone. For one thing, stretching the definition of rock, in 2016, it was only the fourth single by an American rock band to reach that peak since the year 2000. The first, "Butterfly" by Crazy Town, from 2001, is actually rap, influenced more by the Beastie Boys than the Beatles. The other two songs are from establishment favorites Maroon 5. Rising to number one just a few weeks before the Plain White T's track, was the highly sophisticated R&B influenced "Makes Me Wonder," in which lead singer Adam Levine can be seen sporting a bow tie. That particular song shot out of nowhere to number one from the Adult Pop chart. In 2011, the slightly more credible rocker, "Moves Like Jagger," with a guest vocal by Christina Aguilera, benefited greatly from the two stars' (over)exposure on the TV singing contest *The Voice*.

Spare, poignant, and catchy, by every measure "Hey There Delilah" was the more prominent achievement, taking over a year from its release to crash through the barriers erected by radio against rock music at this juncture. Written about a real Delilah (DiCrescenzo), an American athlete, who attended the Grammy Awards on writer Tom Higgenson's tab the year the song was nominated, the song obviously did not break down any of those barriers for other rock bands. The biggest coup the song's success afforded the band was an appearance on *Sesame Street*. "It's a dream," Higgenson acknowledged. "There's going to be some Muppet singing it on the screen."

As for "Delilah," it is a popular misconception that the track star Delilah DiCrescenzo was responsible for the outsized success of the tune bearing her first name. While it's true that DiCrescenzo was the direct inspiration for the song when Higgenson sat down to write it in 2003, shortly after meeting her, the tune's slow and winding path to number one, in 2007, was a direct result of the now most antiquated of social media platforms Myspace!

"It was the third single off the album," Higgenson recalled. "We released 'All That We Needed' and 'Take Me Away' on this little sampler. Back in the day, you would pass around these free samplers from the label, just to try to get people aware of who the hell you are, that we're on tour, just sweating our butts off and doing anything we can to get people to come watch us. We made a video for 'Take Me Away,' which was the label's choice for first single, and it was on Fuse and MTV, too. That stuff was really big for us at the time. So, then it came down to what video should we make next. We put 'Hey There Delilah' up on our Myspace profile page with five or six other songs from the album. And we literally asked our fans what song should we do for our next video? Ninety-six percent of the people voted for 'Hey There Delilah.' So, it was like, okay, the fans have spoken."

Higgenson credits Myspace for kick-starting (so to speak) their career. "Tom from Myspace actually saw us play on a Warped tour and he made us one of the first bands to ever be featured on the front page. This was back when Myspace was really a tastemaker kind of site. At one point, 'Hey There Delilah' was everybody's profile song. On my feed, every third page you'd visit, 'Hey There Delilah' would start playing because everybody was loving that song."

In that sense, the song was a success even before it ever reached the Billboard charts early in 2007. Being on the road almost continually for several years, the members of the band may have been the last to realize they had a certified hit on their hands.

"There was this one moment when we played Summerfest in Milwaukee," Higgenson said. "We're from Chicago. So, we played Summerfest a bunch of times leading up to it, but that summer of 2007, when 'Delilah' was blowing up on the radio, we were backstage all day. We sound checked and then we just sat back until it was time to play. When we went onstage, there were like ten thousand people out there and we kind of had

268 | They're Playing My Song

Figure 36. Tom Higgenson, 2015. Photo: Justin Higuchi, Wikimedia Commons, CC BY 2.0.

a movie moment, like, 'What the hell are all these people doing here? I thought we were last.' And then I realized, that's the power of having a hit song on the radio. That was definitely the moment of going from a local band playing the side stage at Summerfest to headlining one of the main stages and having ridiculous crowds. For ten years, we were grinding it out, right? It was just like every tour would get a little better. Every album would do a little better. It was just this slow and steady grind. And then obviously with 'Delilah,' once that hit, it was like, okay, skyrocket, right? That song definitely made a lot of dreams come true.

"After meeting Delilah, I was like, well, all right, I've got to write a song for this girl," said Higgenson. "Maybe I can use this one guitar part I had. And I literally started playing it. The first verse just poured out exactly as it is, all the way through to the chorus. I didn't really know the girl, you know? So, it was like, what's it like in New York City / Tonight, you look so pretty. And then the second verse—and that's all I had. But the thing is, I knew it was good. I was like, wow, this is really nice. This feels good. Now I'm gonna have to write the whole song. I took my time, over the next six months. There was no rush. It wasn't like we were going into the studio tomorrow or anything. Over the next six months, I'm taking a shower thinking about the song, or I'm sitting around with the guitar, thinking about the song. I just had to make up the rest of it. If I was in this long-distance relationship with somebody, what would I want to say? What would those emotions be? During that whole time, I was also writing the rest of the album. But most songs, I'd spend a day or two and that's it. But because I felt those lyrics were so special, I really had to take my time to make it the perfect story.

"I demoed the whole thing myself on a buddy of mine's digital eight-track recorder. I played everything myself in the basement. I did about ten songs in one day. Just demoing them out real quick. The final song I demoed was 'Hey There Delilah.' By the time I got to that song, after singing nine other songs worth of vocals and harmonies, my voice was just trashed. But in a way, the way I sang fit the song really nicely. It added to the earnestness of it. But I hadn't written all of the bridge yet. When I got to the last line, I had to hum the melody. That's the demo I played for the band, and our manager and everybody was like, 'Dude, that's a great song.'

"When we recorded the song in the studio, everybody had such demo-itis for the way I sang it on the demo. We wanted it to have that same raspy quality. So, when it came time to do the vocal, we were actually sleeping in the studio when we were making the record. After I woke up, I didn't have any coffee, and I did like seven passes without warming up or doing anything. I listen to that recording now and I'm like, this vocal is crazy, but again, I think that added to the sincerity.

"I don't remember when we first played it live. Like I said, the song was written over the course of 2003. We recorded the album in the spring of 2004, and it came out in January of 2005. So, technically there may have been some shows between us recording it and the time it came out, where we may have played it, but honestly, I don't think so because we were still pushing our other two albums. When the album came out, I don't think it was even in the set list right off the bat. 'Cause it was like a slow acoustic song. We usually play the rocking fun songs. We were still playing real small venues where it was, let's turn it up louder so we can get the kids to dance. So 'Delilah' was kind of an afterthought for the live shows.

"On the *All That We Needed* album, it was just an acoustic and vocal, exactly the way I demoed it. When it came time to do the video, we said, okay, let's produce it up a little bit. That's when we went in with Sean O'Keefe, a Chicago producer who did Fall Out Boy. We'd always wanted to do stuff with him. So, we added some strings and a very subtle organ in the chorus and a couple of harmonies and stuff.

"We'd been on the road since 2001, basically nonstop, playing three hundred shows a year. Anytime we weren't playing shows, it was either Christmas or we were in the studio, making the next record. Even when 'Delilah' was slowly climbing the charts, we already kind of knew this song was connecting with people. It was never in doubt. Because it had already been tried and tested. It was all an organic build. We went to play in the UK and the record was not even available there. And the entire crowd would be singing along. It was like every step of the way the song almost did it by itself. We just had to be the ones to go and play it. And then we were able to follow it up with '1, 2, 3, 4' and 'Rhythm of Love,' so for a good five years it was amazing. We were working our asses off but seeing the rewards for it.

"I have all these songwriter friends and their big thing is, this guy wrote, 'Hey There Delilah' by himself—because hit songs these days are cowritten by like eleven people. So, all my songwriter buddies are like, 'Dude, that's awesome,' and they're jealous. I'm sure if I wanted to I'd never have to work a day in my life, and I'd probably be okay. But that's not why I'm here. I love what I do. I'm writing almost every day and I started my own record label. I've got artists that I'm writing with and producing. So yeah, it's like, even if I had all the money in the world, I'd still be doing exactly what I'm doing."

∾

Plain White T's most recent album, Plain White T's, *was released in 2023. "Hey There Delilah" hit the top ten in Canada, Croatia, the Czech Republic, Germany, Ireland, the Netherlands, New Zealand, Scotland, Slovakia, Switzerland, the UK, and the US.*

Stephan Moccio (2015)

"Wrecking Ball"

The thing that every songwriter dreams of is what is known in the trade as "a window of opportunity." That period of time when it seems like every song you write is cut, every cut you deliver is a single, and every single released under your name soars effortlessly up the charts. It's when all the previously closed doors slide open, the phone rings off the hook (or buzzes off your belt or in the folds of your briefcase), and every executive assistant knows your name. The lucky ones find that "window" for a few months, maybe once or twice in a lifetime. As cowriter of Celine Dion's "Your Day Has Come" in 2002, the Miley Cyrus mega-smash "Wrecking Ball" in 2013, and the monstrous hit for the Weeknd from *Fifty Shades of Grey*, "Earned It," in 2014, Canadian-born composer Stephan Moccio's "window of opportunity" has lasted more than ten years.

Not that his last two credits haven't opened it another mile wider. "The phone is ringing off the hook," Moccio agreed. "I mean the president of music at Universal Pictures took a meeting with me. I would say a big part of the meeting was because I was the cowriter on 'Wrecking Ball.' So he was interested to see what I could do for *Fifty Shades of Grey*, because he was a fan of that song. And 'Earned It' has been played more times on radio than 'Wrecking Ball' ever was. At one point I think we had thirty-six thousand spins a week in the US alone. Now, with the success of 'Earned It,' often I'm getting asked to write big movie songs or end credits for films. I've gotten to know all heads at all the major studios and that's been an extraordinary thing. I spent the last eight months coproducing the Weeknd's album and that album is number one around the world. I'm working on three movies now. The only one I can talk about is the new

Julia Roberts film, *The Secret in Their Eyes*, in which I cowrote a song with this girl Maty Noyes. I'm consumed with producing Maty's album right now because I really believe the music that we're creating together is special and I hope people will react to it.

"I never got into music to make money. That's probably the best lesson my parents taught me: Do what you love and the money will follow. At one point, I was broke. But I knew come hell or high water that one day people would hear my melodies; I knew they were that good. Part of the reason for my success in music is because I'm a hard worker, I'm disciplined. I don't take it for granted. I love music. I'm always trying to write a greater song than my last song. And whether that's the case or not it doesn't matter. It's my goal every time. That's what keeps me honest."

That being said, his association with the notorious *Fifty Shades of Grey* and the probably even more notorious Miley Cyrus has not escaped his attention. "It's kind of ironic," he admits. "Because I'm a guy who

Figure 37. Stephan Moccio. Photo: Frank W. Ockenfels III, provided courtesy of Stephan Moccio.

fundamentally just composes beautiful songs and beautiful music. I'm really a classical writer."

As far as "Wrecking Ball" goes, "Sacha, MoZella, and myself did the entire song in one day. I remember it was September 24th, 2012. We came together as three writers unknown to each other, put together by our publishing companies basically to write a song for Beyoncé. That's what got us in the room. But you just can't force that stuff. When we started writing the song, we thought maybe this is not for Beyoncé. None of the regular studios were available, so Sacha's manager ended up finding us a Montessori school, with a white piano. It was just the most unique situation in terms of where to write a song. I guess, a great song could be written anywhere, if it's meant to be."

MoZella performing "Wrecking Ball" at the ASCAP Pop Awards. That's Stephan on piano. "When you're in a situation like that, the first thing you do is say hello to people and chat, but within five or ten minutes of meeting each other, things became highly charged. MoZella was extremely emotional that day. She was very frail because she had broken off her wedding during that week. She almost didn't end up making the session. 'Wrecking Ball' in every way is about MoZella's toxic relationship and then the courage to say, 'I can't go through with this.' So here we are, Sacha and I holding this girl together who was just very emotional, trying to comfort her.

"I don't write lyrics, but I remember we all wanted a strong metaphor as a title and we were just throwing out words. And I remember kind of shyly putting up my hand and saying, 'What about "Wrecking Ball"?' And Sacha went, 'Yeah, "Wrecking Ball," that sounds good.' And MoZella kind of ran with that. It's when she got the line, 'I came in like a wrecking ball.' It was real collaborative. Sacha is a great pianist, so he started off on keyboards and then for some reason he surrendered the piano to me for the rest of the session. MoZella worked with lyrics and melodies while I was at the piano. We demoed it the following day and in a couple of hours we had this beautiful piano vocal demo.

"At one point in the writing session MoZella said, 'I know Miley Cyrus well enough; do you mind if I play it for her?' Of course, Sacha and I are, 'Sure not a problem, it would be great.' And then MoZella a few weeks later ended up playing it for Miley Cyrus. I don't know all the details, but I know MoZella wanted to play it for Miley on a Sunday, because she said, 'If I'm going to get Miley's attention, the best way to get Miley's attention is on a Sunday.' I respect that. There is a psychology sometimes about playing a song for an artist at the right time. If you play it at the wrong time, it can be the best song in the world, but it won't be heard because the artist is not receptive to it. But Miley was really excited about it.

"I don't know Miley at all, so I don't like to say things on her behalf. However, we all know that she was in a relationship with Liam [Hemsworth] at the time and it was clearly public. So she obviously related to the lyric. Miley thought that Luke, being Dr. Luke, should be the producer. And he ran with it, along with his partner, Henry Walters [Cirkut]. They produced the song, so that's when their names came on it as writers. They didn't change the song at all, but they did produce it brilliantly. I mean, if you were to hear the demo, the demo is almost verbatim to the sonics of the song they did. The arrangement was exactly the same key, same tempo, everything.

"We wrote it on September 24th and her vocal was already recorded by December. Within that eight- to ten-week period everyone was telling us how amazing the song was, how amazing it sounded. I didn't really get a chance to hear it until it was released, except once over the phone. Meanwhile, the record company kept on saying, ' "Wrecking Ball" is such a big, big record and we think it's going to be the next single.' And lo and behold, she dropped it by surprise when she did her controversial performance at the MVAs in August 2013. That night it went to the world and became the number one single on iTunes.

"It's one of those global songs that you always wish you were a part of. Luckily, I've been a part of a few of those now. But then when it happens, you try not to pay too much attention to it, because you can drive yourself mental. But I'd be lying if I didn't say we weren't calling people just checking to see the amount of spins it got on radio, because that also dictates chart position. I did kind of check in on that every few days.

"But it's incredible, when you have a song like 'Wrecking Ball' that becomes a social movement. Clearly, the video had a lot to do with it, as well. It was a controversial video. I know everyone has an opinion about it, love it or loathe it. We live in that kind of age, where it affects, for better for worse, the experience of the song. The visual's such a big part and sometimes who's featured on the song is a big part. There's a lot of contributing factors that affect whether a song is going to be heard by the masses. Sadly, as much as I want to believe it, it's not just about the fact that the song's a great song. I mean, there are a lot of great songs that we don't hear, because they just haven't been given that platform.

Stephan Moccio (2015) | 275

"And 'Wrecking Ball,' in my humble opinion, is a great song. If you hear it stripped down to vocal and piano, it's a classical piece of music in a lot of ways. There's a lot of classical influence in it. And when you hear the chordal structure, it's completely there. The sentiment couldn't be more genuine, because we have MoZella, who's pouring her heart and soul out, she's crying half the day. I believe we genuinely wrote a great song with blood, sweat, and tears. We worked for it. However, we were also given the platform that only an artist like Miley could give us, with everything that was going on in her life at the same time just hitting. It all hit at the right time."

Since 2020, Moccio has written and produced thirty-four singles and five solo albums. Since 2016, his protégé, Maty Noyes, has released two EPs and one full-length album. Her best-selling single was her second, "In My Mind," which went to number forty-seven in Czechoslovakia.

Kevin Kadish (2018)

"All About That Bass"

When I first met Kevin Kadish, back before the turn of the twenty-first century, he was toiling in the lower depths of the music business, in the cubicle across the hall from me as an intern at BMG. "I had a record deal at the time," he said, "and I was still doing data entry."

A few years later, when I interviewed him for my book *Working Musicians: Defining Moments from the Road, the Studio, and the Stage*, he was just glimpsing a light at the end of his long personal tunnel toward making a living in music. "I'd have to say that the hardest things to deal with in the music business are all the false promises," he said at the time. "People like to hype you up using words like 'genius' and 'smash,' but frankly these words get to be so overused that after a while they don't really mean anything." After being in and out of bands, and in and out of performing as a solo artist, he was about to become a staff songwriter in Matt Serletic's (Matchbox 20) stable. But it would mean giving up his dream of performing. "I've spent the last four years of my life basically not working so that I could focus on writing songs and honing my craft," he said. "Total dedication is what it takes to make it as a working musician. At the same time, I definitely knew my main priority at that point had to be to get out of debt."

"There are some people who have hits for five years straight and just sort of relax," he said recently. "But for me, it's like every three to five years I'd have a single that sustained me for those three to five years. This single will sustain me for the rest of my life. The single he was talking about was "All About That Bass," one of the top songs of 2014 and a

277

worldwide smash. It came about as the product of a typical workday for a working songwriter.

"I'd have meetings two or three times a week, depending on my schedule," said Kadish. Trainor's publisher had asked Kadish if he would meet with this unknown teenager. Kadish wanted to hear some of her songs first. "Her songs were okay, but I loved her voice." It was not the ditsy Shirelles-meet-Salt-N-Pepa growl you hear on the hit. "If you heard the stuff she did before me, it did not sound like that," Kadish said. "But she did have that swagger and she did have the patois. So, I said, yeah, I'll do a day with her."

It was a day that changed his life.

"We talked for a long time about how we both loved the music from that era. It's rare to find someone who's nineteen who likes fifties music. I had wanted to make a fifties record for probably three years before I ever met her, but nobody really cared to do it. I had the idea of the drum beat and I had a list of titles. I told her the title and she started singing, 'I'm all about that bass,' and I went, 'no treble.' We were off to the races. I think we wrote it in two hours before we started tracking vocals.

"We wrote it in July 2013. Her publisher pitched it to Epic Records. I heard that [label president] L. A. Reid liked it in November, but I didn't know anything else besides that. In February, Meghan called me. She said, 'Are you sitting down? L. A. Reid signed me on the spot for our song and basically wants to release your track and send it to radio.'

"I was like, *that's awesome.* I definitely knew the song was something special because I played it for my wife and my wife was like, 'Can I send it to my sister?' I played it for my sister and she's like, 'Can I send it to my friends?' They never do that, so now I know that if they actually like one of my songs, it's gonna be a good one.

"We started working on her album in February and didn't finish it until September. I didn't work on anything else for six months. My entire life was that record. Soon after the single came out, when Justin Bieber covered it, we knew something weird was going on. She was number one on iTunes and still in the twenties or thirties at radio. The video was a really big part of what broke it. It was very polarizing. This tastemaker music blog, *The Idolator*, did a premiere and they said it got the most views for any artist they ever had. In the meantime, we were writing her album every day and then we get a call. *Entertainment Tonight* wants to come to your studio to interview Meghan. I'm like, *What?* The producer

Figure 38. Kevin Kadish, 2010. Photo: Maxman732, Wikimedia Commons, CC0 1.0.

walks into the room and he says, 'Meghan's song just went to number two on the Billboard Hot 100.' And she started crying.

"All About That Bass" dislodged Taylor Swift's "Shake It Off" from the top of the Hot 100 on September 20, 2014, and stayed for eight weeks. Trainor's album went to number one on January 31, 2015, knocking off Swift's *1989*. "Swift is a size 2, but Trainor can shake it, shake it like she's supposed to.

"There were so many special moments. The whole experience was surreal. Honestly, it still feels surreal today. The first time I saw Meghan perform it live was when she was on tour in Nashville. I was blown away. Everyone knew every word. I kept checking every week and when it stayed number one, I would be baffled but excited. You've got to understand—we were battling head to head with Taylor Swift! The album going number one was pretty amazing, too.

"The Grammy nominations were just mind blowing. I know how hard it is to get a nomination in the big four categories, and we actually got two. I remember the Record of the Year announcement came first, and I was super grateful. But when the Song of the Year nomination came in,

I was in my studio and I kind of lost it. I walked over to my house, like seventy-five feet away, and my wife and I just hugged. It was the greatest honor of my career. Better than the sales, better than the airplay. It was recognition from my peers and the industry heavy hitters on the Grammy committee that I created one of the best pieces of music that year. I was very proud to be recognized for that.

"I talked to a friend in publishing and he said, 'It's not like you wrote the fourth single on Demi Lovato's third record. You wrote a song that changed the way little girls look at themselves in the mirror. This song will be a game changer for you.'

"What I've learned is that you can't predict anything when you release a record. No matter how much the label loves it and spends money on it and you believe the song is a hit and everyone's telling you it's a hit, if the public doesn't react to it, none of it matters. Even if you get the science down of how to do it again, you still can't predict it's going to do the same thing. There's a disconnect because songwriters have no control beyond the writing. I may think the song is something special and think it's a hit but if the label doesn't see it, or the right artist doesn't cut it, nothing comes to fruition. So, seeing something come to fruition was really an interesting experience. I'd had successes and failures with other artists but this was different. This was like being strapped to a rocket ship.

"I've been doing this for a long time so I knew how to deal with it. I think if this happened when I was younger, it would have been different. I'm just happy to have been on the ride for a minute. And I'm happy that I'll be able to make music for the rest of my life."

Other notable songs by Kevin Kadish: "Geek in the Pink" by Jason Mraz, number one country hit "Whiskey Glasses" by Morgan Wallen, and "Stuck" by Stacie Orrico, which hit the top ten in Australia, Germany, Ireland, Japan, the Netherlands, New Zealand, Sweden, Switzerland, and the UK.

Index of Song Titles

1, 2, 3, 4, 271
4th of July, The, ix, 2, 242, 243, 245–247
59th Street Bridge Song, 112
88 Lines About 44 Women, vii, 188, 191, 192, 195

Across the Universe, 224
Aftermath, 144
Age of Aquarius, 132
Ain't No Mountain High Enough, 123, 124
Ain't Nothing Like the Real Thing, 125
Alice in Wonderland, 37
All About That Bass, ix, 277, 279
All Mine, 8
All That We Needed, 271
America, 113
American Pie, vii, 143–145
American Tune, 114
Angel from Montgomery, 167
Angel of Mine, ix, 261, 262
Annie Had a Baby, 45, 51, 102
Annie's Aunt Fanny, 46
Another Day in Paradise, 229
Anyway, Anyhow, Anywhere, 90
Apache, 239

Are You Lonesome Tonight, 166
As I Lay Me Down, 255, 256
At the Hop, 42
At the Zoo, 113

Babe in Arms, 64
Baby Don't Do It, 45
Baby One More Time, 263
Bach, Beethoven, Mozart and Me, 63
Back Room Blood', 54
Backwater Blues, 144
Ball of Confusion, 123
Ballad of the Cuban Invasion, 60
Beehive State, 165
Bells, The, 126
Betcha, By Golly, Wow, 155
Bette Davis Eyes, 55
Big Money, 198
Bitch, 265
Blue Moon, 8
Blueberry Hill, 139
Boom Boom, vii, 15, 18
Borderline, 213, 215, 216
Born to Be Wild, 160
Bowtie Daddy, 103
Boxer, The, 114
Boy in the Bubble, 116
Breaking Up Is Hard to Do, 36

Bridge over Troubled Water, 114
Butterfly, 267
By the Time I Get to Phoenix, 98
Bye Bye Love, 22, 27, 110

Calendar Girl, 36
Can't Explain, 90
Changes, 63
Charlie Freak, 157
Chemistry, 203
Closer to the Heart, 198
Cloud Nine, 123
Cod'ine, 64
Come Live with Me, 24
Come on Over Baby, 265
Country Boy, 22
Crazy Love, 117
Crucifixion, The, 63
Crying My Heart out Over You, 36

Damn, I Wish I Was Your Lover, ix,
    252, 253, 256
Dance with Me Henry, 46
Dangling Conversation, The, 112
Davy the Fat Boy, 165
Day by Day, 132
Deacon Blues, 157
Dear God, 233, 237
Dear One, 5, 7
Dedicated to the One I Love, 48
Diamonds on the Soles of Her Shoes,
    116
Diary, The, 36
Dirty Work, 79
Distant Early Warning, 198
Do the Bop, 42
Do You Believe in Magic?, 92
Do You Know Where You're Going
    To, 54
Don't Call Me Brother, 141
Don't Let the Blues Die, 16
Donald and Lydia, 168, 169

Dr. Wu, 157
Dream On, vii, 151
Dreamer, The, 37
Drowned, 87
Dum Dum, 55

Earned It, 272
Easy to Be Hard, 132
Ebony and Ivory, 75
Eternal Flame, ix, 218, 247–249
Every Beat of My Heart, 44
Everything and Nothing, 53

Face of Appalachia, The, 94
Faith in Something Bigger, 89
Fakin' It, 113
Fantasy, 187
Far from Me, 167
Farewell Blues, 84
Fever, 48
Fifty Ways to Leave Your Lover, 114
Finger Poppin' Time, 43
Flower Lady, The, 63
For Africa, in Africa, 58
Four of Us, The, 94
Frank Mills, 132
Freak Your Boom Boom, 50
Free Girl, 155
Freeway of Love, ix, 219, 220
Friends Again, 96
Frisco, 16
From a Distance, ix, 2, 224–231

Gee, 7, 102
Geek in the Pink, 280
Generation, 67
Genie in a Bottle, 266
Genius of Love, 183, 184, 186
Get It, 45
Gimme Shelter, 81
Go See the Doctor, 241
God's Song, 161

282 | Index of Song Titles

Good Times, 240, 244
Goodnight Irene, 139
Graceland, 2, 116
Grand Designs, 203
Greatest Love of All, The, 155

Hair!, 132
Happy, 82
Happy Happy Birthday Baby, 110
Happy Jack, 89
He's an Indian Cowboy at the Rodeo, 67
Heartbreak Hotel, 76, 165
Hello in There, 167, 168
Her Brains They Rattle and Her
    Bones They Shake, 173
Here She Comes Now, 208
Heroin, 128–130
Hey Jude, 74
Hey There, Delilah, ix, 267, 268, 270,
    271
History Lesson, 208
History Lesson, Part 2, 207, 209–211
Hold On, 229
Holiday, 213, 215, 216
Hoochie Coochie Man, 16
Hound Dog, 143
How Do I Make You, 213, 214
How Will I Know, 219, 220, 222
Hungry Freaks, 103

I, 102
I Ain't Marchin' Anymore, 63
I Am a Rock, 112
I Count the Tears, 34
I Cover the Waterfront, 16
I Don't Know How to Love Him, 132
I Don't Want Nobody Else, 94
I Go Ape, 36
I Left My Heart in San Francisco, 17
I Love the Dead, 150
I Make the Livin', She Makes the
    Livin' Worthwhile, 27

I Only Have Eyes for You, 8
I Think It's Going to Rain Today, 161
I Want to Hold Your Hand, 81, 110
I Want You, 253
I'll Be Missing You, 265
I'm a Man, 31
I'm Edgy, 148
I'm Eighteen, vii, 148
I'm Living in Shame, 123
I'm One, 86
I'm Waiting for My Man, 128
I've Cried Before, 34
I've Got to Be Me, 162
I've Had Her, 63
I've Lost, 5
Immigrant, The, 41
In My Mind, 276
In the Midnight Hour, 143
In the Still of the Night (Cole Porter
    version), 7
In the Still of the Night, vii, 4, 6–9,
    11–14
Into the Groove, 217
It's About Time, 262
It's My Life, 176
It's My Way, 64

Jackass Blues, 26
Java, 178
Jesus Christ, Superstar, vii, 129
Jones Girl, The, 8
Just One Smile, 161

Keep Going Strong, 155
Kid Charlemagne, 157, 160
Kiddio, 16
King of Clowns, 36
Kingfish, 163
Kodachrome, 114

Lady Marmalade, 178
Lashes LaRue, 94

Index of Song Titles | 283

Laughter in the Rain, 40 41
Leopard Skin Pillbox Hat, 242
Let It All Hang Out, 191
Let's Think About Livin', 24
Like a Virgin, ix, 213–217
Lili Done the Zampoogie, 142
Limelight, 198
Little Devil, 36
Liverpool Oratorio, 75
Lonely Avenue, 32
Love Child, 123
Love Will Find a Way, 57
Love Will Keep Us Together, 39 40
Lucky Star, 213, 216

Make Love to Me, 51
Makes Me Wonder, 267
Mama Told Me Not to Come, 161
Manhattan Project, The, 199
Marching Through Georgia, 84
Marie Marie, 246
Mary, Queen of Arkansas, 173
Melody in the Sky, 111
Memories of El Monte, 103
Middletown Dreams, 205
Moratorium, 67
Mother, 131
Mother and Child Reunion, 114
Mother in Law, 178, 179
Mother Nature, 144
Moves Like Jagger, 267, 268
Moving to Montana, 106
Mr. Lee, 110
Mr. Tambourine Man, 133
Mr. Wendall, 257
My Back Pages, 207
My Country 'Tis of Thy People You're
    Dying, 67, 68
My Generation, 89
My Little Town, 114
My Sweet Lord, 149

Mystic Rhythms, 205

Native North American Child, 67
Natural, 257
Needles and Pins, 55
Next Door to An Angel, 36, 37
Night Owl, 9
No More Mr. Nice Guy, 150
Nothing Compares 2 U, 229
Nothing's Gonna Stop Us Now, 221
Now That the Buffalo's Gone, 64, 66,
    68

Oh Carol, 35, 36, 39
Oh No I Don't Believe It, 103, 106
Oh What a Night, 110
On the Love Side, 49
Once in a Lifetime, 184
Our Last Song Together, 39
Over the Rainbow, 143

P. F. Sloan, 100
Paradise, 167
Pearl of the Quarter, 157
Peg, 157
Penguin in Bondage, 106
People Who Died, 37
Pictures of Lily, 89
Piney Wood Hills, 66
Political Science, 165
Poor Man's Daughter, 67
Power and the Glory, The, 63
Proud Mary, 133
Puppet Man, 38
Put a Little Love in Your Heart, vii,
    56–58

Rainy Jane, 38
Rainy Night in Georgia, A, 16
Rapture, 185
Rattlesnake Shake, 152

Reach Out and Touch (Somebody's Hand), 123, 124
Red Lenses, 198
Reelin' in the Years, 157
Relax, 89
Return to Sender, 191
Reuben and Cherise, 118
Rhinestone Cowboy, 40
Rhythm of Love, 271
Rikki Don't Lose That Number, 157
Riot in Cell Block Number, 9, 102
Roadrunner, 191
Roll with Me Henry, 46
Rose Darling, 157
Ruby Tuesday, 81
Run Samson, Run, 36
Runaway Child, Running Wild, 123

Sail Away, 165
Satisfaction, 80, 237
Save the Last Dance for Me, 34
Saving All My Love for You, 54
Say Say Say, 75
School's Out, 150
Sexy Ways, 44, 51
Sh-Boom, 102
Shake It Off, 279
She's a Lady, 95
She's Gone, 9, 11
Sick Things, 150
Six White Horses, 144
Sixteen Reasons, 155
Small Circle of Friends, 62
Solitaire, 39
Someday We'll Be Together, 123
Sound of Silence, The, 112
Southern Nights, xi, 178, 180–182
Spirit in the Night, 173
Stairway to Heaven, 36
Standing on the Inside, 39
Starboy, 67

Starshine, 132
Stone, Sam, 167
Stop the War Now, 123
Stories We Could Tell, 96
Stray Cat Blues, 81
Street Fighting Man, 81
Stuck, 280
Suffer the Little Children, 67
Sunday Morning Coming Down, 49
Sweet Little Vera, 66
Sweet Little You, 36
Switch-a-Roo, 48
Sympathy for the Devil, 81

Take Me Away, 268
Teardrops on Your Letter, 42
Teenager in Love, A, 34
Tell Old Bill, 144
Tennessee, ix, 257, 259
Territories, 199
That's Where the Music Takes Me, 39
There But for Fortune, 63
There Must Be a Better World Somewhere, 34
There's a Future in Fish, Mr. Shine, 95
Tragedy of the Trade, 54
Tom Sawyer, 198
Truckin', 122
Twist, The, xii, 42, 43

Umbrella, 263
Under African Skies, 11
Under My Thumb, 81
Universal Soldier, 64, 66–68
Until It's Time for You to Go, 64, 68
Until You Say You Love Me, 219
Up on the Roof, 53

Vision of Love, 229
Vital Signs, 198, 206

Walk Right In, 147
Walk This Way, 152, 153
Wallflower, The, 46
War, 123
We Close Tonight, 86
We Don't Have to Take Our Clothes
    Off, 220
Weight, The, 56
Welcome, 89
Welcome Back, 97
What a Girl Needs, 265
What a Girl Wants, ix, 263, 266
What the World Needs Now Is Love,
    55
What's Going On, 126
Wheel Bound Man, 211
Whiskey Glasses, 280
Who Are the Brain Police, 103, 106
Who's Zooming Who?, 219
Will You Love Me Tomorrow, 36
Wind Beneath My Wings, The, 228

Wind, The, 110
Wordy Rappinghood, 183–185
Work with Me Annie, 44, 46
Working in the Coal Mine, 178
Working on a Groovy Thing, 38
Wrecking Ball, ix, 272, 274–276

Yesterday, 72
You Are Everything, 155
You Can Call Me Al, 116
You Didn't Have to Be So Nice, 93
You Know My Name, Look up the
    Number, 74
You Make Me Feel Brand New,
    155
You Mean Everything to Me, 36
You Really Got Me, 90
You're a Friend of Mine, 220
Youngblood, 31
Your Day Has Come, 272
Your Precious Love, 124